Unix Topical
Reference

Unix Topical Reference

Georgia B. Faulkner and Karen M. Morris

Writer's Showcase
San Jose New York Lincoln Shanghai

Unix Topical Reference

Writer's Showcase
an imprint of iUniverse, Inc.

For information address:
iUniverse, Inc.
5220 S. 16th St., Suite 200
Lincoln, NE 68512
www.iuniverse.com

ISBN: 0-595-20071-0

CONTENTS

ACKNOWLEDGEMENTS

Special thanks to the Santa Cruz Operation, Inc., for granting us permission to use the "Syntax & Options" sections from the manual pages on the SCO web site.

INTRODUCTION

Georgia and Karen discovered a need for this book after spending many hours searching Unix manuals to locate the command needed to perform a certain function. Since most Unix manuals consist of several detailed volumes, the process of finding a command can be laborious. Therefore, the idea for a topical guide to help the programmer and technical user quickly locate a command was born. We hope this book will assist you in the Unix environment.

append—overview

Methods for attaching or adding input or file contents to the end of a file

cat   display the contents of file to standard output

>>   redirect and append the contents to a file

append

cat   display the contents of one or more files to standard output

cat [-suvte] file

Options

-s
Suppresses warnings about nonexistent files.

-u
Causes the output to be unbuffered.

-v
Causes non-printing characters (with the exception of tabs, new-lines, and form feeds) to be displayed. Control characters are displayed as ^X (<Ctrl>x), where X is the key pressed with the <Ctrl> key (for example, <Ctrl>m is displayed as ^M). The <Del> character (octal 0177) is printed as ^?. Non-ASCII characters (with the high bit set) are printed as M -x, where x is the character specified by the seven low order bits.

-t
Causes tabs to be printed as ^I and form feeds as ^L. This option is ignored if the-v option is not specified.

-e
Causes a "$" character to be printed at the end of each line (prior to the new-line). This option is ignored if the -v option is not set.

Examples

The contents of file1 and file2 displayed to the terminal screen:

```
cat file1 file2
```

>>   redirect and append the contents to a file (create a new file if the file name does not exist)

>> *file*

Examples

attach the output from the l command to the end of file:

```
l >> file
```

archive—overview

Methods for creating archives or back up files

ar	create, modify, and extract files from an archive
cpio	copy files and/or archives in and out
tar	create tape or disk archives by adding files or use to extract tar files

archive

---

ar   create, modify, and extract files from an archive

ar key [keyarg] [posname] file [name]

Options

Unlike command options, the key, which can begin with a "-", is a required part of ar's command line. The valid key is formed with one of the following letters: dmpqrtx.

d
Delete the named files from the archive file.

m
Move the named files to the end of the archive. If a positioning character from the set [abi] is present, then the posname argument must be present and, as in r, specify where the files are to be moved.

p
Print the named files in the archive.

q
Quickly append the named files to the end of the archive file. Optional positioning characters are invalid. The command does not check whether the added members are already in the archive. This option is useful to avoid quadratic behavior when creating a

large archive piece-by-piece. Unchecked, the file can grow exponentially up to the second degree.

r
Replace the named files in the archive file. If the optional character u is used with r, then only those files with dates of modification later than the archive files are replaced. If an optional positioning character from the set abi is used, then the posname argument must be present and specify that new files are to be placed after (a) or before (b or i) posname. Otherwise new files are placed at the end.

t
Print a table of contents of the archive file. If no names are given, all files in the archive are tabled. If names are given, only those files are tabled.

x
Extract the named files. If no names are given, all files in the archive are extracted. In neither case does x alter the archive file.

Valid keyarg characters
Arguments to the key are made with one or more of the characters from the set [abcilsuv]. The meanings for keyarg are as described below.

a
A positioning character used with the m or r key characters. It specifies that new files are to be placed after posname in the archive file.

b

A positioning character used with the m or r key characters. It specifies that new files are to be placed before posname in the archive file.

c

Suppress the message that is produced by default when afile is created.

I

A positioning character used with the m or r key characters. It specifies that new files are to be placed before posname in the archive file.

l

This option is obsolete. It is recognized, but ignored.

s

Force the regeneration of the archive symbol table even if ar(CP) is not invoked with a command that modifies the archive contents. This command is useful to restore the archive symbol table after the strip(CP) command has been used on the archive.

u

When used with the r key character, then only updated versions of files in the archive are used to overwrite the originals.

v

Give a verbose file-by-file description of the making of a new
archive file from the old archive and the constituent files:

* When used with key character t, give a long listing of all information about the files
* When used with any key character from the set [drx], precede
  each file with its filename
* When used with key character p, write filename to stdout

---

cpio   copy files and/or archive in and out

cpio -o [-aBLUvV] [-C bufsize] [-c|-H format]
[-K volumesize] [[-O file[,file...]] [-M message]] [-Pifd,ofd]

cpio -i [-6AbBcdfkmnqrsStTuvV] [-C bufsize] [[-I file[,file...]]
[-M message]] [-Pifd,ofd] [pattern...]

cpio -p [-adlLmruvV] [-Pifd,ofd] directory

Options

There are three main options to cpio which determine its mode of
operation. These modes are used to create an archive (cpio -o),
extract files from an archive (cpio -i), and copy files from one
filesystem to another (cpio -p). There are a number of secondary
options, which are interpreted differently depending on which
mode of operation cpio is in.

-o

copy out) Reads a list of pathnames from the standard input, and copies those files onto the standard output together with pathname and status information. Output is padded to a 512-byte boundary by default.

-i

(copy in) Extracts files from the standard input, which is assumed to be the product of a previous cpio -o. Only files with names that match the wildcard patterns are selected. (See "Using patterns" for details of the notation used.) Extracted files are conditionally created and copied into the current directory tree in accordance with the secondary options described below.

If cpio is used to copy files by a process without appropriate privileges, the access permissions are set in the same fashion that creat() would have set them when given the mode argument, matching the file permissions supplied by the c_mode field of the cpio format. The owner and group of the files will be that of the current user unless the user is root, which causes cpio to retain the owner and group of the files of the previous cpio -o.

NOTE: If cpio -i tries to create a file that already exists and the existing file is the same age or newer, cpio will output a warning message and not replace the file. (The -u option can be used to unconditionally overwrite the existing file.)

-p

(pass) Reads the standard input to obtain a list of pathnames of files that are conditionally created and copied into the destination directory tree based upon the options described below. Archives of text files created by cpio are portable between implementations of UNIX System V.

The following additional options are recognized by cpio. Their interpretation depends on the context selected by the primary option (-o, -i, or -p):

-6
Process a UNIX System Sixth Edition format file. Used only with the -i option.

-a
Reset access times of input files after they have been copied. Access times are not reset for linked files when cpio -pla is specified.

-A
Suppress absolute filenames. A leading "/" character is removed from the filename during copy-in. If a pattern is provided, it should match the relative (rather than the absolute) pathname.

-b
Reverse the order of the bytes within each word. Use only with the -i option.

-B
Block input/output 5,120 bytes to the record. The default buffer size is 512 bytes when this and the -C options are not used. (-B does not apply to the pass option; -B is meaningful only with data directed to or from a character-special device, for example, /dev/rdsk/f0q15dt.)

-c
For portability, write header information in ASCII character form. Always use this option when the origin and destination machines are of different types.

-C bufsize
Block input/output bufsize bytes to the record, where bufsize is replaced by a positive integer. The default buffer size is 512 bytes when this and -B options are not used. (-C does not apply to the pass option; -C is meaningful only with data directed to or from a character-special device, for example, /dev/rmt/c0s0.) When used with the -K option, bufsize is forced to be a 1KB multiple.

-d
Create directories as needed.

-f
Copy in all files except those in patterns. (See the paragraph on cpio –i for a description of patterns.)

-H bin
(binary format). This is a non-portable version of the -c header format.

-H crc
(new character format with checksum) Write checksum information in the header of each file. This option uses the SVR4 extended ASCII header format.

-H newc
(new character format without checksum). Write archives using the SVR4 extended ASCII header format.

-H odc
(old character format) This has the same functionality as -c.

-I file[,file...]
Read the contents of file as input. If file is a character-special device, when the first medium is full, replace the medium and type a carriage return to continue to the next medium. You can perform an unattended multi-archive restore if you specify a comma-separated list of files.

Use only with the -i option.

-k
Attempt to skip corrupted file headers and I/O errors that may be encountered. If you want to copy files from a medium that is corrupted or out of sequence, this option lets you read only those files with good headers. (For cpio archives that contain other cpio archives, if an error is encountered, cpio may terminate prematurely. cpio will find the next good header, which may be one for a smaller archive, and terminate when the smaller archive's trailer is encountered.) Used only with the -i option.

-K volumesize
Specify the size of the media volume. Must be in 1KB blocks. For example, a 1.2MB floppy disk has a volumesize of 1200. Must include the -C option with a bufsize multiple of 1KB. If you specify an incorrect size with -K, the command executes without error,

but cpio generates the message "out of sync: bad magic" when the volume is read. (-K is not available with cpio -i.)
Note that this option is not needed with SCSI tape devices.

-l
Link files rather than copying them whenever possible. Used only with the -p option.

-L Follow symbolic links.
This option requires that you use the -follow option to find(C) when it is used in conjunction with cpio.

-m
Retain previous file modification time. This option is ineffective on directories that are being copied.

-M message
Define a message to use when switching media. When you use the -O or -I options and specify a character-special device, you can use this option to define the message that is printed when you reach the end of the medium. One %d can be placed in the message to print the sequence number of the next medium needed to continue.

-n
Calculate the checksum value for each file read from an archive (the checksum value is equivalent to that produced by the command sum -r). Filetypes other than regular files produce a checksum of 0 (zero). This option is intended to be used in conjunction with the -itv options; the first entry on each output line is the checksum of an archived file.

-O file[,file…]
Direct the output of cpio to file. If file is a character-special device, when the first medium is full, replace the medium and type a carriage return to continue to the next medium. You can change the end-of-media (EOM) message using the -M option.

You can perform an unattended multi-archive backup if you specify a comma-separated list of files. Unless you use SCSI devices, you should specify the volume size using the -K option. Note that cpio assumes that all specified devices have the same volume size.

Use only with the -o option.

-Pifd,ofd
Use file descriptors ifd and ofd for input from and output to a parent process. Any end-of-media (EOM) message is written to ofd rather than to /dev/tty. This option is only useful to programmers who want to write applications that communicate with cpio after a fork(S) and exec(S) by a parent process. The file descriptors must be opened prior to, and remain open on the invocation of cpio by the exec call.

-q
Extract files quickly. cpio extracts only the specified files from the archive and then stops. Shell regular expressions (wildcards) cannot be used in the filenames to be extracted.

-r
Rename files interactively. If the user types a null line, the file is skipped. If the user types a ".", the original pathname will be copied.

-s

Swap bytes within each half word. Use only with the -i option.

-S

Swap halfwords within each word. Use only with the -i option.

-T

Truncate long filenames to 14 characters. Use only with the -i option.

-t

Print a table of contents of the input. No files are created.

-u

Copy unconditionally (normally, an older file will not replace a newer file with the same name).

-v

(verbose) Print a list of filenames. When used with the -t option, the table of contents looks like the output of an ls -l command (see ls(C)).

-V

(special verbose) Print a dot for each file seen. This shows cpio is working without printing filenames.

Examples

find all files from the current directory and archive out to a tape drive

```
find . -print | cpio -ocvdumBO/dev/rct0
```

extract all files from tape drive to the current directory or to the absolute path

```
cpio -icvdumBI/dev/rct0
```

---

tar   create tape or disk archives by adding files or use to extract tar files

tar [key] [files]

Options

One of the following function letters must be specified:

c
Creates a new archive; writing begins at the beginning of the archive, instead of after the last file.

C
Creates a new archive as above, containing compressed files. The files to be archived should be compressed first using compress(C). When the archive is unpacked, tar will pipe the files through uncompress(C), expanding them (if necessary). Note that this

function modifier has no effect on filenames. That is, files stored with a .Z suffix retain them when unpacked, even if they have been uncompressed.

r

The named files are written to the end of an existing archive. This function letter is only valid for appending files to disk archives. When specifying the absolute path of an archive device with the f function modifier, use the n function modifier to indicate that the device is not a magnetic tape.

This function letter cannot be used with tape devices.

t

The names of the specified files are listed each time that they occur on the archive. If no files argument is given, all the names on the archive are listed.

u

The named files are added to the archive if they are not already there, or if they have been modified since last written on that archive.

This function letter cannot be used with tape devices.

x

The named files are extracted from the archive. If a named file matches a directory whose contents had been written onto the archive, this directory is (recursively) extracted. The owner, modification time, and mode are restored (if possible). If no files argument is given, the entire contents of the archive are extracted. Note that if several files with the same name are on the archive, the last one overwrites all earlier ones. There is no way to ask for the nth occurrence of a file.

Function modifiers
The following characters are used in addition to the key function letter:

0,...,9999
This numeric key selects the device on which the archive is mounted. The available numeric keys are defined in the file /etc/default/tar. A list of archive devices and their corresponding numeric keys can be displayed by entering tar without any arguments. The f function modifier is used to specify an archive device which is not in /etc/default/tar.

A
Suppresses absolute filenames by removing leading slash (/) characters from filenames. When used with the c, r, t and u function letters, the A function modifier prevents leading slashes being written to the archive headers. When used with the x function letter to extract files, arguments must be given as pathnames excluding the leading slash.

b
Causes tar to use the next argument as the blocking factor for archive records. The blocking factor is used to calculate the archive block size. This function modifier should only be used with archives on raw devices (see the f function modifier for how to select different devices).

The blocking factor is specified as a multiple of 512 bytes, from 1 (equivalent to an archive block size of 512 bytes) up to a maximum of 20 (equivalent to 10K). If the device is not a tape device, the blocking factor must be specified as an even number from 2 to

20. For example, to use a 9K block size with a floppy disk, specify a blocking factor of 18:
tar cvfb /dev/rfd0 18 file

The block size is determined automatically when reading tape archives.
e
Prevents files from being split across volumes (tapes or floppy disks). If there is not enough room on the present volume for a given file, tar prompts for a new volume. This is only valid when the k function modifier is also specified on the command line.

f
Causes tar to use the next argument as the name of the archive instead of the default device listed in /etc/default/tar. If the name of the file is a dash (-), tar writes to the standard output or reads from the standard input, whichever is appropriate. Thus, tar can be used as the head or tail of a pipeline. tar can also be used to move hierarchies with the command:

cd fromdir; tar cf—. | (cd todir; tar xf -)

F
Causes tar to use the next argument as the name of a file from which succeeding arguments are taken.

k
Causes tar to use the next argument as the size of an archive volume in kilobytes (KB). The minimum value allowed is 250. Very large files are split into "extents" across volumes. When restoring from a multi-volume archive, tar only prompts for a new volume if a split file has been partially restored. To override the archive

length value in the default file, specify 0 as the argument to k on the command line.

l

Tells tar to display an error message if it cannot resolve all of the links to the files being backed up. If l is not specified, no error messages are displayed.

L

Follow symbolic links and archive the contents of the regular files to which they ultimately point with the name of the topmost link. By default, tar archives symbolic links without following them unless you also specify the P function modifier.

m

Tells tar not to restore the modification times. The modification time of the file is the time of extraction.

n

Indicates the archive device is not a magnetic tape. The k function modifier implies this. Listing and extracting the contents of an archive are faster because tar can seek over files it wishes to skip. Sizes are printed in kilobytes instead of tape blocks.

o

Assign the user and group identifiers of the user to the files being extracted rather than those stored on the archive. This is the default behavior of tar. This function modifier cannot be combined with the p function modifier.

p
Extract the files using their original permissions if the user is not the super user. It is possible that the user may be unable to extract files because of the permissions associated with the files or directories being extracted.

The sense of this function modifier is reversed for root; the files will be extracted with user and group ownership by root. This function modifier cannot be combined with the function letter o.

P
Select the historical-compatibility mode of tar; do not archive symbolic links, information about directories, or empty directories. If you specify this function modifier but not the L function modifier, tar issues a warning message when it encounters a symbolic link, skips over the link, and continues with the rest of the files.

q
During extraction causes tar to exit immediately after each file on the command line has been extracted, rather than continuing to look for additional files of the same name.

T
Truncates filenames of greater than 14 characters on extraction. This is used for extracting files from EAFS-type filesystems that support long filenames (up to 255 characters long) to AFS-type filesystems that support maximum 14-character filenames.

v
Normally, tar does its work silently. The v (verbose) function modifier causes tar to display the name of each file it treats, preceded by

the function letter. With the t function, v gives more information about the archive entries than just the name.

w

Causes tar to display the action to be taken, followed by the name of the file, and then wait for the user's confirmation. If a word beginning with "y" is given, the action is performed. Any other input means "no".

Examples

create back up of files in current directory to tape device:

```
tar cvf  /dev/rct0
```

display table of contents of tar archive on tape device:

```
tar tvf /dev/rct0
```

extract tar archive from tape device to current directory:

```
tar xvf /dev/rct0 .
```

combine—overview

Methods for combining the contents of two files

cat   combine two files
join   combine two files based on relationship

combine

cat   display the contents of one or more files to standard output

cat [-suvte] file

Options

-s
Suppresses warnings about nonexistent files.

-u
Causes the output to be unbuffered.

-v
Causes non-printing characters (with the exception of tabs, new-lines, and form feeds) to be displayed. Control characters are displayed as ^X (<Ctrl>x), where X is the key pressed with the <Ctrl> key (for example, <Ctrl>m is displayed as ^M). The <Del> character (octal 0177) is printed as ^?. Non-ASCII characters (with the high bit set) are printed as M -x, where x is the character specified by the seven low order bits.

-t
Causes tabs to be printed as ^I and form feeds as ^L. This option is ignored if the-v option is not specified.

-e
Causes a "$" character to be printed at the end of each line (prior to the new-line). This option is ignored if the -v option is not set.

Examples

The contents of file1 and file2 displayed to the terminal screen:

```
cat file1 file2
```

---

join   join the relations specified by the lines of two files

join [[-a file] | [-v file]] [-e str] [-o list] [-t c]
[[-j[file] field] | [-1 field] [-2 field]] file1 file2

Options

-a file
In addition to the normal output, produces a line for each unpairable line in file, where file is 1 or 2.

-e str
Replaces empty output fields by string str.

-j[file] field
Joins on field (1,2,3...) of file (1 or 2). If file is missing, the same field from each file is used (equivalent to -j1 field -j2 field or -1 field -2 field).

-1 field
Equivalent to -j1 field.

-2 field
Equivalent to -j2 field.

-o list
Each output line comprises the fields specified in list, each element
of which has the form file.field formed from the file number (1 or
2) and the field number (1,2,3...). The list may consist of single or
multiple command line arguments, each element separated by
blanks or commas.

-t c
Uses character c as a field separator. Every appearance of c in a
line is significant.

-v file
Only produce output for each unpairable line in file, where file is
1 or 2.

Examples

join file1 and file2 output to file3:

```
join -a1 -a2 file1 file2 > file3
```

communicate—overview

Methods for communicating from one system to another or between users. Also methods for transferring data between systems

cu	connect to another system
ftp	file transfer protocol
mail	send, read, forward mail messages
mailx	electronic messaging environment
notify	notify for mail
rcp	remote file copy
rlogin	connect to another system
talk	communicate to another user
telnet	connect to another system
uucp	Unix to Unix file copy
vacation	automatic mail message response
wall	communicate to all users
write	communicate to another user

communicate

cu   call up another system, manage conversation as well as file transfers

cu [-dht] [-l line] [-o | -e | -oe] [-s speed] [-x n] telno
cu [-dht] [-l line] [-o | -e | -oe] [-s speed] [-x n] -n
cu [-dht] [-o | -e | -oe] [-s speed] [-x n] -l line [dir]
cu [-dht] [-o | -e | -oe] [-x n] systemname

Options

-s speed
Specifies the transmission speed (150, 300, 600, 1200, 2400, 4800, 9600, 19200, 38400). The default value is "Any" speed which will depend on the order of the lines in the /usr/lib/uucp/Devices file. A speed range can also be specified (for example, -s 1200-4800).

-l line
Specifies a device name to use as the communication line. This can be used to override the search that would otherwise take place for the first available line having the right speed. When the -l option is used without the -s option, the speed of a line is taken from the Devices file. When the -l and -s options are both used together, cu will search the Devices file to check if the requested speed for the requested line is available. If so, the connection will be made at the requested speed; otherwise, an error message will be printed and the call will not be made. The specified device is generally a directly connected asynchronous line (for example, /dev/ttyab) in

which case a telephone number (telno) is not required. The specified device need not be in the /dev directory. If the specified device is associated with an auto dialer, a telephone number must be provided. Use of this option with systemname rather than telno will not give the desired result (see systemname below).

-d
Enables diagnostic tracing.

-h
Emulates local echo, supporting calls to other computer systems which expect terminals to be set to half-duplex mode.

-t
Used to dial an ASCII terminal which has been set to auto answer. Appropriate mapping of carriage-return to carriage-return-line-feed pairs is set.

-x n
Causes diagnostic traces to be printed; it produces a detailed output of the program execution on stderr. The debugging level, n, is a single digit in the range 0 to 9; -x 9 is the most useful value.

-n
For added security, -n will prompt the user to provide the telephone number to be dialed rather than taking it from the command line.

telno
When using an automatic dialer, the argument is the telephone number with equal signs for secondary dial tone or minus signs placed appropriately for delays of 4 seconds.

systemname
A UUCP system name may be used rather than a telephone number. In this case, cu will obtain an appropriate direct line or telephone number from /usr/lib/uucp/Systems. Note: the systemname option should not be used in conjunction with the -l and -s options as cu will connect to the first available line for the system name specified, ignoring the requested line and speed.

dir
The keyword dir can be used with cu -l line, in order to talk directly to a modem on that line, instead of talking to another system via that modem. This can be useful when debugging or checking modem operation. Note: only users with write access to the Devices file are permitted to use cu -l line dir.
In addition, cu uses the following options to determine communications settings:
-o
If the remote system expects or sends 7-bits with odd parity.
-e
If the remote system expects or sends 7-bits with even parity.
-oe
If the remote system expects or sends 7-bits, ignoring parity and sends 7-bits with either parity.
By default, cu expects and sends 8-bit characters without parity. If the login prompt received appears to contain incorrect 8-bit characters, or a correct login is rejected, use the 7-bit options described above.
After making the connection, cu runs as two processes: the transmit process and the receive process. The transmit process reads data from standard input and, except for lines beginning with "~", passes the data to the remote system. The receive process

accepts data from the remote system and, except for lines beginning with "~", passes the data to standard output.

Normally, an automatic XON/XOFF protocol is used to control input from the remote system so the buffer is not overrun.

Lines beginning with "~" have special meanings.

The transmit process interprets the following user-initiated commands:

~.

Terminate the conversation.

~!

Escape to an interactive shell on the local system.

~!cmd...

Run cmd on the local system (via sh -c).

~$cmd...

Run cmd locally and send its output to the remote system.

~+cmd...

Run cmd on the local system but take standard input from the remote system.

~%cd

Change the directory on the local system. Note: ~!cd will cause the command to be run by a sub-shell, probably not what was intended.

~%take there_name [here_name]

Copy file there_name on the remote system to file here_name on the local system. If here_name is omitted, the pathname there_name on the remote system is used by default.

~%put here_name [there_name]

Copy file here_name on the local system to file there_name on the remote system. If there_name is omitted, the pathname here_name on the local system is used by default.

For both ~%take and ~%put commands, as each block of the file is transferred, consecutive single digits are printed to the terminal

~~line

Send the line ~line to the remote system.

~%b

~%break

Transmit a BREAK to the remote system.

~%d

~%debug

Toggles the -x debugging level between 0 and 9.

~t

Prints the values of the termio structure variables for the user's terminal (useful for debugging).

~l

Prints the values of the termio structure variables for the remote communication line (useful for debugging).

~%nostop

Toggles between XON/XOFF input control protocol and no input control. This is useful in case the remote system is one which does not respond properly to the XON and XOFF characters.

The use of ~%put requires *stty(C)* and *cat(C)* on the remote side. It also requires that the current erase and kill characters on the remote system be identical to these current control characters on the local system. Backslashes are inserted at appropriate places.

The use of ~%take requires the existence of *echo(C)* and *cat(C)* on the remote system. Also, tabs mode (see *stty(C)*) should be set on the remote system if tabs are to be copied without expansion to spaces.

The receive process normally copies data from the remote system to its standard output. It may also direct output to local files.
You can construct take and put commands that work between UNIX and non-UNIX systems by sending the appropriate characters to cu. To do this, you will need to know the equivalent of *echo(C)* and *cat(C)* on the non-UNIX system.

For example, to transfer a file named fred from a remote non-UNIX system to the file /tmp/fred on the local UNIX system, construct a command similar to the following:

```
~%
echo '~>':/tmp/fred
cat fred
echo '~>'
```

This creates a file /tmp/fred on the local UNIX system, putting the characters "~>" into it, which tells cu to start receiving data into this file. The file fred is then sent to standard output on the remote machine, and cu therefore receives it. Finally, a "~>" is echoed into the file; this is a signal to cu to stop receiving input. (Remember to replace echo and cat with the equivalent commands for the non-UNIX system.)

You can also append the file from the remote machine to an existing file on the local system:

```
~%
echo '~>>':/tmp/fred
cat fred
echo '~>'
```

This appends the remote file onto the end of the existing file /tmp/fred.

When cu is used on system1 to connect to system2 and subsequently used on system2 to connect to system3, commands on system2 can be executed by using "~~". Executing a tilde command reminds the user of the local system uname. For example, uname can be executed on systems 1, 2, and 3 as follows:

uname
system3
~!uname
system1
~~!uname
system2

In general, "~" causes the command to be executed on the original machine, and "~~" causes the command to be executed on the next machine in the chain.

Exit values

Exit code is zero for normal exit, otherwise, one.

---

ftp   transfer data across network through a command interpreter if FTP server is not on host machine

ftp [-v] [-d] [-i] [-n] [-t] [-g] [host]

Options

-v

(verbose on) forces ftp to show all responses from the remote server, as well as report on data transfer statistics. Normally, this is on by default, unless the standard input is not a terminal.

-n

restrains ftp from attempting auto-login upon initial connection. If auto-login is enabled, ftp will check the .netrc (see below) file in the user's home directory for an entry describing an account on the remote machine. If no entry exists, ftp will prompt for the remote machine login name (default is the user identity on the local machine), and, if necessary, prompt for a password and an account with which to login.

-i

turns off interactive prompting during multiple file transfers.

-d
enables debugging.

-g
disables filename globbing.

-t

enables packet tracing. This option is not currently implemented. The client host with which ftp is to communicate may be specified on the command line. If this is done, ftp will immediately attempt to establish a connection to an FTP server on that host; otherwise, ftp will enter its command interpreter and await instructions from the user. When ftp is awaiting commands from the user the prompt ftp> is provided to the user.

The following commands are recognized by ftp:
! [command [args]]
Invoke an interactive shell on the local machine. If there are arguments, the first is taken to be a command to execute directly, with the rest of the arguments as its arguments.

$ macro-name [args]
Execute the macro macro-name that was defined with the macdef command. Arguments are passed to the macro unglobbed.

account [passwd]
Supply a supplemental password required by a remote system for access to resources once a login has been successfully completed. If no argument is included, the user will be prompted for an account password in a non-echoing input mode.

append local-file [remote-file]
Append a local file to a file on the remote machine. If remote-file is left unspecified, the local filename is used in naming the remote file after being altered by any ntrans or nmap setting. File transfer uses the current settings for type, format, mode, and structure.

ascii
Set the file transfer type to network ASCII. This is the default type.

bell
Arrange that a bell be sounded after each file transfer command is completed.

binary
Set the file transfer type to support binary image transfer.

bye
Terminate the FTP session with the remote server and exit ftp. An end of file will also terminate the session and exit.

case
Toggle remote computer filename case mapping during mget commands. When case is on (default is off), remote computer filenames with all letters in uppercase are written in the local directory with the letters mapped to lowercase.

cd remote-directory
Change the working directory on the remote machine to remote-directory.

cdup
Change the remote machine working directory to the parent of the current remote machine working directory.

chmod [mode] [remote-file]
Change file permissions of remote file.

close
Terminate the FTP session with the remote server, and return to the command interpreter. Any defined macros are erased.

cr
Toggle carriage return stripping during ASCII type file retrieval. Records are denoted by a carriage return/linefeed sequence during ASCII type file transfer. When cr is on (the default), carriage returns are stripped from this sequence to conform with the UNIX single linefeed record delimiter. Records on non-UNIX remote systems may contain single linefeeds; when an ASCII type transfer is made, these linefeeds may be distinguished from a record delimiter only when cr is off.

delete remote-file
Delete the file remote-file on the remote machine.

debug [debug-value]
Toggle debugging mode. If an optional debug-value is specified, it is used to set the debugging level. When debugging is on, ftp prints each command sent to the remote machine, preceded by the string "—>".

dir [remote-directory] [local-file]
Print a listing of the directory contents in the directory, remote-directory, and, optionally, placing the output in local-file. If interactive prompting is on, ftp will prompt the user to verify that the last argument is indeed the target local file for receiving dir output. If no directory is specified, the current working directory on the remote machine is used. If no local file is specified, or local-file is -, output comes to the terminal.

disconnect
A synonym for close.

form format
Set the file transfer form to format. The default format is file.

get remote-file [local-file]
Retrieve the remote-file and store it on the local machine. If the local filename is not specified, it is given the same name it has on the remote machine, subject to alteration by the current case, ntrans, and nmap settings. The current settings for type, form, mode, and structure are used while transferring the file.

glob
Toggle filename expansion for mdelete, mget, and mput. If glob-bing is turned off with glob, the filename arguments are taken literally and not expanded. Globbing for mput is done as in sh(C). For mdelete and mget, each remote filename is expanded separately on the remote machine and the lists are not merged. Expansion of a directory name is likely to be different from expansion of the name of an ordinary file: the exact result depends on the foreign operating system and ftp server, and can be previewed by doing `mls remote-files -'.

Note that mget and mput are not meant to transfer entire direc-tory subtrees of files. That can be done by transferring a tar(C) archive of the subtree (in binary mode).

hash
Toggle hash-sign (#) printing for each data block transferred. The size of a data block is BUFSIZ bytes. BUFSIZ is defined in stdio.h.

help [command]
Print an informative message about the meaning of command. If no argument is given, ftp prints a list of the known commands.

idle
Get/set idle timer on the remote machine.

image
Same as binary.

lcd [directory]
Change the working directory on the local machine. If no directo-ry is specified, the user's home directory is used.

ls [remote-directory] [local-file]
Print an abbreviated listing of the contents of a directory on the remote machine. The listing includes any system-dependent information that the server chooses to include; for example, most UNIX systems will produce output from the command ls -l. (See also nlist.) If remote-directory is left unspecified, the current working directory is used. If interactive prompting is on, ftp will prompt the user to verify that the last argument is indeed the target local file for receiving ls output. If no local file is specified, or if local-file is -, the output is sent to the terminal. Additional options may be specified by quoting the arguments (e.g., ls "-rt dir", will cause a time sorted listing of directory dir to be displayed if the remote operating system is UNIX).

macdef macro-name
Define a macro. Subsequent lines are stored as the macro macro-name; a null line (consecutive newline characters in a file or carriage returns from the terminal) terminates macro input mode. There is a limit of 16 macros and 4096 total characters in all defined macros. Macros remain defined until a close command is executed. The macro processor interprets "$" and "\" as special characters. A "$" followed by a number (or numbers) is replaced by the corresponding argument on the macro invocation command line. A "$" followed by an "i" signals that macro processor that the executing macro is to be looped. On the first pass, "$i" is replaced by the first argument on the macro invocation command line, on the second pass it is replaced by the second argument, and so on. A "\" followed by any character is replaced by that character. Use the "\" to prevent special treatment of the "$".

mdelete [remote-files]
Delete the remote-files on the remote machine.

mdir remote-files local-file
Like dir, except multiple remote files may be specified. If interactive prompting is on, ftp will prompt the user to verify that the last argument is indeed the target local file for receiving mdir output.

mget remote-files
Expand the remote-files on the remote machine and do a get for each filename thus produced. See glob for details on the filename expansion. Resulting filenames will then be processed according to case, ntrans, and nmap settings. Files are transferred into the local working directory, which can be changed with lcd directory; new local directories can be created with`! mkdir directory.

mkdir directory-name
Make a directory on the remote machine.

mls remote-files local-file
Like nlist, except multiple remote files may be specified, and the local-file must be specified. If interactive prompting is on, ftp will prompt the user to verify that the last argument is indeed the target local file for receiving mls output.

mode [mode-name]
Set the file transfer mode to mode-name. The default mode is "stream" mode.

modtime file-name
Show the last modification time of the file on the remote machine.

mput local-files
Expand wildcards in the list of local files given as arguments and do a put for each file in the resulting list. See glob for details of

filename expansion. Resulting filenames will then be processed according to ntrans and nmap settings. The mput command does not allow specifying remote filenames.

newer remote-file [local-file]
Get file if remote file is newer than local file.
nlist [remote-directory] [local-file]
Print a list of the files of a directory on the remote machine. If remote-directory is left unspecified, the current working directory is used. If interactive prompting is on, ftp will prompt the user to verify that the last argument is indeed the target local file for receiving nlist output. If no local file is specified, or if local-file is -, the output is sent to the terminal. Additional options may be specified by quoting the arguments (e.g., nlist "-rt dir", will cause a time sorted listing of directory dir to be displayed if the remote operating system is UNIX).

nmap [inpattern outpattern]
Set or unset the filename mapping mechanism. If no arguments are specified, the filename mapping mechanism is unset. If arguments are specified, remote filenames are mapped during mput commands and put commands issued without a specified remote target filename. If arguments are specified, local filenames are mapped during mget commands and get commands issued without a specified local target filename. This command is useful when connecting to a non-UNIX remote computer with different file-naming conventions or practices. The mapping follows the pattern set by inpattern and outpattern. Inpattern is a template for incoming filenames (which may have already been processed according to the ntrans and case settings). Variable templating is accomplished by including the sequences $1, $2,..., $9 in inpattern. Use "\" to prevent this special treatment of the "$" character. All other

characters are treated literally, and are used to determine the nmap inpattern variable values. For example, given inpattern $1.$2 and the remote filename mydata.data, $1 would have the value "mydata", and $2 would have the value "data". The outpattern determines the resulting mapped filename. The sequences $1, $2,..., $9 are replaced by any value resulting from the inpattern template. The sequence '$0' is replaced by the original filename. Additionally, the sequence [seq1,seq2] is replaced by seq1 if seq1 is not a null string; otherwise it is replaced by seq2. For example, the command nmap $1.$2.$3 [$1,$2].[$2,file] would yield the output filename myfile.data for input filenames myfile.data and myfile.data.old, myfile.file for the input filename myfile, and myfile.myfile for the input filename .myfile. Spaces may be included in outpattern, as in the example:

nmap $1 |sed "s/ *$//" > $1 .
Use the "\" character to prevent special treatment of the "$", "[", "]", and "," characters.

ntrans [inchars [outchars]]
Set or unset the filename character translation mechanism. If no arguments are specified, the filename character translation mechanism is unset. If arguments are specified, characters in remote filenames are translated during mput commands and put commands issued without a specified remote target filename. If arguments are specified, characters in local filenames are translated during mget commands and get commands issued without a specified local target filename. This command is useful when connecting to a non-UNIX remote computer with different file-naming conventions or practices. Characters in a filename matching a character in inchars are replaced with the corresponding character in outchars. If the character's position in

inchars is longer than the length of outchars, the character is deleted from the filename.

open host [port]
Establish a connection to the specified host FTP server. An optional port number may be supplied, in which case, ftp will attempt to contact an FTP server at that port. If the auto-login option is on (default), ftp will also attempt to automatically log the user in to the FTP server (see below).

prompt
Toggle interactive prompting. Interactive prompting occurs during multiple file transfers to allow the user to selectively retrieve or store files. If prompting is turned off (default is on), any mget or mput will transfer all files, and any mdelete will delete all files.

proxy ftp-command
Execute an ftp command on a secondary control connection. This command allows simultaneous connection to two remote ftp servers for transferring files between the two servers. The first proxy command should be an open, to establish the secondary control connection. Enter the command proxy ? to see other ftp commands executable on the secondary connection. The following commands behave differently when prefaced by proxy: open will not define new macros during the auto-login process, close will not erase existing macro definitions, get and mget transfer files from the host on the primary control connection to the host on the secondary control connection, and put, mput, and append transfer files from the host on the secondary control connection to the host on the primary control connection. Third party file transfers depend upon support of the ftp protocol PASV command by the server on the secondary control connection.

put local-file [remote-file]
Store a local file on the remote machine. If remote-file is left unspecified, the local file name is used after processing according to any ntrans or nmap settings in naming the remote file. File transfer uses the current settings for type, format, mode, and structure.

pwd
Print the name of the current working directory on the remote machine.

quit
A synonym for bye.

quote arg1 arg2...
The arguments specified are sent, verbatim, to the remote FTP server.

recv remote-file [local-file]
A synonym for get.

reget
Retrieve a file restarting at the end of the local-file.

restart
Restart the transfer of a file from a particular byte-count.

rhelp [command-name]
Request help from the remote FTP server. If a command-name is specified, it is supplied to the server as well.

rstatus [file-name]
With no arguments, show status of remote-machine. If file-name
is specified, show status of file-name on remote machine.

rename [from] [to]
Rename the file from on the remote machine, to the file to.

reset
Clear reply queue. This command re-synchronizes command/reply
sequencing with the remote ftp server. Resynchronization may be
necessary following a violation of the ftp protocol by the remote
server.

rmdir directory-name
Delete a directory on the remote machine.

runique
Toggle storing of files on the local system with unique filenames.
If a file already exists with a name equal to the target local filename for a get or mget command, a .1 is appended to the name.
If the resulting name matches another existing file, a .2 is appended to the original name. If this process continues up to .99, an
error message is printed, and the transfer does not take place. The
generated unique filename will be reported. Note that runique will
not affect local files generated from a shell command (see below).
The default value is off.

send local-file [remote-file]
A synonym for put.

sendport
Toggle the use of PORT commands. By default ftp will attempt to use a PORT command when establishing a connection for each data transfer. The use of PORT commands can prevent delays when performing multiple file transfers. If the PORT command fails, ftp will use the default data port. When the use of PORT commands is disabled, no attempt will be made to use PORT commands for each data transfer. This is useful for certain FTP implementations which do ignore PORT commands but, incorrectly, indicate they were accepted.

size file-name
Return size of file-name on remote machine.

status
Show the current status of ftp.

site [command]
Get/set site specific information from/on remote machine.

struct [struct-name]
Set the file transfer structure to struct-name. By default, stream structure is used.

sunique
Toggle storing of files on remote machine under unique filenames. Remote ftp server must support ftp protocol STOU command for successful completion. The remote server will report unique name. Default value is off.

system
Show the type of operating system running on the remote machine.

tenex
Set the file transfer type to that needed to talk to TENEX machines.

trace
Toggle packet tracing. This option is not currently implemented.

type [type-name]
Set the file transfer type to type-name. If no type is specified, the current type is printed. The default type is network ASCII.

umask [mask]
Set user file-creation mode mask on the remote site. If mask is omitted, the current value of the mask is printed.

user user-name [password] [account]
Identify yourself to the remote FTP server. If the password is not specified and the server requires it, ftp will prompt the user for it (after disabling local echo). If an account field is not specified, and the FTP server requires it, the user will be prompted for it. If an account field is specified, an account command will be relayed to the remote server after the login sequence is completed if the remote server did not require it for logging in. Unless ftp is invoked with auto-login disabled, this process is done automatically on initial connection to the FTP server.

verbose
Toggle verbose mode. In verbose mode, all responses from the FTP server are displayed to the user. In addition, if verbose is on, when a file transfer completes, statistics regarding the efficiency of the transfer are reported. By default, verbose is on.

? [command]
A synonym for help.

Command arguments which have embedded spaces may be quoted with quote (") marks.

Examples

connect to remote system:

```
ftp system
```

help for a specific command from the ftp prompt:

```
ftp> help command
```

help from the ftp prompt:

```
ftp> help
```

---

mail   send, read and forward mail messages

Sending mail
mail [-s subject] address...

mail [-s subject] [-h hops] [-U] -r address

Receiving mail
mail -e
mail [-HinN] [-F] [-u user]
mail -f [-HinN] [-F] [file]

Options

-e
Test for presence of mail. mail prints nothing and exits with a successful return code if there is mail to read.

-f filename
Read messages from filename instead of mailbox. If no filename is specified, the mbox is used.

-F
Record the message in a file named after the first recipient. The name is taken from the address on the To: line in the mail header. This overrides the record variable, if set (see "Internal variables".)

-h hops
The number of network hops made so far. This is provided for network software to avoid infinite delivery loops. (See addsopt under "Internal variables".)

-H
Print header summary only.

-i

Ignore interrupts. (See ignore under "Internal variables".)

-n

Do not initialize from the system default .mailrc file.

-N

Do not print initial header summary.

-r address

Pass address to network delivery software. All tilde commands are disabled. (See addsopt under "Internal variables".)

-s subject

Set the subject header field to subject.

-t

Allow use of tilde escapes when standard input is not a tty.

-u user

Read user's mailbox. This is only effective if user's mailbox has read/write permissions granted for the invoker's group or general (others).

-U

Convert UUCP-style addresses to internet standards. This overrides the conv variable. (See addsopt under "Internal variables".)

Examples

read mail in mailbox:

```
mail
```

send message to user:

```
mail user
```

list mail commands:

```
?
```

---

mailx   send and receive messages electronically

The mailx command with the pathname /usr/bin/mailx is a link to /bin/mail.

---

notify   automatic response

notify -y
notify [-n]

Options

-y
Install mail notification facility.

-n
Remove mail notification facility.

If invoked with no arguments, notify reports whether automatic mail notification is activated or not.

---

rcp   copy files between two machines

rcp [-p] file1 file2
rcp [-p] [-r] file...directory

Options

If the -r option is specified and any of the source files are directories, rcp copies each subtree rooted at that name; in this case the destination must be a directory.

By default, the mode and owner of file2 are preserved if it already existed; otherwise, the mode of the source file modified by the umask on the destination host is used. (See umask(C) for a description of umasks.) The -p option causes rcp to attempt to preserve (duplicate) in its copies the modification times and modes of the source files, ignoring the umask.

If path is not a full path name, it is interpreted relative to your login directory on rhost. A path on a remote host may be quoted (using \, ", or ´) so that the metacharacters are interpreted remotely. See sh(C) for quoting rules.

rcp does not prompt for passwords; if the user account requires a password, your current local user name must exist on rhost and allow remote command execution via rcmd(TC).

If an account has no password, any user can use rcmd or rcp commands to access that account. In this case, an entry in /etc/hosts.equiv or in a .rhosts file is not required.

rcp handles third-party copies, where neither source nor target files are on the current machine. Hostnames may also take the form "rname@rhost" to use rname rather than the current user name on the remote host.

Examples

copy file1 to host system file2:

```
rcp file1 system:file2
```

---

rlogin   connect users terminal to another system

rlogin rhost [-ec] [-8] [-E] [-L] [-l username]
/usr/hosts/rhost [-ec] [-8] [-E] [-L] [-l username]

Options

Each host has a file /etc/hosts.equiv which contains a list of rhost's with which it shares account names. (The host names must be the standard names as described in rcmd(TC).) When you rlogin as the same user on an equivalent host, you do not need to give a password. Users may also have a private equivalence list in a file .rhosts in their login directories. Each line in this file should contain an rhost and a username separated by a space, giving additional cases where logins without passwords are to be permitted. If the originating user is not equivalent to the remote user, then a login and password will be prompted for on the remote machine as in login(M). To avoid some security problems, the .rhosts file must be owned by either the remote user or root.

The remote terminal type is the same as your local terminal type (as given in your environment TERM variable). The terminal or window size is also copied to the remote system if the server supports the option, and changes in size are reflected as well. All echoing takes place at the remote site, so that (except for delays) the rlogin is transparent. Flow control via <Ctrl>s and <Ctrl>q and flushing of input and output on interrupts are handled properly. The optional argument -8 allows an eight-bit input data path at all times; otherwise parity bits are stripped except when the remote side's stop and start characters are other than <Ctrl>s/<Ctrl>q. The argument -L allows the rlogin session to be run without any output post-processing, (for example, stty -opost.)
A line of the form "~." disconnects from the remote host, where "~" is the default escape character.

A line of the form "~susp" suspends the login session (only if you are using the Korn shell). "susp" is your "suspend" character, usually "^Z", (CTRL-Z). See stty(C).

An escape character other than "~" may be specified with the -e option. There is no space separating this option flag and the argument character. The -E option specifies that no character is to be recognized as the escape character.

Examples

connect to system:

```
rlogin system
```

---

talk   talk to another user by copying lines from your terminal to another user's terminal

talk person [ttyname]

Options

If you wish to talk to someone on you own machine, then person is just the person's login name. If you wish to talk to a user on another host, then person is of the form user@host.

If you want to talk to a user who is logged in more than once, the ttyname argument may be used to indicate the appropriate terminal name, where ttyname is of the form "ttyXX".

When first called, it sends the message
    Message from TalkDaemon@his_machine...talk:
    connection requested by
    your_name@your_machine. talk: respond

with: talk your_name@your_machine
to the user to whom you wish to talk.

At this point, the recipient of the message should reply by typing:

talk your_name@your_machine

It does not matter from which machine the recipient replies, as long as his login-name is the same. Once communication is established, the two parties may type simultaneously, with their output appearing in separate windows. Typing <Ctrl>L will cause the screen to be reprinted, while your erase and kill characters will behave normally. In addition, <Ctrl>W is defined as a word-kill character. To exit, just type your interrupt character; talk then moves the cursor to the bottom of the screen and restores the terminal to its previous state.

Permission to talk may be denied or granted by use of the mesg(C) command. At the outset talking is allowed. Certain commands, in particular nroff and pr(C) disallow messages to prevent messy output.

Examples

talk to user:

```
talk user
```

telnet   connect to another system using telnet protocol (can be invoked in command mode) *telnet [-8] [-E] [-L] [-a] [-d] [-e escape_char] [-l user] [-n tracefile] [-r] [host [port]]*

Options

-8
Use an eight bit data path. This will cause an attempt to negotiate the BINARY option on both input and output.

-E
Option stops any character from being recognized as an escape character.

-L
Use an eight bit data path on output. This causes the BINARY option to be negotiated on output.

-a
Automatic login into the remote system. If the remote system understands the ENVIRON option, then the variable LOGNAME will be sent to the remote system. This option may also be used with the open command.

-d
Toggles socket level debugging (useful only to root). Sets the initial value of the debug toggle to "TRUE".

-e [escape_char]
Sets the initial TELNET escape character to escape_char. If escape_char is omitted, then there will be no pre-defined escape character.

-l user
When connecting to the remote system and if the remote system understands the ENVIRON option, then user will be sent to the remote system as the value for the variable LOGNAME. This option may also be used with the open command.

-n tracefile
Opens tracefile for recording the trace information. (See the set-tracefile command below.)

-r
Use a user interface similar to rlogin(TC). In this mode, the escape character is set to the tilde (~) character, unless modified by the -e flag.

host
Indicates the host's official name: an alias or the Internet address of a remote host. host may be specified as an IP source-route. This takes the form of [!]@addr@addr@addr:dest. If the source-route is prefixed with the "!" character, it is interpreted as a strict source route. Otherwise, it is interpreted as a loose source route. See the IP specification for more information about source routing. Note: This exists primarily for debugging or for use when network connectivity is problematic. Use of source-routing is not normally recommended.

port
Indicates a port number (that is, the address of an application). If a number is not specified, the default TELNET port will be used. Once a connection has been opened, TELNET will enter the "input mode". TELNET will attempt to enable the TELNET LINEMODE option. If this fails, then TELNET will revert to one of two input modes: either the "character at a time" mode or the old "line by line" mode, depending on what the remote system supports.

When LINEMODE is enabled, character processing will be done on the local system while under the control of the remote system. When input editing or character echoing is to be disabled, the remote system will relay that information. The remote system will also relay changes to any special characters that happen on the remote system, so that they can take effect on the local system.

In the character at a time mode, most entered text will be sent immediately to the remote host for processing.

In the old line by line mode, all text will be echoed locally, but (normally) only completed lines will be sent to the remote host. The "local echo character" (initially "^E") may be used to enable and disable the local echo mode; normally, this would be used only for entering passwords so that the password will not be echoed.

If the LINEMODE option is enabled or if the localchars toggle is "TRUE" (the default value for the old line by line mode; see below), the user's quit, intr, and flush characters will be trapped locally and sent as TELNET protocol sequences to the remote machine. If LINEMODE had been enabled at any earlier time, then the user's susp and eof characters will also be sent as TEL-NET protocol sequences; quit will be sent as a TELNET ABORT instead of <Break>. There are options (see toggle autoflush and toggle autosynch below) which cause this action to flush any subsequent output to the terminal (until the remote host acknowledges the TELNET sequence) and to flush previous terminal input (in the case of quit and intr).

While connected to a remote host, the telnet command mode may be entered by typing the TELNET <Esc> (initially "^]").

When in command mode, the normal terminal editing conventions will be available.

The following TELNET commands are available, but only enough of each command need be typed to uniquely identify it (this is also true for arguments pertaining to the mode, toggle, set, unset, slc, environ, and display commands).

close
Close a TELNET session and return to command mode.

display argument...
Displays all, or some, of the set and toggle values (see description below).

mode [type]
Depending on the state of the TELNET session, the type argument is one of several available options. The remote host will be asked for permission to go into the requested mode. If the remote host is capable of entering that mode, the requested mode will be entered.

character
Disable the TELNET LINEMODE option; or, if the remote side does not understand the TELNET LINEMODE option, then enter the character at a time mode.

line
Enable the TELNET LINEMODE option; or, if the remote side does not understand the TELNET LINEMODE option, then attempt to enter the old line by line mode.

isig
-isig
Attempt to enable (disable) the TRAPSIG mode of the TELNET LINEMODE option. This requires that the LINEMODE option be enabled.

edit
-edit
Attempt to enable (disable) the EDIT mode of the LINEMODE option. This requires that the LINEMODE option be enabled.

softtabs
-softtabs
Attempt to enable (disable) the SOFT_TAB mode of the LINEMODE option. This requires that the LINEMODE option be enabled.

litecho
-litecho
Attempt to enable (disable) the LIT_ECHO mode of the LINEMODE option. This requires that the LINEMODE option be enabled.

?
Prints out help information for the mode command.
open host [user] [[—] port] [-a] [-l user]
Open a connection to the named host. If no port number is specified, telnet will attempt to contact a TELNET server at the default port. The host specification may be either a host name (see hosts(SFF)) or an Internet address specified in the "dot notation" (see inet(SLIB)). The -l or the -a option may be used to specify the user name to be passed to the remote system via the ENVIRON option. When connecting to a non-standard port, telnet will omit the automatic initiation of any TELNET options. When the port number is preceded by a minus sign, the initial option negotiation will be done as follows: After establishing a connection, the file .telnetrc in the user's home directory will be opened. Lines beginning with a "#" will be treated as comment lines; blank lines will be

ignored. Lines that begin without whitespace will be the start of a machine entry. The first thing on the line will be the name of the machine to which this host is being connected. The rest of the line—and successive lines which begin with whitespace—will be assumed to be telnet commands and will be processed as if they had been entered manually in response to the telnet command prompt.

quit
Close any open TELNET session and exit telnet. When in command mode, an End-of-File (EOF) will also close a session and exit.

send arguments
Sends one (or more) special character sequences to the remote host. The following are the arguments which may be specified (more than one argument may be specified at a given time):

abort
Sends the TELNET ABORT (ABORT processes) sequence.

ao
Sends the TELNET AO (Abort Output) sequence which should cause the remote system to flush all output from the remote system to the user's terminal.

ayt
Sends the TELNET AYT (Are You There?) sequence; the remote system may or may not choose to respond to this transmission.

brk
Sends the TELNET BRK (Break) sequence which may have significance to the remote system.

ec
Sends the TELNET EC (Erase Character) sequence which should cause the remote system to erase the last character entered.

el
Sends the TELNET EL (Erase Line) sequence which should cause the remote system to erase the line currently being entered.

eof
Sends the TELNET EOF (End Of File) sequence.

eor
Sends the TELNET EOR (End Of Record) sequence.

escape
Sends the current TELNET escape character (initially "^]").

ga
Sends the TELNET GA (Go Ahead) sequence, which probably has no significance to the remote system.

getstatus
If the remote side supports the TELNET STATUS command, getstatus will send the subnegotiation request that the server send its current option status.

ip
Sends the TELNET IP (Interrupt Process) sequence, which should cause the remote system to abort the currently running process.

nop
Sends the TELNET NOP (No Operation) sequence.

susp
Sends the TELNET SUSP (Suspend process) sequence.

synch
Sends the TELNET SYNCH sequence. This sequence causes the remote system to discard all previously typed (but not yet read) input. This sequence will be sent as TCP urgent data (and may not work if the remote system is a 4.2 BSD system; if it does not work, a lowercase "l" may be echoed on the terminal).

?
Prints out help information for the send command.

set argument value
unset argument value
The set command will set any one of a number of TELNET variables to a specific value or to "TRUE". The special value off will turn off the function associated with this variable; this is equivalent to using the unset command. The unset command will disable (or set to "FALSE") any of the specified functions. The values of variables may be interrogated with the aid of the display command. The variables which may be set or unset—but not toggled—are listed here. In addition, any of the variables for the toggle command may be explicitly enabled or disabled using the set and unset commands.

echo
This is the value (initially "^[") which, when in the line by line mode, will toggle between doing local echoing of entered characters (for normal processing) and suppressing echoing of entered characters (for example, for entering a password).

eof
If telnet is operating in LINEMODE or in the old line by line mode, entering this character as the first character on a line will cause this character to be sent to the remote system. The initial value of the "eof" character is taken to be the terminal's eof character.

erase
If telnet is in localchars mode (see "toggle" localchars below), and if telnet is operating in the character at a time mode, then when this character is entered, a TELNET EC sequence (see send ec above) will be sent to the remote system. The initial value for the erase character is taken to be the terminal's erase character.

escape
This is the TELNET escape character (initially "^]") which causes entry into the TELNET command mode when connected to a remote system.

flushoutput
If telnet is in localchars mode (see toggle localchars below) and the flushoutput character is entered, a TELNET AO sequence (see send ao above) will be sent to the remote host. The initial value for the flush character is taken to be the terminal's flush character.

interrupt
If TELNET is in localchars mode (see toggle localchars below) and the interrupt character is entered, a TELNET IP sequence (see send ip above) will be sent to the remote host. The initial value for the interrupt character is taken to be the terminal's intr character.

kill

If TELNET is in localchars mode (see toggle localchars below), and if TELNET is operating in the character at a time mode, then when this character is entered, a TELNET EL sequence (see send el above) will be sent to the remote system. The initial value for the kill character is taken to be the terminal's kill character.

lnext

If TELNET is operating in LINEMODE or in the old line by line mode, then this character is taken to be the terminal's lnext character. The initial value for the lnext character is taken to be the terminal's
lnext character.

quit

If TELNET is in localchars mode (see toggle localchars below) and the quit character is entered, a TELNET BRK sequence (see send brk above) will be sent to the remote host. The initial value for the quit character is taken to be the terminal's quit character.

reprint

If TELNET is operating in LINEMODE or in the old line by line mode, then this character is taken to be the terminal's reprint character. The initial value for the reprint character is taken to be the terminal's reprint character.

start

If the TELNET TOGGLE-FLOW-CONTROL option has been enabled, then this character is taken to be the terminal's start character. The initial value for the start character is taken to be the terminal's start character.

stop
If the TELNET TOGGLE-FLOW-CONTROL option has been enabled, then this character is taken to be the terminal's stop character. The initial value for the stop character is taken to be the terminal's stop character.

forw1
If TELNET is in the localchars mode, then this character is taken to be an alternate end of line character.

forw2
If TELNET is in the localchars mode, then this character is taken to be an alternate end of line character.

ayt
If TELNET is in the localchars mode, then this character is taken to be the alternate AYT character.

susp
If TELNET is in the localchars mode or if the LINEMODE is enabled and the suspend character is entered, a TELNET SUSP sequence (see send susp above) will be sent to the remote host. The initial value for the suspend character is taken to be the terminal's suspend character.

tracefile
This is the file to which the output generated by the netdata command will be written.

worderase
If TELNET is operating in LINEMODE or in the old line by line mode, then this character is taken to be the terminal's worderase

character. The initial value for the worderase character is taken to be the terminal's worderase character.

?

Displays the legal set and unset commands.

slc [state]

The slc command (Set Local Characters) sets (or changes) the state of the special characters when the TELNET LINEMODE option has been enabled. The "Special Characters" are characters that get mapped to TELNET commands sequences (like ip or quit) or line-editing characters (like erase and kill). By default, the "local special characters" are exported.

export

Switch to the local defaults for the "special characters". The local default characters are those of the local terminal at the time when telnet was started.

import

Switch to the remote defaults for the "special characters". The remote default characters are those of the remote system at the time when the TELNET connection was established.

check

Verify the current settings for the current "special characters". The remote side is requested to send all the current special character settings; if there are any discrepancies with the local side, the local side will switch to the set of remote values.

?

Prints out help information for the slc command.

environ [arguments [...]

The environ command manipulates the variables that may be sent through the TELNET ENVIRON option. The initial set of variables is taken from the user's environment; with only the LOGNAME and DISPLAY variables being exported.

The valid arguments for the environ command are:

define variable value

Define the variable to have a value of value. Any variables defined by this command are automatically exported. The value may be enclosed in single or double quotes so that tabs and embedded spaces may be included.

undefine variable

Remove variable from the list of environment variables.

export variable

Mark the variable to be exported to the remote side.

unexport variable

Mark the variable to not be exported unless explicitly requested by the remote side.

list

List the current set of environment variables. Those marked with a "*" will be sent automatically; any other variables will be sent only if requested explicitly.

send variable

Send environment variable.

?
Prints out help information for the environ command.

toggle arguments [...]
Toggle various flags (between "TRUE" and "FALSE") that control how TELNET responds to events. These flags may be set explicitly to "TRUE" or "FALSE" using the set and unset commands listed above. More than one argument may be specified. The state of these flags may be interrogated with the aid of the display command.
The valid arguments are:

autoflush
If autoflush and localchars are both "TRUE", then when the ao or the quit characters are recognized (and transformed into TELNET sequences; see set above for details), TELNET will refuse to display any data on the user's terminal until the remote system acknowledges (via a TELNET TIMING MARK option) that it has processed those TELNET sequences. The initial value for this toggle is "TRUE" if the terminal user had not executed an stty noflsh; otherwise "FALSE" (see stty(C)).

autosynch
If autosynch and localchars are both "TRUE", then when either the intr or quit character is entered (see set above for descriptions of the intr and quit characters), the resulting TELNET sequence sent will be followed by the TELNET SYNCH sequence. This procedure should cause the remote system to begin throwing away all previously entered input until both of the TELNET sequences have been read and acted upon. The initial value of this toggle is "FALSE".

binary
Enable or disable the TELNET BINARY option on both the input and output.

inbinary
Enable or disable the TELNET BINARY option on input.

outbinary
Enable or disable the TELNET BINARY option on output.

crlf
If this toggle value is "TRUE", then Carriage Returns will be sent as "<CR><LF>". If this is "FALSE", then Carriage Returns will be sent as "<CR><NUL>". The initial value for this toggle is "FALSE".

crmod
Toggle the Carriage Return mode. When this mode is enabled, most Carriage Return characters received from the remote host will be mapped into a Carriage Return followed by a Line Feed. This mode does not affect those characters entered by the user, but only those received from the remote host. This mode is not very useful unless the remote host only sends Carriage Return, but never any Line Feeds. The initial value for this toggle is "FALSE".

debug
Toggles the socket level debugging mode (useful only to root). The initial value for this toggle is "FALSE".

localchars
If this is "TRUE", then the flush, interrupt, quit, erase, and kill characters (see set above) are recognized locally and then transformed

into appropriate TELNET control sequences (respectively ao, ip, brk, ec, and el; see send above). The initial value for this toggle is "TRUE" in old line by line mode and "FALSE" in character at a time mode.

When the LINEMODE option is enabled, the value of localchars is ignored and assumed to always be "TRUE". If LINEMODE has ever been enabled, then quit will be sent as abort; eof and suspend will be sent as eof and susp; (see send above).

netdata
Toggles the display of all network data (in hexadecimal format). The initial value for this toggle is "FALSE".

options
Toggles the display of some internal telnet protocol processing which pertain to TELNET options. The initial value for this toggle is "FALSE".

prettydump
When the netdata toggle is enabled and if prettydump is enabled, the output from the netdata command will be reorganized into a more user-friendly format. Spaces will be put between each character in the output and the beginning of any TELNET escape sequence will be preceded by a "*" to aid in locating them.

skiprc
Toggle does not process ~/.telnetrc file. The initial value for this toggle is "FALSE".

termdata
Toggles printing of hexadecimal terminal data. The initial value for this toggle is "FALSE".

?

Displays the legal toggle commands.

<Ctrl>Z

Suspend telnet. This command will work only when the user is using csh(C) or ksh(C).

! [command]

Execute a single command in a subshell on the local system. If command is omitted, then an interactive subshell will be invoked.

status

Show the current status of telnet. This includes the peer to which one is connected, as well as the current mode.

? [command]

Get help. When no command is specified, telnet will print a summary for the help command. If a command is specified, telnet will print the help information for just that command.

Environment variables

The telnet command uses at least the following environment variables: HOME, SHELL, LOGNAME, DISPLAY, and TERM. Other environment variables may be propagated to the other side via the TELNET ENVIRON option.

Examples

connect to system:

```
telnet system
```

uucp   copy files from one Unix system to another Unix system

uucp [-c \ -C] [-d \ -f] [-jmr] [-g grade] [-n user] [-s file] [-x debug_level] source-file...destination-file
uulog [-s system] [-x]
uulog -f system [-number] [-x]
uuname [-l] [-c]

Options

uulog- query a log of uucp or uuxqt transactions

uuname- list names of systems known to uucp

uucp copies files named by the source-file arguments to the desti-nation-file argument. A filename may be a pathname on your machine, or may have the form:

system-name!pathname
where system-name is taken from a list of system names that uucp knows about. The system-name may also be a list of names such as

system-name!system-name!...!system-name!pathname
in which case an attempt is made to send the file via the specified route, to the destination. See "Limitations" below for restrictions. Care should be taken to ensure that intermediate nodes in the route are willing to forward information.

The shell metacharacters "?", "*" and [...] appearing in pathname will be expanded on the appropriate system.
Pathnames may be one of:

A full pathname.
A pathname preceded by ~user where user is a login name on the specified system and is replaced by that user's login directory.

A pathname preceded by ~/destination where destination is appended to /usr/spool/uucppublic; this destination will be treated as a filename unless more than one file is being transferred by this request or the destination is already a directory. To ensure that destination is a directory, follow the destination with a "/". For example, ~/dan/ as the destination will make the directory /usr/spool/uucppublic/dan if it does not exist and put the requested file(s) in that directory.
Anything else, which gets prefixed by the current directory.

If the result is an erroneous pathname for the remote system, the copy will fail. If the destination-file is a directory, the last part of the source-file name is used.

If a simple ~user destination is inaccessible to uucp, data is copied to a spool directory and the user is notified by mail(C).

uucp preserves execute permissions across the transmission and gives 0666 read and write permissions (see chmod(C)).

The following options are interpreted by uucp:

-c

Do not copy local file to the spool directory for transfer to the remote machine (default).

-C
Force the copy of local files to the spool directory for transfer.

-d
Make all necessary directories for the file copy (default).

-f
Do not make intermediate directories for the file copy.

-g grade
grade is a single letter/number; lower ASCII sequence characters will cause the job to be transmitted earlier during a particular conversation.

-j
Print the job identification ASCII string on standard output. This job identification can be used by uustat to obtain the status or terminate a job.

-m
Send mail to the requester when the copy is completed.
The -m option will only work when sending files or receiving a single file. Receiving multiple files specified by special shell characters "?", "*", [...] will not activate the -m option.

-n user
Notify user on the remote system that a file was sent.

-r
Do not start the file transfer, just queue the job.

-s file
Report status of the transfer to file. Note that the file must be a full pathname.

-x debug_level
Produce debugging output on standard output. The debug_level is a number between 0 and 9; higher numbers give more detailed information. uulog writes the status of uucp and uuxqt(ADM) transactions to the standard output. (It queries the transaction log files /usr/spool/uucp/.Log/uucico/system, or /usr/spool/uucp/.Log/uuxqt/system respectively.) By default, information is written about all known systems.

uulog has the following options:

-s system
Print information about file transfer operations for system only.

-f system
Continuously monitors the file transfer log for system and displays the output using tail -f. (You must press DELETE or BREAK to exit.)

-number
Indicates that tail should show number lines at a time. Used with the -f option.

-x
Look in the uuxqt log file for the given system, instead of the uucico log file (the default).

uuname lists the names of systems known to uucp. It takes the following options:

-c
Returns the names of systems known to cu instead of uucp. (The two lists are the same, unless your machine is using different Systems files for cu and uucp. See sysfiles(F).)

-l
Returns the local system name

Examples

copy file1 from system1 to file2 on system2:

```
uucp system1!file1 system2!file2
```

---

vacation   respond automatically to incoming mail messages from a canned file

vacation [-a alias] [-d] [-e exemption-file] [-f forward-id]
[-i forward-id] [-j] [-l logfile] [-M canned_msg_file]
[-m savefile]

vacation -n

Options

-a alias
The -a option allows you to add an additional name to check for
to allow a vacation message to be delivered. This is useful if multiple mailboxes are forwarded to one mailbox, or if a user's
account on one machine is forwarded to another machine.
Multiple -a options may be specified.

-d
The day's date will be appended to the filename specified by -m.

-e exemption-file
Specify a filename which contains a list of usernames to whom a
vacation message is not to be sent.

-f forwarding-id
The mail will be forwarded to this user id in addition to being
stored in the user's mailbox.

-i forwarding-id
The mail will be forwarded to this user id instead of being stored
in the user's mailbox. If both -f and -i are given, the mail will not
be stored in the user's mailbox.

-j
Do not check whether the recipient appears in the To:, Cc: or Bcc:
headers. In other words, send replies to users even if the mail is
not directly addressed to your login name or an alias for it.

-l logfile
File to keep track of which originators have already seen the
canned response. If not specified, it defaults to $HOME/.maillog.
The log file prevents the originator from seeing the vacation message multiple times.

-M canned_msg_file
File to send back as the canned response. Any occurrences of the
string $SUBJECT in the message file will be replaced with the subject
of the message being responded to. If canned_msg_file is not specified, it defaults to /usr/share/lib/mail/std_vac_msg, which contains:
Subject: AUTOANSWERED!!!
I am on vacation. I will read (and answer if necessary) your e-mail
message when I return.
This message was generated automatically and you will receive it
only once, although all messages you send me while I am away
WILL be saved.

-m savefile
Normally, the user's mailbox is used to store the mail. This option
allows a different filename to be specified. If the file cannot be
written, the user's mailbox will be used.

-n
Remove the vacation processing. It is equivalent to:
mail -F " "

---

wall   broadcast message from file or standard input to all logged
in users

/etc/wall [-g group] [file]

Options

wall is used to warn all users, for example, prior to shutting down the system.

If a group is specified using the -g option, wall sends a message only to that group.

The sender should be root to override any protections that users may have set on their terminal lines using mesg(C).

Examples

send "meeting in five minutes" to all users:

```
wall "meeting in five minutes"
```

---

write   display message to another user by copying batch lines from your screen to another screen

write user [tty]

Options

The write command copies lines from your terminal to that of another user. When first called, it sends the message:

Message from your-logname your-tty...

The recipient of the message should write back at this point. Communication continues until an end-of-file is read from the terminal or an interrupt is sent. At that point, write displays:

(end of message)

on the other terminal and exits.

If you want to write to a user who is logged in more than once, the tty argument may be used to indicate the appropriate terminal.

Permission to receive messages from other users of the system may be granted or denied by use of the mesg(C) command. By default, users are not allowed to receive messages (this is for security). This may be altered by issuing the mesg command from the .login script.

If the character "!" is found at the beginning of a line, write calls the shell to execute the rest of the line as a command. Output from the command is sent to the terminal; it is not sent to the remote user.

The following protocol is suggested for using write: when you first write to another user, wait for him or her to write back before starting to send. Each party should end each message with a distinctive signal ((o) for "over" is conventional), indicating that the other may reply; (oo) for "over and out" is suggested when conversation is to be terminated.

Return values
A return value of 0 indicates successful completion; a value of 1 indicates that an error occurred.

Examples

send message to user's screen:

```
write user
```

compare—overview

Methods for comparing files and/or directories

bdiff	compare two large files
cmp	compare two files displaying byte and line number
comm	compare two files displaying columnar listing
diff	compare two files
diff3	compare three files
diffmk	compare file versions
dircmp	compare two directories
sdiff	compare two files displaying side-by-side listing
uniq	compare lines within a file

compare

---

bdiff   compare files that are too large for diff to find differences between two files

bdiff file1 file2 [n] [-s]

Options

n
The number of lines bdiff splits each file into for processing. The default value is 3500. This is useful when 3500-line segments are too large for diff.

-s
Suppresses printing of bdiff diagnostics. Note that this does not suppress printing of diagnostics from diff.
If file1 (or file2) is a dash (-), the standard input is read.
The output of bdiff is exactly that of diff. Line numbers are adjusted to account for the segmenting of the files, and the output looks as if the files had been processed whole.

Examples

display differences between file1 and file2:

```
bdiff file1 file2
```

cmp   compare two files and display the byte and line number where the difference occurred

cmp [-l] [-s] file1 file2

Options

-l
Prints the byte number (decimal) and the differing bytes (octal) for each difference.

-s
Returns an exit code only, 0 for identical files, 1 for different files, and 2 for inaccessible or missing files.
cmp understands the—option delimiter.
This command should be used to compare binary files; use diff(C) or diff3(C) to compare text files.

Examples

compare file1 and file2:

```
cmp file1 file2
```

comm   compare two files and display column one containing lines only in first file, column two containing lines only in second file, and column three containing lines in both files

comm [-123] file1 file2

Options

comm reads file1 and file2, which should be ordered according to the collating sequence defined by the current locale (see sort(C)), and produces a three-column output: lines only in file1; lines only in file2; and lines in both files. The filename "-" means the standard input.

Flags 1, 2, or 3 suppress printing of the corresponding column. Thus comm -12 prints only the lines common to the two files; comm -23 prints only lines in the first file but not in the second; comm -123 is a no-op (does nothing).

comm understands the—option delimiter

Examples

compare file1 and file2:

```
comm file1 file2
```

diff   find difference between two files

diff [-br] [-c | -C n |-e | -f | -h] file1 file2

Options

-b
Ignores trailing blanks (spaces and tabs) and cause other strings of blanks to compare equal.

-c
Produces output in a form that provides three lines of context.

-C n
Produces output in a form that provides n lines of context.

-e

Produces a script of a, c, and d commands for the editor ed, which will recreate file2 from file1.

-f
Produces a similar script to -e, not useful with ed, and in the opposite order.

-h
Makes diff do a fast, less-rigorous job. This works only when changed stretches are short and well separated, but the files can be of unlimited length.

-r

Applies diff recursively to files and directories when file1 and file2 are directories.

Exit Values

Exit status is 0 for no differences, 1 for some differences, 2 for errors

Examples

display differences between file1 and file2:

```
diff file1 file2
```

---

diff3   find disagreeing ranges of text between three files

diff3 [-ex3] file1 file2 file3

Options

-e

Write a script for the editor ed(C) on the standard output that will incorporate into file1 all changes between file2 and file3, that is, the changes that normally would be flagged ==== and ====3.

-x
Write an ed script on the standard output to incorporate changes
flagged with ====.

-3
Write an ed script on the standard output to incorporate changes
flagged with ====3.

Examples

list differences between file1, file2, and file3:

```
diff3 file1 file2 file3
```

---

diffmk　compare two versions of a file creating a third version
that includes change marks for nroff and troff

/usr/ucb/diffmk oldfile newfile markedfile

Options

diffmk can also be used in conjunction with the proper troff
requests to produce program listings with marked changes. In the
following command line:
diffmk old.c new.c marked.c ; nroff reqs marked.c | pr

the file reqs contains the following troff requests:
.pl 1
.ll 77

.nf
.eo
.nh

which eliminate page breaks, adjust the line length, set no-fill mode, ignore escape characters, and turn off hyphenation, respectively.

If the characters | and * are inappropriate, you might run marked-file through sed to globally change them.

Examples

compare oldversion and newversion creating markedversion:

```
diffmk version1 version2 version3
```

---

dircmp   compare two directories and display various information about the directory contents

dircmp [-ds] [-wn] dir1 dir2

Options

-d
Performs a full diff(C) on each pair of like-named text files if they are not identical. If files differ that are neither text files nor empty, dircmp prints only the name and type (see file(C)).

-s
Suppresses output of identical filenames.

-wn
Prints the name of the files and directories being compared in two columns; each column is assigned a width of n/2. dircmp truncates pathnames that are too long to fit in a column. The default value of n is 72.

If the -d option is not specified, dircmp compares only text and empty files that are common to both directories

Examples

compare directory1 to directory2:

```
dircmp dir1 dir2
```

sdiff   produce a side-by-side listing of two files and indicate which lines are different

sdiff [options...] file1 file2

Options

-w n
Uses the next argument, n, as the width of the output line. The default line length is 130 characters.

-l
Only prints the left side of any lines that are identical.

-s
Does not print identical lines.

-o output
Uses the next argument, output, as the name of a third file that is created as a user-controlled merging of file1 and file2. Identical lines of file1 and file2 are copied to output. Sets of differences, as produced by diff(C), are printed where a set of differences share a common gutter character. After printing each set of differences, sdiff prompts the user with a % and waits for one of the following user-entered commands:

l
Appends the left column to the output file.

r
Appends the right column to the output file.

s
Turns on silent mode; does not print identical lines.

v
Turns off silent mode.

e l
Calls the editor with the left column.

e r
Calls the editor with the right column.

e b
Calls the editor with the concatenation of left and right.

e
Calls the editor with a zero length file.

q
Exits from the program. On exit from the editor, the resulting file is concatenated on the end of the output file.

Examples

display file1 and file2 indicating differences:

```
sdiff file1 file2
```

---

uniq   compare adjacent lines in a file and remove duplicate lines

uniq [-c | -d | -u] [-f fields] [-s chars] [-n] [+n] [input [output]]

Options

-n
The first n fields together with any blanks before each are ignored. A field is defined as a string of nonspace, nontab characters separated by tabs and spaces from its neighbors.

+n
The first n characters are ignored. Fields are skipped before characters.

-f fields
Same as -n, where n is fields.

-s chars
Same as +n, where n is chars.

Examples

remove adjacent duplicate lines from file:

```
uniq file file.new
```

compile-overview

Method for compiling files

make   execute a comand file called "makefile" or "Makefile"

compile

make   execute commands in a makefile to update one or more computer programs allowing a programmer to maintain and regenerate groups of programs

make [-f makefile] [-eiknpPqrstuw] [-b | -B] [names] [macro definitions]

Options

-f makefile
Description file name. makefile is assumed to be the name of a description file.

-e
Environment variables override assignments within makefiles.

-i
Ignore error codes returned by invoked commands. This mode is entered if the fake target name .IGNORE appears in the description file.

-k
Abandon work on the current entry if it fails, but continue on other branches that do not depend on that entry.

-n
No execute mode. Print commands, but do not execute them. Even lines beginning with an @ are printed.

-p
Print out the complete set of macro definitions and target descriptions.

-P
Update in parallel more than one target at a time. The number of targets updated concurrently is determined by the environment variable PARALLEL and the presence of .MUTEX directives in makefiles.

-q
Question. The make command returns a zero or non-zero status code depending on whether the target file is or is not up-to-date.

-r
Do not use the built-in rules.

-s
Silent mode. Do not print command lines before executing. This mode is also entered if the fake target name .SILENT appears in the description file.

-t
Touch the target files (causing them to be up-to-date) rather than issue the usual commands.

-u
Unconditionally make the target, ignoring all timestamps.

-w
Suppress warning messages. Fatal messages will not be affected.

-b
Compatibility mode for old makefiles; this is the default mode.

-B
Turn off compatibility mode for old makefiles.

Special targets
.DEFAULT
If a file must be made but there are no explicit commands or relevant built-in rules, the commands associated with the name .DEFAULT are used if it exists.

.IGNORE
Same effect as the -i option.

.MUTEX:
Serialize the updating of specified targets (see "Parallel make" below).

.PRECIOUS
Dependents of this target will not be removed when quit or interrupt are hit.

.SILENT
Same effect as the -s option.

Examples

lines from a sample makefile:

```
ARFILES = armast.o artrx.o
TXFILES = txmast.o txtrx.o
AR_MAIN.4ge:  ARMAIN.4gl $(ARFILES)  $(TXFILES)
c4gl   -o     AR_MAIN.4ge:  $(ARFILES)    $(TXFILES)
$(SRC)/library/lib.a
strip AR_MAIN.4ge
INSTALL:
mv AR_MAIN.4ge  /ar/executables
```

compress—overview

Methods for condensing a file

compress	condense a file and store in file.Z
uncompress	restore a file condensed with compress
pack	condense a file and store in file.z
unpack	restore a file condensed with pack
pcat	view a packed file
zcat	restore a file condensed with compress and keep the .Z file intact

compress

compress   condense a file and store the result in file.Z

compress [-cdfFqv] [-H | -b bits] [file | -P fd]

Options

compress deals with input and output files depending on the arguments specified:

file
compress reads file, compresses it, and places the output in a file of the same name with the suffix .Z appended. If the standard output is redirected (for example, into a pipe), compress sends its output to the standard output.

-P fd
compress reads a list of filenames from the pipe associated with the file descriptor fd. One filename is read from each successive 1K block of data in the pipe. Each filename is null terminated. Filenames are read until a null character is encountered at the beginning of a block or the pipe is closed. Each file is then compressed. The output files have the same name as, and overwrite, the original files. This option can also be used with uncompress.

The following options are available from the command line:

-b bits
Specifies the maximum number of bits to use in encoding.

-c
Writes output on the standard output and does not remove original file.

-d
Decompresses a compressed file.

-f
Overwrites previous output file. Writes output file even if compression saves no space.

-F
Overwrites previous output file. Writes output file even if compression saves no space.

-H
Compresses a file by approximately a further 20% based on the LZH algorithm. uncompress(C) automatically detects when files have been compressed with this option and processes them accordingly.

-q
Generates no output except error messages, if any.

-v
Prints the name of the file being compressed, and the percentage of compression achieved. With uncompress, the name of the uncompressed file is printed.

Limitations

The -P option is provided for internal use by tar(C).

The -v option is not compatible with the -c option.

compress uses a version of Lempel-Ziv encoding to reduce the redundancy of information stored in files. A variable length sequence of bits is used to represent each character string encountered in the file; in general, the more frequently the string occurs, the less bits are used to represent it. The ratio of the size of the compressed file to the size of the uncompressed original depends on the type of file. Database files tend to shrink dramatically, while short files or some binaries may shrink very little.

Decompression is controlled by a two byte magic number at the start of a compressed file: this is 1F 9D for a standard (Lev Zimpel Welch) compressed file, and 1F A0 for a LZH (Lev Zimpel Huffman) compressed file. Implementations of compress on other systems may not recognize LZH compressed files.

Examples

condense file1 and store the result in file.Z:

```
compress file1
```

---

uncompress   restore a file condensed using compress command

uncompress [-cfFqv] [file | -P fd]

Options

uncompress restores a previously compressed file to its uncompressed state and removes the compressed version.

-P fd
compress reads a list of filenames from the pipe associated with the file descriptor fd. One filename is read from each successive 1K block of data in the pipe. Each filename is null terminated. Filenames are read until a null character is encountered at the beginning of a block or the pipe is closed. Each file is then compressed. The output files have the same name as, and overwrite, the original files. This option can also be used with uncompress

The following options are available from the command line:

-b bits
Specifies the maximum number of bits to use in encoding.

-c
Writes output on the standard output and does not remove original file.

-d
Decompresses a compressed file.

-f
Overwrites previous output file. Writes output file even if compression saves no space.

-F
Overwrites previous output file. Writes output file even if compression saves no space.

-H
Compresses a file by approximately a further 20% based on the LZH algorithm. uncompress(C) automatically detects when files have been compressed with this option and processes them accordingly.

-q
Generates no output except error messages, if any.

-v
Prints the name of the file being compressed, and the percentage of compression achieved. With uncompress, the name of the uncompressed file is printed.

Examples

restore file1 from file1.Z:

```
uncompress file1
(the .Z is implied)
```

---

pack   condense a file and store the result in file.z

pack [-f] [—] name...

Options

pack uses Huffman (minimum redundancy) codes on a byte-by-byte basis.

The -f option forces packing of all files to ensure consistency in a directory.

If the "-" argument is used, an internal flag is set that causes pack to display information about the file compression. Additional occurrences of "-" in place of name will cause the internal flag to be set and reset.

The amount of compression obtained depends on the size of the input file and the character frequency distribution. Because a decoding tree forms the first part of each .z file, it is usually not worthwhile to pack files smaller than three blocks, unless the character frequency distribution is very scattered, which may occur with printer plots or pictures.

Typically, text files are reduced to 60-75% of their original size. Load modules, which use a larger character set and have a more uniform distribution of characters, show little compression, the packed versions being about 90% of the original size.

Examples

condense file1 and store in file1.z:

```
pack file1
```

unpack   restore a file condensed with the pack command

unpack name...

Options

unpack expands files created by pack. For each file name specified in the command, a search is made for a file called name.z (or just name, if name ends in .z). If this file appears to be a packed file, it is replaced by its expanded version. The new file has the .z suffix stripped from its name, and has the same access modes, access and modification dates, and owner as those of the packed file.

Examples

restore file1.z to file1:

```
unpack file1
```

pcat   view a packed file

pcat name...

Options

pcat does for packed files what cat(C) does for ordinary files. The specified files are unpacked and written to the standard output. Enter pcat name.z or just pcat name to view the packed file name.z.

Examples

view packed file1.z

```
pcat file1
```

---

zcat   uncompress a file condensed with compress to standard output and keep the .Z file intact

zcat file

Options

The following options are available from the command line:

-b bits
Specifies the maximum number of bits to use in encoding.

-c
Writes output on the standard output and does not remove original file.

-d
Decompresses a compressed file.

-f
Overwrites previous output file. Writes output file even if compression saves no space.

-F
Overwrites previous output file. Writes output file even if compression saves no space.

-H
Compresses a file by approximately a further 20% based on the LZH algorithm. uncompress(C) automatically detects when files have been compressed with this option and processes them accordingly.

-q
Generates no output except error messages, if any.

-v
Prints the name of the file being compressed, and the percentage of compression achieved. With uncompress, the name of the uncompressed file is printed.

Examples

uncompress file1.Z to standard output and do not change file1.Z:

```
zcat file1.Z
```

concatenate—overview

Method for joining more than one file

cat   display content of file to standard output

concatenate

cat   display contents of file to standard output

cat [-u] [-s] [-v] [-t] [-e] file...

Options

-s
Suppresses warnings about nonexistent files.

-u
Causes the output to be unbuffered.

-v
Causes non-printing characters (with the exception of tabs, new-lines, and form feeds) to be displayed. Control characters are displayed as ^X (<Ctrl>x), where X is the key pressed with the <Ctrl> key (for example, <Ctrl>m is displayed as ^M). The <Del> character (octal 0177) is printed as ^?. Non-ASCII characters (with the high bit set) are printed as M -x, where x is the character specified by the seven low order bits.

-t
Causes tabs to be printed as ^I and form feeds as ^L. This option is ignored if the -v option is not specified.

-e
Causes a "$" character to be printed at the end of each line (prior to the new-line). This option is ignored if the -v option is not set.

Examples

display file1 to standard output:

```
cat file1
```

copy—overview

Methods for duplicating a file

cp   copy a file or files
cut   copy from one location and place in a new location
dd   copy an input file to output with conditional and
            conversion capabilities
rcp   copy a file or files when one exists on a remote system
            see backup

copy

cp   copy a file to a new file name or a different directory. Also copy multiple files to a different directory

cp [-fip] source_file target_file

cp [-fip] source_file1 source_file2...target

cp -R [-fip] source_file1 source_file2...target

cp -r [-fip] source_file1 source_file2...target

Options

-f
If the destination file exists but is not writeable, it is unlinked before copying is performed. Any hard links to the file are lost. (This option forces cp to overwrite existing files.)

-i
Before attempting to copy to an existing file, cp prompts for confirmation. The copy operation is not performed unless the user types an affirmative.

-p
When copying, cp tries to transfer the following characteristics from each source file to the corresponding destination file:

Time of last modification and access

User and group ID

File permission bits

-r
Copies file hierarchies recursively.

-R
Copies file hierarchies recursively. Also permits copying of device nodes and named pipes. (The copy of a device node or pipe is assigned the file permissions of the source file, subject to the user's UMASK setting, unless the -p option is applied).

Examples

copy file1 to file2:

```
cp file1 file2
```

copy file1 from /usr1 to /usr2 when current directory is /usr1:

```
cp file1 /usr2
(result:  file1 will exist in /usr1 and /usr2)
```

copy file1 from /usr1 to /usr2 when current directory is /usr2:

```
cp /usr1/file1 .
(result:  file1 will exist in /usr1 and /usr2)
```

cut   copy from one location and place in a new location

cut -b list [-n] [file...]

cut -c list [file...]

cut -f list [-d char] [-s] [file...]

Options

The list is a comma-separated list of integers (in increasing order).
It can be tab or blank-separated if it is enclosed in quotes. A dash
(-) can be used to indicate ranges, for example:

1,3,7
fields 1, 3, and 7

2-4,8
fields 2, 3, 4, and 8

-4,10
equivalent to 1-4,10

2-
equivalent to the second through last field
cut understands the following options:

-b list
list specifies byte positions. For example, -b 1-100 cuts the first 100 bytes of each line. Each selected byte will be output unless explicitly suppressed by the -n option).

-c list
list specifies character positions. For example, -c 1-72 would keep the first 72 characters of each line.

-f list
list specifies fields assumed to be separated in the file by a delimiter character (see -d). For example, -f 1,7 copies the first and seventh field only. Lines with no field delimiters will be passed through intact (useful for table subheadings), unless -s is specified.

-d char
The character following -d is the field delimiter (-f option only). Default is Tab. Space or other characters with special meaning to the shell must be quoted.

-n
Do not split characters. Used in conjunction with the -b option as in the following example:

cut -b 1-100 -n file
Here 1 is the low byte and 100 is the high byte. If the low byte is not the first byte of a character, its value will be decremented by 1 so that the first byte of a character is selected. Similarly, if the specified high byte is not the last byte of a character, its value will be decremented by 1 so that the selected byte becomes the last byte of the character prior to the character selected on the command line.

-s

If the -f option is used, -s suppresses lines with no delimiter characters. Unless specified, lines with no delimiters will be passed through untouched.

One of the options -b, -c or -f must be specified.

Examples

cut data in column 1-100 located in file1 and place it in file.new:

```
cut -c1-100 file1 >  file.new
```

---

dd　copy an input file to output with conditional and conversion capabilities

dd [option=value]...

Options

if=file

Input filename; standard input is default.

of=file

Output filename; standard output is default. This option truncates an existing file to zero bytes in length unless conv=notrunc is specified.

ibs=n

Input block size is n bytes (default is BSIZE block size).

obs=n
Output block size (default is BSIZE block size).

bs=n
Sets both input and output block size, superseding ibs and obs. If no conversion is specified, it is particularly efficient since no in-core copy needs to be done.

cbs=n
Conversion buffer size.

skip=n
Skips n input records before starting copy. (The records are read but not output.)

seek=n
Seeks n records from beginning of output file before copying.

lseek=n
Same as skip, but seeks over the records (that is, uses lseek(S)) instead of reading them.

oseek=n
As for seek.

files=n
Specify the number of input files to concatenate. This option effectively causes a sequence of n EOFs to be ignored. (It is generally only useful for tape.)

conv=block
Convert ASCII to unblocked ASCII.

conv=unblock
Convert unblocked ASCII to ASCII.

count=n
Copies only n input records.

conv=ascii
Converts EBCDIC to ASCII.

conv=ebcdic
Converts ASCII to EBCDIC.

conv=ibm
Slightly different map of ASCII to EBCDIC.

conv=immap
Input is to be memory mapped. (Input must be a regular file or block special device.)

conv=lcase
Maps alphabetic characters to lowercase.

conv=mmap
Input and output are to be memory mapped. (Both input and output must be a regular file or block special device.)

conv=ommap
Output is to be memory mapped. (Both input and output must be a regular file or block special device.)

conv=ucase
Maps alphabetic characters to uppercase.

conv=swab
Swaps every pair of bytes.

conv=noerror
Does not stop processing on an error.

conv=notrunc
Do not truncate the output file. dd preserves existing blocks in the output file that are not written to explicitly.

conv=sync
Pads every input record to ibs.

conv=...,...
Several comma-separated conversions.
Where sizes are specified, a number of bytes is expected. A number may end with k, b, or w to specify multiplication by 1024, 512, or 2 respectively; a pair of numbers may be separated by x to indicate a product.
cbs is used only if ascii, ebcdic, or ibm conversion is specified. In the former case, cbs characters are placed into the conversion buffer, converted to ASCII, and trailing blanks trimmed and newline added before sending the line to the output. In the latter two cases, ASCII characters are read into the conversion buffer, converted to EBCDIC, and blanks added to make up an output record of size cbs.

After completion, dd reports the number of whole and partial input and output blocks.

Examples

copy file1 to file2 converting all lowercase to uppercase:

```
dd if=file1 of=file2 conv=ucase
```

---

rcp   copy a file or files to or from a remote system

rcp [-p] file1 file2

rcp [-p] [-r] file...directory

Options

If the -r option is specified and any of the source files are directories, rcp copies each subtree rooted at that name; in this case the destination must be a directory.

By default, the mode and owner of file2 are preserved if it already existed; otherwise, the mode of the source file modified by the umask on the destination host is used. (See umask(C) for a description of umasks.) The -p option causes rcp to attempt to preserve (duplicate) in its copies the modification times and modes of the source files, ignoring the umask.

If path is not a full path name, it is interpreted relative to your login directory on rhost. A path on a remote host may be quoted (using \, ", or ´) so that the metacharacters are interpreted remotely. See sh(C) for quoting rules.

rcp does not prompt for passwords; if the user account requires a password, your current local user name must exist on rhost and allow remote command execution via rcmd(TC).

If an account has no password, any user can use rcmd or rcp commands to access that account. In this case, an entry in /etc/hosts.equiv or in a .rhosts file is not required.

rcp handles third-party copies, where neither source nor target files are on the current machine. Hostnames may also take the form "rname@rhost" to use rname rather than the current user name on the remote host.

Examples

copy file1 from system1 to system2 current directory when current system is system2:

```
rcp:system1/file1 .
```

count—overview

Methods for displaying file size information

size	display number of file bytes
sum	display file checksum and number of file blocks
wc	display number of file bytes, words, and lines

count

size   display number of file bytes

size [-F -f -n -o -V -x] files

Options

If size cannot calculate either segment or section information, it prints an error message and stops processing the file.

-F
Prints out the size of each loadable segment, the permission flags of the segment, then the total of the loadable segment sizes. If there is no segment data, size prints an error message and stops processing the file.

-f
Prints out the size of each allocatable section, the name of the section, and the total of the section sizes. If there is no section data, size prints out an error message and stops processing the file.

-n
Prints out non-loadable segment or non-allocatable section sizes. If segment data exists, size prints out the memory size of each loadable segment or file size of each non-loadable segment, the permission flags, and the total size of the segments. If there is no segment data, size prints out, for each allocatable and non-allocatable section, the memory size, the section name, and the total size

of the sections. If there is no segment or section data, size prints an error message and stops processing.

-o
Prints numbers in octal, not decimal.

-V
Prints the version information for the size command on the standard error output.

-x
Prints numbers in hexadecimal; not decimal.

Examples

display hexadecimal number of bytes of file1:

```
size -x file1
```

---

sum   display file checksum and number of file blocks (512 bytes)

sum [-lr] [file...]

Options

-l
Print a long (32-bit) checksum. (The default is to print a short (16-bit) checksum.)

-r
Use an alternate (older) algorithm to compute the checksum. This alternate algorithm is sensitive to the order of the bytes in the data; the standard algorithm is not.
sum is typically used to validate data after being transported across unreliable media. It is also useful when you want to reduce the contents of a file into a representative value.

Examples

display the checksum and number of blocks for file1:

sum file1

---

wc   display number of file bytes, words, and lines contained in a file. This command is useful in conjuction with other commands which produce output that needs to be counted.

wc [-lw] [-c | -m] [file...]

Options

The options -l, -w, and -c or -m may be used in any combination to specify that a subset of newline characters, words, and bytes or characters (respectively) are to be reported. The default options are -lwm.

The order and number of output columns are not affected by the order and number of options. There is always at most one column in the following order: number of newline characters, words, bytes, and filename. The filename is not present if one or no filename is given on the command line.

If more than one filename is given on the command line, the final line contains the total number of newline characters, words and bytes in all files, and is labeled with the word total in the filename column.

Examples

display the number of lines in file1:

```
wc -l file1
```

display the number of files/directories in the current directory: (count includes the . directory)

```
l | wc -l
```

date—overview

Methods for printing or setting the date

ca   print a calendar for a month or year
calendar display lines in the calendar file with the current date
date   print or set the date

date

cal   print a calendar for a month or year to standard output

cal [[month] year]

Options

The cal command prints a Gregorian calendar for the specified year. If a month is also specified, a calendar for that month only is printed. If no arguments are specified, the current, previous, and following months are printed, along with the current date and time. The year must be a number between 1 and 9999; month must be a number between 1 and 12 or enough characters to specify a particular month. For example, May must be given to distinguish it from March, but S is sufficient to specify September. If only a month string is given, only that month of the current year is printed.

Examples

print a calendar for November, 2005:

```
cal 11 2005
```

calendar   display lines in the user-defined calendar file (current directory) with the current date

calendar [—]

Options

calendar consults the file calendar in the user's current directory and mails the user lines that contain today's or tomorrow's date. Most reasonable month-day dates, such as Sep. 14, september 14, and 9/14, are recognized, but not 14 September, or 14/9.

On weekends, "tomorrow" extends through Monday. Lines that contain the date of a Monday will be sent to the user on the previous Friday. This is not true for holidays.

When an argument is present, calendar does its job for every user who has a file calendar in his login directory. Normally this is done daily, in the early morning, under the control of cron(C).

---

date   display or set the date with format options

date [-u] [+format]

date [-u] [MMDDhhmm[YY] | -t [CC]YYMMDDhhmm[.SS]]

Options

If no argument is given, or if the output format is specified following +, the current date and time are printed as defined by the locale. Otherwise, you may set the date and time if you are the super user.
date normally performs its calculations taking care of the conversion to and from local standard and daylight time.

The -u option, if specified, causes operations to be performed as if the current time zone is Greenwich Mean Time (the environment variable TZ is set to GMT0).

When setting the date and time, you can specify it in the form MMDDhhmm[YY] where:

MM
month (01-12)

DD
day of month (01-31)

hh
hour in the 24-hour system (00-23)

mm
minute (00-59)

YY
last 2 digits of the year (optional)
If you use the -t option, you can also optionally specify the century and the second using the form [CC]YYMMDDhhmm[.SS] where:

CC
century (00-99)

SS
second (00-59)
For example, date 10080045 sets the date to Oct 8, and the time to 12:45 AM, if the local language is set to English. The current year is taken by default if no year is specified.

If the argument begins with +, the output of date is under the control of the user. The format for the output is similar to that of the first argument to printf(S). All output fields are of fixed size (zero padded if necessary). Each field descriptor begins with a percent sign "%" and is replaced in the output by its corresponding value. A single percent sign may be output if it is quoted with another percent sign, that is, by specifying "%%". All other characters are copied to the output without change. The string is always terminated with a newline character. Extra newlines may be produced using the descriptor "%n".

Field descriptors

%%
quoted percent sign

%a
abbreviated weekday, as defined by the locale (for example, Sun to Sat)

%A
full weekday name, as defined by the locale

%b
abbreviated month name, as defined by the locale

%B
full month name, as defined by the locale

%c
current date and time, as defined by the locale

%C
century as a decimal number, 00 to 99

%d
day of month, 01 to 31

%D
date as MM/DD/YY

%e
day of month as a decimal number, in range 01 to 31 (in a two
digit field with numbers less than 10 preceded by a zero)

%h
abbreviated month, as defined by the locale (for example, Jan to
Dec)

%H
hour, 00 to 23

%I
hour (12-hour clock), 01 to 12

%j
day of the year, 001 to 366

%m
month of year, 01 to 12

%M
minute, 00 to 59

%n
inserts a newline character

%p
equivalent of AM or PM for current locale

%r
time in AM/PM notation

%S
second, 00 to 59

%t
inserts a tab character

%T
time as hh:mm:SS

%u
week day as a decimal number, with Monday represented by day 1

%U
week number of the year (Sunday as the first day of the week) as a decimal number in the range 00 to 53. (All days in a new year preceding the first Sunday are considered to be in week 0.)

%V
week number of the year (Monday as the first day of the week) as a decimal number in the range 01 to 53. If the week containing January 1 has four or more days in the new year, then it is

considered week 1; otherwise it is week 53 of the previous year, and the next week is week 1.

%w
day of the week, with Sunday represented by 0

%W
week number of the year (Monday as the first day of the week) as a decimal number in the range 00 to 53. (All days in a new year preceding the first Sunday are considered to be in week 0.)

%x
current date, as defined by the locale

%X
current time, as defined by the locale

%y
year (offset from %C) as a decimal number in the range 00 to 99

%Y
year (including century), as decimal numbers

%Z
timezone name, or no characters if no timezone exists

Examples

display the current date and time:

```
date
```

set a variable $DAT_ENV to date in mm/dd/yyyy format:

```
DATE_ENV=`date '+%Y%m%d'`          ;export DATE_ENV
```

delete—overview

Methods for removing files or directories

rm   remove a file or files
rmdir   remove an empty directory, directory with files,
            or recursive directories and files

delete

rm   remove a file or multiple files from the existing directory or a specified directory

rm [-firR] file...

Options

rm will not delete directories unless the -r option is used.

The following options are recognized:

-f
When invoked with the -f option rm does not prompt the user for confirmation for files on which the user does not have write permission. The files are simply removed. Any previous occurrences of the -i option on the command line are ignored. This option only applies if rm is invoked with its standard input attached to a terminal.
If -f is not specified and the user does not have write permission on the target file, the user is prompted for confirmation. The file's name and permissions are printed and a line is read from the standard input. If that line begins with a "y" the file is deleted; otherwise it remains.

-i
The -i (interactive) option causes rm to ask whether to delete each file, and if the -r or -R option is in effect, whether to examine each directory.

-r

The -r (recursive) option causes rm to recursively delete the entire contents of the any directories specified, and the directories themselves. Symbolic links encountered with this option will not be traversed. Note that the rmdir(C) command is a safer way of removing directories.

-R

Equivalent to -r.

The special option "—" can be used to delimit options. For example, a file named "-f" could not be removed by rm because the hyphen is interpreted as an option; the command rm -f would do nothing, since no file is specified. Using rm—-f removes the file successfully

Examples

delete files file1, file2, and file3:

```
rm file1 file2 file3
```

---

rmdir   remove an empty directory, directory with files, or recursive directories and files

rmdir [-p] [-s] dirname...

Options

rmdir takes the following options:

-p
recursively remove the directory dirname and those of its parent directories that become empty when a subdirectory is removed. (For example, if a series of empty nested directories exist, the -p option removes the deepest subdirectory and all its parent directories until a non-empty directory is reached.) A message is printed on standard output if the whole path is removed or part of the path remains for some reason.

-s
suppress the message printed on standard error when -p is in effect.
rmdir will refuse to remove the root directory of a mounted filesystem

Examples

delete directory directory1 only if it is empty:

```
rmdir  directory1
```

delete directory directory1 and its contents recursively:

```
rm -r  directory1
```

directory—overview

Methods for creating, removing, and navigating within directory structures

cd	change directory
mkdir	make a new directory
pwd	print working directory
rmdir	remove a directory
	directory summary

directory

---

cd   change current directory to be the specified directory

cd [directory]

Options

Wildcard designators will work with the cd command.

Built-in versions
cd is built in as part of the shell since the new working directory must be set in the current shell.
Both ksh(C) and csh(C) recognize cd ~user to mean change to the home directory of a specified user. The command cd ~ changes to the directory specified by the environment variable HOME.

ksh(C) and sh(C) implement the following cd functionality:

If the specified directory does not exist and it does not begin with /, ".", or "..", cd searches for a match to directory in the colon-separated list of pathnames held by the environment variable CDPATH. The working directory is set to the first match found. Note that ksh(C) includes the following extensions to cd:

The absolute pathname of the old working directory is saved in the environment variable OLDPWD; PWD is set to the absolute pathname of the new working directory.

The command cd—changes the working directory to the value of OLDPWD. The pathname of the new working directory is written to the standard output if successful.

The version of cd built into the Bourne, C, and Korn shells supports the -L and -P flags for following logical or physical paths. The default behavior for ksh(C) is to follow logical paths. The default behavior for csh(C) and sh(C) is to follow physical paths.

Software storage objects (SSOs) preserve the traditional directory structure and filenames by using symbolic links to point to the real files which are maintained in the /var and /opt/var directory hierarchies (see hierarchy(M)). Using the -L option to the version of cd built into the Bourne and C shells allows you to traverse the traditional directory structure while hiding the details of the implementation of SSOs.

Examples

change directory to /usr1 from any other directory:

```
cd /usr1
```

change directory to the parent of the current directory:

```
cd ..
```

change directory to user home directory:

```
cd
```

change directory to /usr1/directory2 from current directory of /usr1:

```
cd directory2
```

change to parent directory of parent directory (two levels up):

```
cd ../..
```

---

mkdir   make a new directory

mkdir [-ep] [-m mode] dirname...

Options

mkdir accepts the following options:

-e
For historical compatibility, mkdir changes the ownership of the new directory to the real user ID (RUID) and the real group ID (RGID). The -e option says to use the effective user ID (EUID) and effective group ID (EGID) instead.

-m mode
This option allows users to specify the mode to be used for new directories. Choices for modes can be found in chmod(C).

-p
With this option, mkdir creates dirname by creating all the non-existing parent directories first. Any intermediate directories that do not exist are created with mode 777 altered by umask(C). However, to ensure that mkdir does not fail, the user execute and write permissions are always set.

Examples

create the directory directory2 in the current directory:

```
mkdir directory2
```

created the directory /usr1/directory2 from any directory:

```
mkdir /usr1/directory2
```

---

pwd   print the name of the current working directory

pwd

Options

pwd prints the absolute pathname of the current working directory. cd(C) sets the environment variable PWD to this pathname.

Examples

display current directory path:

pwd

---

rmdir   remove an empty child directory from the parent directory

rmdir [-p] [-s] dirname...

Options

rmdir takes the following options:

-p
recursively remove the directory dirname and those of its parent directories that become empty when a subdirectory is removed. (For example, if a series of empty nested directories exist, the -p option removes the deepest subdirectory and all its parent directories until a non-empty directory is reached.) A message is printed on standard output if the whole path is removed or part of the path remains for some reason.

-s
suppress the message printed on standard error when -p is in effect.
rmdir will refuse to remove the root directory of a mounted filesystem.

Examples

remove the empty directory /usr1/directory2 when current directory is /usr1:

```
rmdir directory2
```

remove the directory /usr1/directory2 and its contents when current directory is /usr1:

```
rm -r  directory2
```

---

directory summary

The directory structure is a tree of top-down directories with the root directory at the highest level. Each directory created under the root directory is a subdirectory which may contain many subdirectories and files.   The tree structure is the pathname that must be used to reference the location of a file or directory. Environment variables may be created to easily reference pathnames. Certain directory structures which are used frequently should be included in the .profile $PATH variable to automate the reference process.

display—overview

Methods for displaying text to a terminal screen

clear   clear screen
echo   display text to screen

display

clear   remove text from screen leaving the command prompt in upper left hand corner

clear [term]

Options

The clear command clears the screen. If term is not specified, the terminal type is obtained from the TERM environment variable. Standard output may be redirected to another terminal to clear its screen. You must have write permission on the other terminal for the command to take effect. The term parameter must be supplied if the terminal is of a different type than the one from which the command is issued.

If a video terminal does not have a clear screen capability, newlines are output to scroll the screen clear. If the standard output is a hardcopy, the paper is advanced to the top of the next page.

Examples

clear screen:

```
clear
```

echo   display text to the screen

echo [-n] [arg]...

Options

echo also understands C-like escape conventions; beware of conflicts with the shell's use of "\":

\a
alert character (for example, ASCII BEL)

\b
backspace

\c
ignore all subsequent arguments, and do not output a newline

\f
form-feed

\n
new line

\r
carriage return

\t
tab

\v
vertical tab

\\
backslash

\0n
The 8-bit character whose ASCII code is a 1, 2 or 3-digit octal
number n. For example:

echo \07
echoes <Ctrl>g

echo \007
also echoes <Ctrl>g

echo \065
echoes the number "5"

echo \0101
echoes the letter "A"
For the octal equivalents of each character, see ascii(M).
The echo command is useful for producing diagnostics in command files and for sending known data into a pipe.

A version of this command is built into ksh(C) and sh(C).

Examples

display this is a test to the screen:

```
echo "this is a test"
```

duplicates—overview

Method for removing duplicates

uniq   remove duplicate lines of a file duplicates

duplicates

uniq   compare adjacent lines in a file and remove duplicate lines

uniq [-c | -d | -u] [-f fields] [-s chars] [-n] [+n] [input [output]]

Options

Note that repeated lines must be adjacent in order to be found; see sort(C). If the -u flag is used, just the lines that are not repeated in the original file are output. The -d option specifies that one copy of just the repeated lines is to be written. The normal mode output is the union of the -u and -d mode outputs.

The -c option supersedes -u and -d and generates an output report in default style but with each line preceded by a count of the number of times it occurred.

The other arguments specify skipping an initial portion of each line in the comparison:

-n
The first n fields together with any blanks before each are ignored. A field is defined as a string of nonspace, nontab characters separated by tabs and spaces from its neighbors.

+n
The first n characters are ignored. Fields are skipped before characters.

-f fields
Same as -n, where n is fields.

-s chars
Same as +n, where n is chars.

Examples

remove adjacent duplicate lines from file:

```
uniq file file.new
```

editors—overview

Methods for editing files

ed	text editor
edit	text editor
ex	line text editor
vi	text editor

editors

ed edit file with the standard text editor

ed [—] [-p string] [file]

red [—] [-p string] [file]

Options

red is a restricted version of ed. It will only allow editing of files in the current directory. It prohibits executing sh(C) commands via the ! command. red displays an error message on any attempt to bypass these restrictions.

In general, red does not allow commands like !date or !sh.

Furthermore, red will not allow pathnames in its command line. For example, the command red /etc/passwd causes an error when the current directory is not /etc.

The options to ed are:

-

Suppresses the printing of character counts by the e, r, and w commands, of diagnostics from e and q commands, and the "!" prompt after a ! shell command.

-p
Allows the user to specify a prompt string.

ed supports formatting capability. After including a format speci-fication as the first line of file and invoking ed with your terminal in stty-tabs or sttytab3 mode (see stty(C)), the specified tab stops will automatically be used when scanning file. For example, if the first line of a file contained: <:t5,10,15 s72:> tab stops would be set at columns 5, 10, and 15, and a maximum line length of 72 would be imposed.

NOTE: While inputing text, tab characters are expanded to every eighth column as the default.

Commands to ed have a simple and regular structure: zero, one, or two addresses followed by a single-character command, possi-bly followed by parameters to that command. These addresses specify one or more lines in the buffer. Every command that requires addresses has default addresses, so that the addresses can very often be omitted.

In general, only one command may appear on a line. Certain com-mands allow the input of text. This text is placed in the appropri-ate place in the buffer. While ed is accepting text, it is said to be in input mode. In this mode, no commands are recognized; all input is merely collected. Input mode is left by entering a period (.) alone at the beginning of a line.

ed supports a limited form of regular expression notation; regular expressions are used in addresses to specify lines and in some com-mands (for example, s) to specify portions of a line that are to be substituted. A regular expression specifies a set of character strings. A member of this set of strings is said to be matched by the regular expression. The regular expressions allowed by ed are constructed in accordance with the guidelines detailed in regexp(M).

To understand addressing in ed, it is necessary to know that there is a current line at all times. Generally speaking, the current line is the last line affected by a command; the exact effect on the current line is discussed under the description of each command. Addresses are constructed as follows:

The character "." addresses the current line.

The character "$" addresses the last line of the buffer.

A decimal number n addresses the n-th line of the buffer.

'x addresses the line marked with the mark name character x, which must be a lowercase letter. Lines are marked with the k command described below.

A regular expression enclosed by slashes (/) addresses the first line found by searching forward from the line following the current line toward the end of the buffer and stopping at the first line containing a string matching the regular expression. If necessary, the search wraps around to the beginning of the buffer and continues up to and including the current line, so that the entire buffer is searched.

A regular expression enclosed in question marks (?) addresses the first line found by searching backward from the line preceding the current line toward the beginning of the buffer and stopping at the first line containing a string matching the regular expression. If necessary, the search wraps around to the end of the buffer and continues up to and including the current line. See also the last paragraph before "Files" below.

An address followed by a plus sign (+) or a minus sign (-) followed by a decimal number specifies that address plus or minus the indicated number of lines. The plus sign may be omitted.

If an address begins with "+" or "-", the addition or subtraction is taken with respect to the current line; for example, -5 is understood to mean .-5.

If an address ends with "+" or "-", then 1 is added to or subtracted from the address, respectively. As a consequence of this rule and of rule 8 immediately above, the address "-" refers to the line preceding the current line. (To maintain compatibility with earlier versions of the editor, the character "^" in addresses is entirely equivalent to "-".) Moreover, trailing "+" and "-" characters have a cumulative effect, so "—" refers to the current line less 2.

For convenience, a comma (,) stands for the address pair 1, $, while a semicolon (;) stands for the pair . , $.

Commands may require zero, one, or two addresses. Commands that require no addresses regard the presence of an address as an error. Commands that accept one or two addresses assume default addresses when an insufficient number of addresses is given; if more addresses are given than such a command requires, the last address(es) are used.

Typically, addresses are separated from each other by a comma. They may also be separated by a semicolon. In the latter case, the current line (.) is set to the first address, and only then is the second address calculated. This feature can be used to determine the starting line for forward and backward searches (see rules 5 and 6 above). The second address of any two-address sequence must correspond to a line that follows, in the buffer, the line corresponding to the first address.

In the following list of ed commands, the default addresses are shown in parentheses. The parentheses are not part of the address.

It is generally illegal for more than one command to appear on a line. However, any command (except e, f, r, or w) may be suffixed by p or by l, in which case the current line is either printed or listed, respectively, as discussed below under the p and l commands.

(.)a

text

.

The append command reads the given text and appends it after the addressed line; dot is left at the address of the last inserted line, or, if there were no inserted lines, at the addressed line. Address 0 is legal for this command: it causes the appended text to be placed at the beginning of the buffer.

(.)c

text

.

The change command deletes the addressed lines, then accepts input text that replaces these lines; dot is left at the address of the last line input, or, if there were none, at the first line that was not deleted.

(. , .)d
The delete command deletes the addressed lines from the buffer. The line after the last line deleted becomes the current line; if the lines deleted were originally at the end of the buffer, the new last line becomes the current line.

e file
The edit command causes the entire contents of the buffer to be deleted, and then the named file to be read in; dot is set to the last line of the buffer. If no filename is given, the currently remembered filename, if any, is used (see the f command). The number of characters read is typed. file is remembered for possible use as a default filename in subsequent e, r, and w commands. If file begins with an exclamation (!), the rest of the line is taken to be a shell command. The output of this command is read for the e and r commands. For the w command, the file is used as the standard input for the specified command. Such a shell command is not remembered as the current filename.

E file
The Edit command is like e, except the editor does not check to see if any changes have been made to the buffer since the last w command.
f file

If file is given, the filename command changes the currently remembered filename to file; otherwise, it prints the currently remembered filename.

(1 , $)g/regular-expression/command list
In the global command, the first step is to mark every line that matches the given regular expression. Then, for every such line, the given command list is executed with "." initially set to that line. A single command or the first of a list of commands appears on the same line as the global command. All lines of a multiline list except the last line must be ended with a "\"; a, i, and c commands and associated input are permitted; the "." terminating input mode may be omitted if it would be the last line of the command list. An empty command list is equivalent to the p command. The g, G, v, and V commands are not permitted in the command list. See also "Limitations" and the last paragraph before "Files" below.

(1 , $)G/regular-expression/
In the interactive Global command, the first step is to mark every line that matches the given regular expression. Then, for every such line, that line is printed, dot (.) is changed to that line, and any one command (other than one of the a, c, i, g, G, v, and V commands) may be input and is executed. After the execution of that command, the next marked line is printed, and so on. A newline acts as a null command. An ampersand (&) causes the re-execution of the most recent command executed within the current invocation of G. Note that the commands input as part of the execution of the G command may address and affect any lines in the buffer. The G command can be terminated by entering an INTER-RUPT (pressing the <Del> key).

h
The help command gives a short error message that explains the reason for the most recent ? diagnostic.

H
The Help command causes ed to enter a mode in which error messages are printed for all subsequent ? diagnostics. It will also explain the previous diagnostic if there was one. The H command alternately turns this mode on and off. It is initially off.

(.)i

text

.

The insert command inserts the given text before the addressed line; dot is left at the address of the last inserted line, or if there were no inserted lines, at the addressed line. This command differs from the a command only in the placement of the input text. Address 0 is not legal for this command.

(. , .+1)j
The join command joins contiguous lines by removing the appropriate newline characters. If only one address is given, this command does nothing.

(.)kx
The mark command marks the addressed line with name x, which must be a lowercase letter. The address 'x then addresses this line. Dot is unchanged.

(. , .)l
The list command prints the addressed lines in an unambiguous
way. Some non-printable characters are printed in the following
format:

\\, \a, \b, \f, \r, \t, \v
All other non-printable characters are printed in octal, and long
lines are folded. An l command may be appended to any command other than e, f, r, or w. The $ character marks the end of
each line.

(. , .)ma
The move command repositions the addressed line(s) after the line
addressed by a. Address 0 is legal for a and causes the addressed
line(s) to be moved to the beginning of the file. It is an error if
address a falls within the range of moved lines. Dot is left at the
last line moved.

(. , .)n
The number command prints the addressed lines, preceding each
line by its line number and a tab character. Dot is left at the last
line printed. The n command may be appended to any command
other than e, f, r, or w.

(. , .)p
The print command prints the addressed lines. Dot is left at the
last line printed. The p command may be appended to any command other than e, f, r, or w; for example, dp deletes the current
line and prints the new current line.

P

The editor will prompt with a "*" for all subsequent commands. The P command alternately turns this mode on and off. It is initially off.

q

The quit command causes ed to exit. No automatic write of a file is done.

Q

The editor exits without checking if changes have been made in the buffer since the last w command.

($)r file

The read command reads in the given file after the addressed line. If no filename is given, the currently remembered filename, if any, is used (see e and f commands). The currently remembered filename is not changed unless file is the very first filename mentioned since ed was invoked. Address 0 is legal for r and causes the file to be read at the beginning of the buffer. If the read is successful, the number of characters read is typed. Dot is set to the address of the last line read in. If file begins with "!", the rest of the line is taken to be a shell command whose output is to be read. Such a shell command is not remembered as the current filename.

(. , .)s/regular-expression/replacement or

(. , .)s/regular-expression/replacement/g or

(. , .)s/regular-expression/replacement/n n=1-512

The substitute command searches each addressed line for an occurrence of the specified regular expression. In each line in which a match is found, all nonoverlapped matched strings are replaced by replacement if the global replacement indicator g appears after the command. If the global indicator does not appear, only the first occurrence of the matched string is replaced. It is an error for the substitution to fail on all addressed lines. Any character other than space or newline may be used instead of "/" to delimit regular-expression and replacement. Dot is left at the address of the last line on which a substitution occurred.

The n character represents any number between one and 512. This number indicates the instance of the pattern to be replaced on each addressed line.

An ampersand (&) appearing in replacement is replaced by the string matching the regular-expression on the current line. The special meaning of the ampersand in this context may be suppressed by preceding it with a backslash. The characters \n, where n is a digit, are replaced by the text matched by the n-th regular subexpression of the specified regular expression enclosed between "\(" and "\)". When nested parenthesized subexpressions are present, n is determined by counting occurrences of "\(" starting from the left. When the character "%" is the only character in replacement, the replacement used in the most recent substitute command is used as the replacement in the current substitute command. The "%" loses its special meaning when it is in a replacement string of more than one character or when it is preceded by a "\".

A line may be split by substituting a newline character into it. The newline in the replacement must be escaped by preceding it with a "\". Such a substitution cannot be done as part of a g or v command list.

(. , .)ta
This command acts just like the m command, except that a copy
of the addressed lines is placed after address a (which may be 0).
Dot is left at the address of the last line of the copy.

u
The undo command nullifies the effect of the most recent command that modified anything in the buffer, namely the most recent
a, c, d, g, i, j, m, r, s, t, v, G, or V command.

(1 , $)v/regular-expression/command list
This command is the same as the global command g except that
the command list is executed with dot initially set to every line
that does not match the regular expression.

(1 , $)V/regular-expression/
This command is the same as the interactive global command G
except that the lines that are marked during the first step are those
that do not match the regular expression.

(1 , $)w file
The write command writes the addressed lines into the named file.
If the file does not exist, it is created with mode 666 (readable and
writeable by everyone), unless the umask setting (see sh(C)) dic-
tates otherwise. The currently remembered filename is not
changed unless file is the very first filename mentioned since ed
was invoked. If no filename is given, the currently remembered
filename, if any, is used (see e and f commands), and dot remains.
If the command is successful, the number of characters written is
displayed. If file begins with an exclamation (!), the rest of the line
is taken to be a shell command to which the addressed lines are

supplied as the standard input. Such a shell command is not remembered as the current filename.

($)=

The line number of the addressed line is typed. Dot is unchanged by this command.

!shell command

The remainder of the line after the "!" is sent to the UNIX shell (sh(C)) to be interpreted as a command. Within the text of that command, the unescaped character "%" is replaced with the remembered filename. If a "!" appears as the first character of the shell command, it is replaced with the text of the previous shell command. Thus, "!!" will repeat the last shell command. If any expansion is performed, the expanded line is echoed. Dot is unchanged.

(.+1)

An address alone on a line causes the addressed line to be printed. A RETURN alone on a line is equivalent to .+1p. This is useful for stepping forward through the editing buffer a line at a time.

If an interrupt signal (ASCII DEL or BREAK) is sent, ed prints a question mark (?) and returns to its command level.

ed has size limitations: LINE_MAX characters per line, LINE_MAX characters per global command list, 64 characters per filename, and 128K characters in the buffer. (See getconf(C) for information on LINE_MAX.) The limit on the number of lines depends on the amount of user memory.

When reading a file, ed discards ASCII NUL characters and all characters after the last newline. Files (for example, a.out) that contain characters not in the ASCII set (bit 8 on) cannot be edited by ed.

If the closing delimiter of a regular expression or of a replacement string (for example, "/") would be the last character before a newline, that delimiter may be omitted, in which case the addressed line is printed. Thus, the following pairs of commands are equivalent:

s/s1/s2 s/s1/s2/p
g/s1 g/s1/p
?s1 ?s1?

Examples

edit file:

```
ed file
```

---

edit   edit file with a command orientated editor, variant of ex

edit [-lLrR] [-C l -x] [-s l -v] [-c command] [-t tag] [-w size]
[file…]

Options

edit is a variant of ex recommended for new or casual users who wish to use a command-oriented editor. It operates precisely as ex with the following options automatically set:

novice
ON

report
ON

showmode
ON

magic
OFF

These options can be turned on or off using the set command.
Refer to the vi(C) manual page for a complete description of ex
commands.

Examples

edit file:

```
edit file
```

---

ex   edit file with a line editor that is the root of all editors

*ex [-lLrR] [-C | -x] [-s | -v] [-c command] [-t tag] [-w size] [
file...]*

Options

-c command
Execute the specified commands at start up. Individual commands can be separated by vertical bar characters "|".

-C
Equivalent to the -x option except that ex assumes files are encrypted.

-l
Sets the showmatch and lisp options when editing LISP source files.

-L
Lists the names of all files that may be recovered after an editor or system crash. Use the -r option to recover the files.

-r
Recovers the last saved version of the named files after an editor or system crash.

-R
Sets read-only mode; the files may be viewed but not altered.

-s
Selects batch mode; suppresses prompts and some other messages, ignores the setting of the environment variables EXINIT and TERM, and overlooks the presence of any .exrc file. (See the section "Environment variables".)

-t tag

Edits the file containing the tag string and positions the editor at its definition; equivalent to an initial :t tag command. For a description of tags see ctags(C).

-v

Invokes the vi(C) visual editor.

-w size

Sets the default window size. This is useful for dialup sessions when a small window may be used.

-x

Encrypt the file as it is being written. The file will require a corresponding key to be read. See crypt(C) for information about encryption.

Examples

edit file:

```
ex file
```

---

vi   edit a file with full screen display-orientated text editor based on ex

vi [-option...] [command...] [filename...]

See Appendix B for more detail

Options

-x

Encryption option; when used, the file is encrypted as it is being written and requires an encryption key to be read. vi makes an educated guess to determine if a file is encrypted or not.
Refer to the crypt(C) page for information about restrictions on the availability of encryption options.

-C

Encryption option; the same as -x except that vi assumes files are encrypted. Refer to the crypt(C) page for information about restrictions on the availability of encryption options.

-c command

Begins editing by executing the specified editor command (usually a search or positioning command).

-t tag

Equivalent to an initial tag command; edits the file containing tag and positions the editor at its definition.

-r file

Used in recovering after an editor or system crash; retrieves the last saved version of the named file.

-l

Specific to editing LISP; sets the showmatch and lisp options.

-L
Lists the names of all files saved as a result of an editor or system crash. Files may be recovered with the -r option.

-wn
Sets the default window size to n; useful on dialups to start in small windows.

-R
Sets a read-only option so that files can be viewed but not edited. The editing buffer
vi performs no editing operations on the file that you name during invocation. Instead, it works on a copy of the file in an "editing buffer". When vi is invoked with a single filename argument, the named file is copied to a temporary editing buffer. The editor remembers the name of the file specified at invocation, so that it can later copy the editing buffer back to the named file. The contents of the named file are not affected until the changes are copied back to the original file.

Modes of operation
Within vi there are three distinct modes of operation:

Command Mode
Within command mode, signals from the keyboard are interpreted as editing commands.

Insert Mode
Insert mode can be entered by typing any of the vi insert, append, open, substitute, change, or replace commands. In insert mode, letters typed at the keyboard are inserted into the editing buffer.

ex Escape Mode

The vi and ex editors are one and the same editor differing mainly in their user interface. In vi, commands are usually single keystrokes. In ex, commands are lines of text terminated by a <Return>. vi has a special "escape" command that gives access to many of these line-oriented ex commands. To use the ex escape mode, type a colon (:). The colon is echoed on the status line as a prompt for the ex command. An executing command can be aborted by pressing INTERRUPT. Most file manipulation commands are executed in ex escape mode (for example, the commands to read in a file and to write out the editing buffer to a file).

Special keys

There are several special keys in vi. The following keys are used to edit, delimit, or abort commands and command lines.

<Esc>

Returns to vi command mode or cancels partially formed commands.

<Return>

Terminates ex commands when in ex escape mode; also starts a newline when in insert mode.

INTERRUPT

Often the same as the <Del> or RUBOUT key on many terminals; generates an interrupt, telling the editor to stop what it is doing; aborts any command that is executing.

/

Specifies a string to be searched for. The slash appears on the status line as a prompt for a search string. The question mark (?)

works exactly like the slash key, except that it is used to search backward in a file instead of forward.

:

Prompts for an ex command. You can then type in any ex command, followed by an <Esc> or <Return>, and the given ex command is executed.

The following characters are special in insert mode:

<Bksp>
Backs up the cursor one character on the current line. The last character typed before the <Bksp> is removed from the input buffer, but remains displayed on the screen.

<Ctrl>U
Moves the cursor back to the first character of the insertion and restarts insertion.

<Ctrl>V
Removes the special significance of the next typed character. Use <Ctrl>V to insert control characters. Linefeed and <Ctrl>J cannot be inserted in the text except as newline characters. Both <Ctrl>Q and <Ctrl>S are trapped by the operating system before they are interpreted by vi, so they too cannot be inserted as text.

<Ctrl>W
Moves the cursor back to the first character of the last inserted word.

<Ctrl>T
During an insertion, with the autoindent option set and at the beginning of the current line, this inserts shiftwidth whitespace.

<Ctrl>@

If entered as the first character of an insertion, this is replaced with the last text inserted, and the insertion terminates. Only 128 characters are saved from the last insertion. If more than 128 characters were inserted, then this command inserts no characters. A <Ctrl>@ cannot be part of a file, even if quoted.

Examples

edit file:

```
vi file
```

recover file when edit interrupted:

```
vi -r file
```

within vi editor, display special characters:

```
:set list
```

file management—overview

Methods for creating, concatenating, and updating files

create:
touch   create an empty file
>   redirect output to a file

concatenate:
cat   concatenate a file from two or more files

update:
touch   update access and modification date and time

file management—create

touch create an empty file with current date and time

touch [-acm] [-r ref_file] [-t [[CC]YY]MMDDhhmm[.ss]] file...

touch [-acm] [MMDDhhmm[yy]] file...

Options

-a
Update the access time only. The modification time is not changed unless the -m option is also specified.

-c
Silently prevent touch from creating a file if it does not already exist.

-m
Update the modification time only. The access time is not changed unless the -a option is also specified.

-r
Use the access and modification times of the file ref_file instead of the current time.

-t
Use the specified time instead of the current time. The form of the specified time is [[CC]YY]MMDDhhmm[.ss]:

CC
first two digits of the year (the century minus one) [19-20];

YY
last two digits of the year [00-99]

MM
month [01-12]

DD
day [01-31]

hh
hour [00-23]

mm
minute [00-59]

ss
second [00-61]; the values 60 and 61 are used for leap seconds
If neither -a nor -m is given, touch updates both the access and
modification times (equivalent to specifying -am).

Examples

create empty file:

```
touch file1
```

> redirect input, out to named file—create if file does not exist;
overwrite if does (empties file if blank input is used)

```
>
```

Options

There are no options for this command.

Examples

create file2 from top of file1:

```
head file1 > file2
```

file management—concatenate

cat   add the contents from two or more files

cat [-u] [-s] [-v] [-t] [-e] file...

Options

-s
Suppresses warnings about nonexistent files.

-u
Causes the output to be unbuffered.

-v
Causes non-printing characters (with the exception of tabs, new-lines, and form feeds) to be displayed. Control characters are displayed as ^X (<Ctrl>x), where X is the key pressed with the <Ctrl> key (for example, <Ctrl>m is displayed as ^M). The <Del> character (octal 0177) is printed as ^?. Non-ASCII characters (with the high bit set) are printed as M -x, where x is the character specified by the seven low order bits.

-t
Causes tabs to be printed as ^I and form feeds as ^L. This option is ignored if the -v option is not specified.

-e
Causes a "$" character to be printed at the end of each line (prior to the new-line). This option is ignored if the -v option is not set.

Examples

add contents of file1 to file2 and display on the terminal screen:

```
cat file1 file2
```

add contents of file1 to file2 and put results in file3:

```
cat file1 file2 > file3
```

file management—update

---

touch update the date and time of access and modifications of a
file

touch [-acm] [-r ref_file] [-t [[CC]YY]MMDDhhmm[.ss]] file...

touch [-acm] [MMDDhhmm[yy]] file...

Options

-a
Update the access time only. The modification time is not changed
unless the -m option is also specified.

-c
Silently prevent touch from creating a file if it does not already
exist.

-m
Update the modification time only. The access time is not changed
unless the -a option is also specified.

-r
Use the access and modification times of the file ref_file instead of
the current time.

-t
Use the specified time instead of the current time. The form of the
specified time is [[CC]YY]MMDDhhmm[.ss]:

CC
first two digits of the year (the century minus one) [19-20];

YY
last two digits of the year [00-99]

MM
month [01-12]

DD
day [01-31]

hh
hour [00-23]

mm
minute [00-59]

ss
second [00-61]; the values 60 and 61 are used for leap seconds
If neither -a nor -m is given, touch updates both the access and
modification times (equivalent to specifying -am).

Examples

change date and time on file:

```
touch file
```

format—overview

Methods for formatting files

nroff	format document
troff	typeset document
pr	format file

format

---

nroff   format a document for display or output to a printer

*/usr/ucb/nroff [-ehiqz] [-Fdir] [-mname] [-nN] [-olist] [-raN] [-sN]
[-Tname] [-uN] [file...]*

Options

The following options may appear in any order, but must appear
before the files.

-e
Produce equally-spaced words in adjusted lines, using full terminal resolution.

-h
Use output TAB characters during horizontal spacing to speed
output and reduce output character count. TAB settings are
assumed to be every 8 nominal character widths.

-i
Read the standard input after the input files are exhausted.

-q
Invoke the simultaneous input-output mode of the rd request.

-Fdir
Search directory dir for font tables instead of the system-dependent default.

-mname
Prepend the macro file /usr/ucblib/doctools/tmac/name to the input files.

-nN
Number first generated page N.

-olist
Print only pages whose page numbers appear in the comma-separated list of numbers and ranges. A range N-M means pages N through M; an initial -N means from the beginning to page N; and a final N- means from N to the end.

-raN
Set register a (one-character) to N.

-sN
Stop every N pages. nroff will halt prior to every N pages (default N=1) to allow paper loading or changing, and will resume upon receipt of a NEWLINE.

-Tname
Prepare output for a device of the specified name. Known names are:

37 Teletype Corporation Model 37 terminal – this is the default.

lp | tn300 GE TermiNet 300, or any line printer or terminal without half-line capability.

300   DASI-300.

300-12 DASI-300—12-pitch.

300S | 300s DASI-300S.

300S-12 | 300s-12 DASI-300S.

382 DASI-382 (fancy DTC 382).

450 DASI-450 (Diablo Hyterm).

450-12 DASI-450 (Diablo Hyterm)—12-pitch.

832 AJ 832.

-uN
Set emboldening factor for the font mounted on position 3 to N. Emboldening is accomplished by overstriking the specified number of times.

-z
Suppress formatted output. The only output will consist of diagnostic messages from nroff and messages output with the .tm request.

Examples

format file:

```
nroff file
```

---

troff   typeset document with formatting requests and macros

/usr/ucb/troff [-afiz] [-Fdir] [-mname] [-nN] [-olist] [-raN] [-sN] [-Tdest] [-uN] [file] . . .

Options

The following options may appear in any order, but they all must appear before the first file.

-a
Send a printable approximation of the formatted output to the standard output file.

-f
Do not print a trailer after the final page of output or cause the postprocessor to relinquish control of the device.

-i
Read the standard input after the input files are exhausted.

-z
Suppress formatted output. Only diagnostic messages and messages output using the .tm request are output.

-Fdir
Search the directory dir for font width tables instead of the system-dependent default directory.

-mname
Prepend the macro file /usr/ucblib/doctools/tmac/name to the input files. Note: most references to macro packages include the leading m as part of the name; for example, the man macro package resides in /usr/ucblib/doctools/tmac/an.

-nN
Number first generated page N.

-olist
Print only pages whose page numbers appear in the comma-separated list of numbers and ranges. A range N-M means pages N through M; an initial -N means from the beginning to page N; and a final N- means from N to the end.

-raN
Set register a (one-character) to N.

-sN
Stop the phototypesetter every N pages. On some devices, troff produces a trailer so you can change cassettes; resume by pressing the typesetter's start button.

-Tdest
Prepare output for typesetter dest. The following values can be supplied for dest:

aps   Autologic APS-5. This is the default value.

uN   Set the emboldening factor for the font mounted in position
3 to N. If N is missing, then set the emboldening factor to 0.

Examples

typeset file:

```
troff file
```

---

pr   format and print contents of a file

pr [options] [files]

Options

-a
Prints multi-column output across the page.

-d
Double-spaces the output.

-eck
Expands input tabs to character positions k+1, 2*k+1, 3*k+1, etc.
If k is 0 or is omitted, default tab settings at every 8th position are
assumed. Tab characters in the input are expanded into the appropriate number of spaces. If c (any non-digit character) is given, it is
treated as the input tab character (default for c is the tab character).

-f
Uses form feed character for new pages (default is to use a sequence of linefeeds). Pauses before beginning the first page if the standard output is associated with a terminal.

-F
Uses a form feed character for new pages.

-h
Uses the next argument as the header to be printed instead of the filename.

-ick
In output, replaces white space wherever possible by inserting tabs to character positions k+1, 2*k+1, 3*k+1, etc. If k is 0 or is omitted, default tab settings at every 8th position are assumed. If c (any non-digit character) is given, it is treated as the output tab character (default for c is the tab character).

+k
Begins printing with page k (default is 1).

-k
Produces k-column output (default is 1). The options -e and -i are assumed for multi-column output.

-l n
Sets the length of a page to n lines (default is 66).

-m
Merges and prints all files simultaneously, one per column (overrides the -k, and -a options).

-nck

Provides k-digit line numbering (default for k is 5). The number occupies the first k+1 character positions of each column of normal output or each line of -m output. If c (any non-digit character) is given, it is appended to the line number to separate it from whatever follows (default for c is a tab).

-o k

Offsets each line by k character positions (default is 0). The number of character positions per line is the sum of the width and offset.

-p

Pauses before beginning each page if the output is directed to a terminal (pr will ring the bell at the terminal and wait for a carriage return).

-r

Prints no diagnostic reports on failure to open files.

-sc

Separates columns by the single character c instead of by the appropriate number of spaces (default for c is a tab).

-t

Prints neither the 5-line identifying header nor the 5-line trailer normally supplied for each page. Quits printing after the last line of each file without spacing to the end of the page.

-w k

Sets the width of a line to k character positions (default is 72 for equal-width multi-column output, no limit otherwise).

Examples

format and print file:

```
pr file
```

link—overview

Methods for linking files and/or directories

ld   link editor
ln   link files or directories

link

ld   combine object files, relocate them if needed, and resolve any external symbols

ld [options] filename [[options] filename]

Options

The following options are recognized by ld, and are common to producing both COFF and ELF binaries. Some options listed here (for example, -a or -r), although common to both formats, have slightly different meanings depending on the format of the object files being linked. Refer to the sections "Linking COFF binaries" and "Linking ELF binaries" for format-specific options.

-a
Create an absolute (executable) file and give errors for undefined references. For COFF objects, this is the default except when the -r option is also used. If -r is used, then -a allocates memory for common symbols. For ELF objects, this option is available in static mode only and is the default. This option can not be combined with -r when the ELF objects are linked.

-b [elflcofflibcs2]
The default is to invoke /bin/ld and scan the object files to be linked in order to determine the file format for the resulting binary. See "Generating COFF vs. ELF binaries." If any one of the option arguments, elf, coff and ibcs2, is specified, ld will not

scan the object files. The file format is that requested through the option:

-b coff
Invoke /usr/ccs/bin/coff/ld to produce an COFF binary.

-b elf
Invoke /usr/ccs/bin/elf/ld to produce an ELF binary.

-b ibcs2
Invoke /usr/ccs/bin/coff/ld to produce an COFF binary.
When linking ELF object files in dynamic mode this option can also be used without an option argument in addition to -belf -dy. A -b option without an argument instructs ld not to do special processing for relocations that reference symbols in shared objects when creating an executable. Without the -b option, the link editor will create special position-independent relocations for references to functions defined in shared objects and will arrange for data objects defined in shared objects to be copied into the memory image of the executable by the dynamic linker at run time. With the -b option, the output code may be more efficient, but it will be less sharable.

-e epsym
Set the default entry point address for the output file to be the address of epsym.

-lx
Search a library libx.a (and also libx.so if any user specified objects are in ELF format), where x is up to nine characters. When COFF objects are linked, or when the -Bstatic option is in effect, ld searches each directory specified in the library search path for a

file libx.a. The directory search stops at the first directory containing libx.a. In dynamic mode, that is, when ELF objects are linked and the -Bstatic option is not in effect, ld searches for both libx.so and libx.a and chooses libx.so if both libx.so and libx.a are found. If no libx.so is found, then ld accepts libx.a. A library is searched when its name is encountered, so the order of the -l, -B and -L is significant. By default, libraries are located in LIBDIR or LLIB-DIR.

-L dir
Change the algorithm of searching for libx.a (and libx.so when applicable). Search libraries in directories dir (in order) first before the standard directories LIBDIR and LLIBDIR (see the -YP option) are searched. This option is effective only if it precedes the -l option on the command line.

-m [mem_map]
Produce a memory map of the input/output sections and send the map to standard output. For COFF objects, the memory map can also be saved to the file mem_map.

-o name
Set the output filename to name instead of a.out.

-r
Retain relocation entries in the output object file and combine relocatable object files to produce one relocatable object file. This option should be used if the output file is to be used as input file in a subsequent ld run. The link editor will not complain about unresolved references, and the output file will not be executable. This option cannot be used in dynamic mode or with -a when ELF objects are linked.

-Rarg[,arg,...]
Set runtime-behavior characteristics. The option accepts a comma-separated list of arguments. Note that there is no space between -R and its arguments. Each argument is one of the accepted values for the -a, -b, or -X flags of cc(CP), and should match the flags used when the objects were compiled. The default is -Rxpg4plus,elf,a for the ELF ld, and -Rxpg4plus,coff,a for the COFF ld. The ELF ld ignores -Rcoff and -Ribcs2; the COFF ld ignores -Relf.
Multiple -R arguments may be given; the last argument of each type (-a, -b, or -X) is the one used. For example, -Ransi,a -Rxpg4,coff is equivalent to -Rxpg4,coff,a.

-s
Strip symbolic information from the output file. The debug and line sections and their associated relocation entries will be removed. Except for relocatable files or shared objects, the symbol table and string table sections will also be removed from the output object file.

-u symbol
Designate the specified symbol as an undefined symbol in the symbol table. This is useful for loading entirely from an archive library, since initially the symbol table is empty and an unresolved reference is needed to force the loading of the first routine. The placement of this option on the ld line is significant; it must be placed before the library which defines the symbol.

-V
Output a message giving information about the version of ld being used.

-Y[LPU],dir
Change the default standard directories used for finding libraries. Do not combine either -YL or -YU with -YP.

-YL,dir
Replace the first default directory which ld searches, LIBDIR, by dir.

-YU,dir
Replace the second default directory which ld searches, LLIBDIR, by dir.

-YP,dir
Replace the default standard directories which ld searches by the colon-separated directory list, dir.
Linking COFF binaries
The following options are also available for linking COFF binaries:

-f fill
Set the default fill pattern for "holes" within an output section as well as initialized .bss sections. The argument fill is a two-byte constant.

-M
Output a message for each multiply-defined external definition.

-N
Put the text section at the beginning of the text segment rather than after all header information, and put the data section immediately following text in the core image.

-strict
Suppress the generation of the symbols edata, etext and end which are aliases, used for compatibility with previous releases, to the symbols _edata, _etext and _end. This prevents name space pollution when linking object files compiled in any one of ANSI, POSIX, or X/OPEN environments (see -a ansi, -a posix and -a xpg4 options to the cc(CP) command).

-t
Turn off the warning about multiply-defined symbols that are not the same size.

-VS num
Use num as a decimal version stamp identifying the a.out file that is produced. The version stamp is stored in the optional header.

-x
Do not preserve local symbols in the output symbol table; enter external and static symbols only. This option saves some space in the output file.

-z
Do not bind anything to address zero. This option will allow runtime detection of null pointers. See also -z in "Linking ELF binaries."
Linking ELF binaries
The following options are also available for linking ELF binaries:

-B arg
where arg can be any one of the following:

dynstat

dynstat can be either dynamic or static. These options govern library inclusion. The argument dynamic is valid in dynamic mode only (-belf -dy). These options may be specified any number of times on the command line as toggles: if -Bstatic is given, no shared objects will be accepted until -Bdynamic is seen. See also the -l option.

export[=list | :filename]
hide[=list | :filename]
where list is a comma separated sequence of symbol names. filename contains a list of symbol names, one symbol name per line. Any line beginning with a # character and blank lines are ignored. Normally, when building a shared object, ld makes all global and weak names defined in the shared object visible outside of the object itself (exported). When building an executable, it makes visible only those names used by the shared objects with which the executable is linked. All other names are hidden. This behavior can be modified with -Bhide and -Bexport.

When building a shared object, -Bexport is the default. All global and weak definitions are exported. -Bexport with a set of symbol names instructs ld to hide all global and weak definitions, except those in the specified set. -Bhide means to hide all global and weak definitions. -Bhide with a set of symbol names means to export all global and weak definitions, except for those in the set of names.

When building an executable, -Bhide is the default. Only those names referenced by the shared objects with which the executable is linked are exported. -Bhide with a set of symbol names instructs ld to export all global and weak definitions, except those in the specified set. Names in a -Bhide list that are referenced by the shared objects with which the executable is linked, are ignored, that is, they are exported. -Bexport means to export all global and weak definitions. -Bexport with a set of symbol names means to hide all global and weak definitions except those in the set of names and those referenced by the shared objects with which the executable is linked.

If -Bhide and -Bexport are used together, one of the options must contain a set of symbol names and the other must not. In this case, the option without the symbol set is ignored. Neither -Bhide nor -Bexport may be used with -dn.

sortbss
All uninitialized global variables within a module will be assigned contiguous addresses. This is the way these variables were assigned by the COFF version of the link editor.

symbolic[=list | :filename]
where list is a comma separated sequence of symbol names. filename contains a list of symbol names, one symbol name per line. Any line beginning with a # character and blank lines are ignored. When building a shared object, if a definition for a named symbol exists, bind all references to the named symbol to that definition. If no list of symbols is provided, bind all references to symbols to definitions that are available; ld will issue warnings for undefined symbols unless -z defs overrides. Normally, references to global symbols within shared objects are not bound until run time, even if definitions are available, so that definitions of the same symbol in an executable or other shared objects can override the object's own definition.

-d yn
ld uses static linking only when yn is n; otherwise, by default, or when yn is y, ld uses dynamic linking.

-G
In dynamic mode only, produce a shared object. Undefined symbols are allowed unless the -z defs option is specified.

-h name
In dynamic mode only, when building a shared object, record name in the object's dynamic section. name will be recorded in executables that are linked with this object rather than the shared object's pathname. Accordingly, name will be used by the dynamic linker as the pathname of the shared object to search for at run time.

-I name
When building an executable, use name as the pathname of the interpreter to be written into the program header. The default in static mode is no interpreter; in dynamic mode, the default is the name of the dynamic linker, /usr/lib/libc.so.1. Either case may be overridden by -I. exec(S) will load this interpreter when it loads the a.out and will pass control to the interpreter rather than to the a.out directly.

-M mapfile
In static mode only, read mapfile as a text file of directives to ld. Because these directives change the shape of the output file created by ld, use of this option is strongly discouraged.

-Q yn
If yn is y, an identification string is added to the .comment section
of the output file to identify the version of the link editor used to
create the file. This will result in multiple instances of such when
there have been multiple linking steps, such as when using ld -r.
This is identical with the default action of the cc(CP) command. If
yn is n (the default), the version information is suppressed.

-z defs
Force a fatal error if any undefined symbols remain at the end of
the link. This is the default when building an executable. It is also
useful when building a shared object to assure that the object is
self-contained, that is, that all its symbolic references are resolved
internally.

-z nodefs
Allow undefined symbols. This is the default when building a
shared object. It may be used when building an executable in
dynamic mode and linking with a shared object that has unresolved references in routines not used by that executable. This
option should be used with caution.

-z text
In dynamic mode only, force a fatal error if any relocations against
non-writable, allocatable sections remain.

Environment variables
There are two environment variables that can be used to specify
alternate library search directories when ELF objects are linked.
One is LD_LIBRARY_PATH and the other is LD_RUN_PATH.

The environment variable LD_LIBRARY_PATH may be used to specify library search directories. In the most general case, it will contain two directory lists separated by a semicolon:

dirlist1;dirlist2

Thus, if ld is called with the following occurrences of -L:

ld...-Lpath1...-Lpathn...-lx

then the search path ordering for the library x (libx.so or libx.a) is:

dirlist1 path1 . . .pathn dirlist2 LIBPATH

LD_LIBRARY_PATH is also used to specify library search directories to the dynamic linker at run time. That is, if LD_LIBRARY_PATH exists in the environment, the dynamic linker will search the directories it names before its default directory for shared objects to be linked with the program at execution.

Additionally, the environment variable LD_RUN_PATH (which also contains a directory list) may be used to specify library search directories to the dynamic linker. If present and not empty, it is passed to the dynamic linker by ld via data stored in the output object file.

---

ln   link files so that any changes to a file are effective regardless of the name used to reference it

ln [-s] [-f] sourcefile targetfile
ln [-s] [-f] sourcefile...targetdirectory

Options

The -s option causes ln to create symbolic links. A symbolic link contains the name of the file to which it is linked; this file does not need to exist prior to the symbolic link. Symbolic links may span file systems and may refer to directories.

When ln is given two arguments, and the second argument does not exist, ln creates a directory entry called targetfile that is a link to sourcefile.

If the last argument is the name of a directory, ln creates a new entry in the directory for each sourcefile given. The name of each new entry will be the basename of the corresponding sourcefile.

If the -f option is not specified and the target filename already exists, the link is not created. If the -f option is specified, the existing file is unlinked before the new link is created.

Examples

link file1 to file2:
```
ln file1 file2
```

listings—overview

Method for listing commands

man   online manual pages

listings

man   view online help files that access manual pages that are also in the hardcopy Reference Manuals of the system

man [-a | -f] [-bcw] [-d dir] [-p pager] [-t proc] [-T term] [section] title

man -e command...

man -k keyword...

Options

-a
ALL mode. Incompatible with -f option. Display all manual pages with matching titles. This option is equivalent to specifying MODE=ALL in /etc/default/man.

-b
Leave blank lines in output. Entries are normally padded with blank lines for line printer purposes; without this option, man filters out excess blank lines and does not display more than 2 consecutive blank lines.

-c
Invoke col(C) if the display does not support character formatting. Note that col is invoked automatically by man unless the terminal

(defined by -T term) is one of the following: 300, 300s, 450, 37, 4000a, 382, 4014, tek, 1620, or X.

-d dir

Specify directory dir to be added to the search path for entries. You can specify several directories to be searched by separating the directory names with colons (:) on the command line.

-e command...

Attempt to locate and display the names and short descriptions of manual pages related to the given commands. The commands may be separated by commas, or by spaces if the list is enclosed in quotes. The full name of command must be given; however, man is insensitive to its case.

man -e is equivalent to the whatis(C) command.

-f

FIRST mode. Display only the first matching title. Incompatible with -a option. This option is equivalent to specifying MODE=FIRST in /etc/default/man.

-k keyword...

Output the name and short description of each manual page that has at least one of the specified keywords in its short description. The search is insensitive to case, and matches on parts of words. For example, a search for the keyword "compile" will match on "Compiler". The keywords may be separated by commas, or by spaces if the list is enclosed in quotes.

man -k is equivalent to the apropos(C) command.

-p pager
Select a paging program pager to display the entry. Paging systems such as more(C), pg(C), cat(C), or any custom pagers that you may have are valid arguments for this option.
The default pager, pg, set in /etc/default/man, may be overridden by setting the environment variable PAGER to the name of a suitable paging program. The pager defined by -p overrides both of these.

-t proc
Indicate that if an unprocessed manual page is available, it is to be passed to proc for formatting. proc can be any command script in /usr/man/bin or an absolute filename of a text processing program elsewhere on the system.

-T term
Format the entry and pass the given term value to the processing program, then print it on the standard output (usually, the terminal), where term is the terminal type (see term(M) and the explanation below).

-w
Print on the standard output only the pathnames of the entries

Examples

get information/syntax for the cat command:

```
man cat
```

login—overview

Methods for signing on, signing off, switching to another user, and displaying user information

exit	sign off as a user
finger	display user information
id	list user and group information
login	sign on
logname	display your user name
su	switch to another user

login

exit sign off from the current user login. Multiple logins will exit back to the previous user with each exit, with the final exit resulting in signing off the system.

exit [returnCode]

Options

Terminates the process, returning returnCode to the system as the exit status. If returnCode isn't specified then it defaults to 0.

Examples

exit from the current user login:

```
exit
```

finger display user information

finger [-bfilpqsw] [login1 [login2...]]

Options

-b
Briefer long output format of users.

-f
Suppresses the printing of the header line (short format).

-i
Quick list of users with idle times.

-l
Forces long output format.

-p
Suppresses printing of the .plan files.

-q
Quick list of users.

-s
Forces short output format.

-w
Forces narrow format list of specified users.

Examples

display general user information for user "user1":

```
finger user1                              .
```

---

id list user and group information

id [-l] [-s] [user]

id -G [-n] [user]

id -g [-n] [-r] [user]

id -u [-n] [-r] [user]

id -u [-n] [-r | -l] [user]

Options

The -s flag is for backwards compatibility and has no effect.

With the -l option, id also outputs the Login User ID (LUID) of the caller.

In the second form, the id command writes three lines of information on the standard output. The first line contains the effective group ID, and the second the real group ID; the last line contains a space-separated list of supplemental groups. Normally the output is in numeric form, but specifying the -n flag shows the ID's in name form.

The third form of id writes the effective group ID of the invoking process, or of the given user in numeric form. The -n flag causes output to be the name of the group, and the -r flag shows the real group ID.

The final form of id writes the effective user ID of the invoking process, or of the given user in numeric form. Again, the -n flag causes the output to be in name form; the -r flag shows the real user ID, and the -l flag shows the login user ID.

When id is given the optional user name, the real, effective and login ID's are always the same. The user and group ID's are taken from the password database entry for that user. The supplemental group list is taken to be all the entries in the group database for that user, the supplemental group list of a process being a subset of these.

Examples

list groups:

```
id -a
```

login   sign on

login [-cf] [name [env-var]]
login [-c] [-r remotehost remotename localname]...

Options

login asks for a user name (if not supplied as an argument), and, if appropriate, the user's password and a dialup password. (For information on dialup passwords, refer to passwd(C)). Echoing is turned off (where possible) during the typing of the passwords, so it will not appear on the written record of the session.

If the user makes a mistake in the login procedure the user will receive the message "Login incorrect" and a new login prompt will appear. The number of login attempts the user is allowed is configurable. If the user makes too many unsuccessful login attempts, the user or the terminal can be locked out.

If the login sequence is not completed successfully within a configurable period of time (for example, one minute), the user is returned to the "login:" prompt or silently disconnected from a dial-in line.

The -c option must be specified to enable accounting for logins that use pseudo-ttys (over a network or on an mscreen(M)). It can also be used safely for ordinary logins.

The -f option enables user login directly without requesting for a password. For instance, login -f name.

The form of the command that uses the -r option is used for remote logins across a network. The remote login must supply parameters in the order indicated; these are the name of the remote host from which the login is being attempted, the user's name on the remote host, and the user's name on the local host (on which the login process is running). This form of the login command is intended for use by network software rather than users.

After a successful login, accounting files (/etc/utmp and /etc/wtmp) are updated, the user is notified if they have mail, and the start-up shell files (.profile for the Bourne shell or .login for the C-shell) if any, are executed.

Login sets the user's supplemental groups list. If the file .supp-groups is in the user's home directory, the supplemental groups list is taken from this. The .suppgroups file contains a list of group names, one per line. Groups are verified before they are added to the supplemental group list.

To be able to use a group, a user must either be explicitly listed in that group in /etc/group, or the group must have the group ID listed for the user in the /etc/passwd file. If no .suppgroups file is found, the supplemental groups list is set from the /etc/group file plus the login group ID.

If the hushlogin feature is enabled in /etc/default/login and a file named .hushlogin exists in the user's home directory, login suppresses the printing of the last successful and last unsuccessful login times and the copyright messages. login also sets the environment variable HUSHLOGIN to TRUE, so the system and user initialization files are aware a hushlogin is taking place and can suppress output as appropriate (typically the message of the day, and the calling of mail(C) and news(C) are suppressed). The .hushlogin file itself does not need to contain anything; it only needs to exist.

login checks /etc/default/login for the following definitions of the form DEFINE=value:

ALTSHELL
If ALTSHELL is set to YES or if it is not present in /etc/default/login, then the SHELL environment variable is set to whatever shell is specified in the user's /etc/passwd entry. If ALT-SHELL is set to NO, then the SHELL environment variable is set

only if the shell is defined in the /usr/lib/mkuser directory (which is list of recognized shells).

CONSOLE

The CONSOLE=device entry means that root can only log in on the device listed. For example, CONSOLE=/dev/tty01 restricts root logins to the first console multiscreen device.

ALLOWHUSH

The ALLOWHUSH entry is used to enable or disable the hushlogin feature on a system-wide basis. If ALLOWHUSH=YES, login checks for the existence of a .hushlogin file in the user's home directory. If the file exists, the environment variable HUSHLOGIN is set to TRUE and a quiet login takes place. If ALLOWHUSH=NO or ALLOWHUSH=YES and there is no .hushlogin file in the user's home directory, the environment variable HUSHLOGIN is set to FALSE and the normal login messages appear. If there is no ALLOWHUSH entry, the HUSHLOGIN environment variable is not set and the normal login messages appear.

IDLEWEEKS

If a password has expired, the user is prompted to choose a new one. If it has expired beyond IDLEWEEKS, the user is not allowed to log in, and must consult system administrator. This works in conjunction with passwd(C).

OVERRIDE

This allows root to log in on the console even if the Protected Password database entry for root is corrupted. login checks /etc/default/login to see if there is an entry similar to the following,

which identifies the tty to be used when doing an override login for root:
OVERRIDE=tty01

PASSREQ
If PASSREQ=YES, a password is required. Users who do not have a password will be forced to select one. PASSREQ=NO allows users to have accounts without passwords.

REUSEUID
The REUSEUID entry is used by unretire(ADM) and rmuser(ADM).

SUPATH
If a user's UID is 0 (that is, if this is the super user), the PATH variable is set to SUPATH, if SUPATH is specified in /etc/default/login. It is not advisable for SUPATH to include the current directory symbol ".". Note that an empty directory ("::" or ":" at the beginning or end) is equivalent to ".".

ULIMIT
This variable defines the maximum allowable file size. The default value used by the kernel is specified in the file mtune(F) as 2,097,151 blocks, or approximately 1GB. This value can be changed using configure(ADM); however, for login sessions, a lower value specified in /etc/default/login overrides the kernel default value.

UMASK
This is the default file creation mask (see umask(C)).
login initializes the user and group IDs and the working directory, then executes a command interpreter (usually sh(C)) according to

specifications found in the /etc/passwd file. Argument 0 of the command interpreter is a dash (-) followed by the last component of the interpreter's pathname. The basic environment (see environ(M)) is initialized to:

HOME= user-login-directory
SHELL=last field of passwd entry
MAIL=/usr/spool/mail/user-login-name
Possible HUSHLOGIN=TRUE or FALSE

Initially, umask is set to octal 022 by login.

---

logname   display your user name

logname

Options

logname returns the user's login name as found in /etc/utmp. If no login name is found, logname displays an error message on the standard error and returns a non-zero exit status.

---

su   switch to another user. If required for user, the system will prompt for a password entry.

su [—] [name [arg...]]

Options

To use su, the appropriate password must be supplied (unless you are already the super user). If the password is correct, su will execute a new shell with the user ID, group ID, and supplemental group list set to those of the specified user. The new shell also has the kernel and subsystem authorizations of the specified user, although the LUID is not changed. (su only sets the LUID if it has not already been set. For example, the init(M) process does not have an LUID; when the system goes to multiuser mode, scripts invoked by init use su to set the LUID for those commands that require it.) The new shell is defined by the program field in /etc/passwd; /bin/sh is run by default if no program is specified. (This may not be true for Network Information Service (NIS) since program could be specified on the NIS server.)

To restore normal user ID privileges, press EOF <Ctrl>d to exit the new shell.

Any additional arguments given on the command line are passed to the program invoked as the shell. When using programs like sh(C), an arg of the form -c string executes string via the shell and an arg of -r gives the user a restricted shell. You must specify a username with the -c option; for example, su root -c scoadmin. When you exit the system administration shell, you will no longer be root.

The following statements are true only if the optional program named in the shell field of the specified user's password file entry is like sh. If the first argument to su is a "-", the environment is changed to what would be expected if the user actually logged in as the specified user. This is done by invoking the program used as the shell with an arg0 value whose first character is "-", thus causing first the system's profile (/etc/profile) and then the specified user's profile (.profile in the new $HOME directory) to be executed. Otherwise, the environment is passed along with the possible exception of $PATH, which is set to /bin:/etc:/usr/bin for root. The "-" option should never be used in /etc/rc scripts.

Note that if the optional program used as the shell is /bin/sh, the user's .profile can check arg0 for -sh or -su to determine if it was invoked by login(M) or su, respectively. If the user's program is other than /bin/sh, then .profile is invoked with an arg0 of -program by both login and su.

The file /etc/default/su can be used to control several aspects of how su is used. Several entries can be placed in /etc/default/su:

SULOG
Name of log file to record all attempts to use su. Usually /usr/adm/sulog. If this is not set, no logfile is kept. (See below.)
PATH
The PATH environment variable to set for non-root users. If not set, it defaults to :/bin:/usr/bin. The current PATH environment variable is ignored.

SUPATH
The PATH environment variable to set for root. If not set, it defaults to /bin:/etc:/usr/bin. The current PATH is ignored.

CONSOLE
Attempts to use su to change to the root account are logged to the named device, independently of SULOG.

For example, if you want to log all attempts by users to become root, edit the file /etc/default/su. In this file, place a string similar to:
    SULOG=/usr/adm/sulog

This causes all attempts by any user to switch user IDs to be recorded in the file /usr/adm/sulog. This filename is arbitrary. The su logfile records the original user, the UID of the su attempt, and the time of the attempt. If the attempt is successful, a plus sign (+) is placed on the line describing the attempt. A minus sign (-) indicates an unsuccessful attempt.

Examples

switch to user2:

```
su user2
```

move—overview

Method for renaming a file or moving data or a file to a new location

mv   rename a file or move a file to a new location

move

---

mv   rename a file or move a file to a different location

mv [-fi] source_file target_file

mv [-fi] source_file...target_directory

Options

If the destination file already exists, it is removed before source_file is copied. If the permissions of the destination file do not permit writing and the standard input is a terminal, or the -i option was specified, mv prints the destination pathname and the mode (see chmod(S)) and prompts for confirmation. If you type "y", the move takes place; otherwise mv does not move the file and continues to the next source_file.

In the second form, mv moves each source_file to a new destination directory. The destination path is formed for each file by concatenating the target_directory, a slash, and the basename of the source_file.

The -f option suppresses all prompting.

mv attempts to preserve the following characteristics of each file moved:

the time of last data modification and time of last access

the user ID and group ID

the file mode

mv can move directories, even across filesystems.

Examples

rename file1 to file2:

```
mv file1 file2
```

delete file1 from the current directory and place it in the directory /usr1 with the name file1:

```
mv file1 /usr1
```

delete file1 from the current directory and place the contents in the directory /usr1 with the name file2:

```
mv file1 /usr1/file2
```

print—overview

Methods for printing files

banner	output characters in large letters
cancel	cancel print job
lp	print
lpmove	move a print job
lpsched	start print spooler
lpshut	stop print spooler
lpstat	status of print spooler
pr	print formatted file

print

banner display text in large letters on standard output

banner strings

Options

There are no options for this command.

Examples

banner OUT:

```
#######    #        #    #######
#       #  #        #          #
#       #  #        #         #
 #######    #######         #
```

cancel a print job on the printer

cancel request-id...[printer...]
cancel [request-id...] printer...

Options

The cancel command cancels printer requests that were made by the lp(C) command. The arguments may be request-ids, printer names, or a list of both. (Request-ids are the print job identification codes returned by lp(C). A complete list of printer names can be found using lpstat(C).)

Specifying a request-id cancels the associated request even if it is currently printing. Specifying a printer cancels the request that is currently printing on that printer. In either case, the cancellation of a request that is currently printing frees the printer to print its next available request.

Examples

cancel print job 1234 on printer1:

```
cancel printer1-1234
```

---

lp   print to a print spooler or service which sends the job to the appropriate printer

lp [options] files

lp -i request-id [options]

Options

-c
Make a temporary copy of the files to be printed. Any subsequent changes to the files are not printed. If -c is not specified, any changes to the file may appear in the printed output.

-d
dest
Print this request using dest as the printer or class of printers. Requests for specific destinations may not be accepted under certain conditions (for example, printer not available or not capable), (see accept(ADM) and lpstat(C)). By default, dest is set to the value of the environment variable LPDEST if this has been set. Otherwise, the default destination for the computer system is used if one exists. Default destination names vary between systems (see lpstat(C)).

-f
form-name [-d any]
Print the request on the form form-name. The LP print service ensures that the form is mounted on the printer. The request is rejected (see lpforms(ADM)):

if form-name is requested with a printer destination that cannot support the form

if form-name has not been defined for the system

if the user is not allowed to use the form

The -d any option sends the request to any printer that has the requested form mounted and can handle all the other needs of the print request.

-H argument
Deal with a request (specified using the -i option) according to one of the following possible settings of argument:

hold
Do not print the request until notified. If already printing, stop the request. Other print requests will go ahead of a held request until it is resumed.

resume
Resume a held request. If it was printing when held, it will be the next request printed, unless subsequently overridden by an immediate request.

immediate
(Available only to root and lp administrators.) Print the request next. If more than one request is assigned as immediate, the requests are printed last-in first-out. If another request is currently printing on the desired printer, you must hold it to allow the immediate request to print.

-L argument
The following arguments are understood by this option:

local
Send the request to the printer attached to the terminal (see lprint(C) for more information about terminal printing).

spooler
    Send the request to the default printer.

live=device
Enable printing from the standard input to the device special file
or text file device. The file /usr/spool/lpd/lock must exist for this to
work. This option may not be combined with any other option.

-m
Send mail (see mail(C)) after the files have been printed. By
default, no mail is sent upon normal completion of the print
request.

-n number
Print number copies of the output (default is 1).

-o options
Specify one or more printer-dependent or class-dependent options
as a comma-separated list. For local printers, -o can be specified
more than once. For remote printers, -o can only be specified once
and the list of options must be enclosed in double quotation
marks (").

The standard(ADM) printer interface program recognizes the following options:

cpi=sdn|pica|elite|compressed

Print the request with the character pitch set to:

sdn
a scaled decimal number; its units are indicated by appending a letter "i" (for characters per inch) or "c" (for characters per centimeter). If no units are specified, they are assumed to be characters per inch.

pica
10 columns per inch

elite
12 columns per inch

compressed
as many columns as the printer can handle

There is no standard number of columns per inch for printers; see the terminfo(F) database for the default character pitch for your printer.

This option cannot be used with the -f option.

length=sdn
Print a request with pages that are sdn long. sdn is a scaled decimal number; its units are indicated by appending a letter "i" (for inches) or "c" (for centimeters). If no units are specified, sdn is assumed to be a absolute number of lines. For example, length=66 indicates a page length of 66 lines, length=11i indicates a page length of 11 inches, and length=27.94c indicates a page length of 27.94 centimeters.

This option cannot be used with the -f option.

lpi=sdn
Print a request with the line pitch set to sdn. sdn is a scaled decimal number; its units are indicated by appending a letter "i" (for
lines per inch) or "c" (for lines per centimeter). If no units are
specified, they are assumed to be lines per inch.

This option cannot be used with the -f option.

nobanner
Do not print a banner page with a request. (The administrator can
disallow this option at any time.)

nofilebreak
Do not insert a form feed between the files given if submitting a
job to print more than one file.

stty=stty-option-list
Set the printer with a list of stty(C) options. You must enclose the
list in single quotes if it contains whitespace.

width=sdn
Print the output of this request with a page-width of sdn. sdn is a
scaled decimal number; its units are indicated by appending a letter "i" (for inches) or "c" (for centimeters). If no units are specified, sdn is assumed to be a absolute number of columns.

This option cannot be used with the -f option.

**The following options to -o are recognized by other interface pro-
grams if the printer has the required capability:**

ascii
allow ASCII source to be printed as PostScript by filtering it through /usr/spool/lp/bin/text2post

cdn
select condensed characters

double
select double sided printing

dq
select draft quality printing

land
select landscape printing

land2
select alternate landscape printing

lower
select the lower paper feed tray

lm=n
set the left margin to column n

lq
select letter quality printing

manual
select the manual feed tray

nlq
select near letter quality printing

port
select portrait printing

postscript
select PostScript printing; note that the printer interface scripts can auto-detect PostScript source files that begin with the sequence "%!" or "<Ctrl>D%!"

raw
select raw printing; needed to print PostScript files on certain PostScript printers

rm=n
set the right margin to column n

upper
select the upper paper feed tray

-P page-list
Print the page(s) specified in page-list. This option can be used only if there is a filter available to handle it; otherwise, the print request will be rejected.

The page-list may consist of range(s) of numbers, single page numbers, or a combination of both. The pages will be printed in ascending order.

-q priority-level
Assign priority-level to this request in the printing queue. The values of priority-level range from 0, the highest priority, to 39, the lowest priority. If a priority is not specified, the default for the print service is used, as assigned by the printer administrator.

-R
Remove file after sending it.

-s
Suppress messages from lp such as "request id is...".

-S character-set [-d any]
Print this request using the specified character-set. The request is rejected if a form has been specified that requires a different character-set.

If the print-wheel specified is not one listed by the administrator as acceptable for the printer involved in this request, the request is rejected unless the print wheel is already mounted on the printer.

The -d any option sends the request to any printer that can select the character set and can handle all the other needs of the request.

-S print-wheel [-d any]
Print this request using the specified print-wheel. The request is rejected if a form has been specified that requires a different print-wheel.

If the character-set specified is not one defined in the terminfo database for the printer (see terminfo(F)) or is not an alias defined by the administrator, the request is rejected.

The -d any option sends the request to any printer that has the print wheel mounted and can handle all the other needs of the request.

-t title Print title on the banner page of the output. The default is no title.

-T type [-r]
Tell the print service to print the request on a printer that supports files of the specified content type. If no printer accepts this type directly, a filter will be used to convert the file contents into an acceptable type. If the -r option is specified, a filter will not be used.

The request is rejected:

if -r is specified but no printer accepts the type directly

if the type is not acceptable to any printer, either directly or with a filter

-w
Write a message on the terminal after the files have been printed. Mail is sent instead if the user has logged out or the terminal cannot be written to (because mesg(C) has been set with the n option).

-y mode[,mode...]
Print a request according to the printing modes listed. The allowed values for mode are locally defined. This option can be used only if there is a filter available to handle it; if there is no filter, the print request will be rejected.

Examples

print file:

```
lp file
```

print file to printer1:

```
lp -dprinter1 file
```

---

lpmove

move print job from one printer to another

/usr/lib/lpmove requests dest

/usr/lib/lpmove dest1 dest2

Options

There are no options for this command.

Examples

move print job 1234 from printer1 to printer2:

```
lpmove printer1-1234 printer2
```

lpsched start the print spooler or service process

/usr/lib/lpsched [-d] [-f int] [-n int] [-r int] [-s]

Options

-d
Debug mode; log all messages between lp and lpsched to /usr/spool/lp/logs/messages, log all requests submitted to /usr/spool/lp/logs/requests, and log all commands executed by lpsched to /usr/spool/lp/logs/exec.

-f int
Increase the number of slow filters that can run concurrently by int (see lpfilter(ADM)).

-n int
Increase the number of notifications that can run concurrently by int (see the -m and -w options of lp(C)).

-r int
Increase the margin of reserved file descriptors used by the scheduler by int.

-s
Do not trap most signals; disables interrupt, hangup, quit, terminate, child, and alarm signals.

Examples

start the print spooler:

```
lpsched
```

---

lpshut   stop the print spooler or service

/usr/lib/lpshut

Options

There are no options for this command.

Examples

stop print spooler:

```
lpshut
```

---

lpstat   display status of the print spooler or services including user's print jobs

lpstat options [request-id | printer | class…]

Options

-a [list]
Print acceptance status (with respect to lp) of destinations for requests (see accept(ADM)). list is a list of intermixed printer names and class names; the default is all.

-c [list]
Print class names and their members. list is a list of class names; the default is all.

-d
Print the system default destination for lp.

-f [list] [-l]
Print a verification that the forms in form-list are recognized by the lp print service. The -l option will list the form descriptions.

-o [list] [-l]
Print the status of output requests. list is a list of intermixed printer names, class names, and request-ids; the default is all. The -l option gives a more detailed status of the request.

-p [list] [-D] [-l]
Print the status of printers named in list. If the -D option is given, a brief description is printed for each printer in list. If the -l option is given, a full description of each printer's configuration is given, including the form mounted, the acceptable content and printer types, a printer description, the interface used, and the number of banner pages.

-r

Print the status of the lp request scheduler.

-s

Print a status summary, including the system default destination, a list of class names and their members, a list of printers and their associated devices, a list of all forms currently mounted, and a list of all recognized character sets and print wheels.

-S [list] [-l]

Print a verification that the character sets or the print wheels specified in list are recognized by the lp print service. Items in list can be character sets or print wheels; the default for the list is all. If the -l option is given, each line is appended by a list of printers that can handle the print wheel or character set. The list also shows whether the print wheel or character set is mounted or specifies the built-in character set into which it maps.

-t

Print all status information.

-u [list]

Print status of output requests for users. list is a list of login names. The default is all.

-v [list]

Print the names of printers and the path names of the devices associated with them. list is a list of printer names. The default is all.

Examples

status for all printers:

```
lpstat -t
```

status of print jobs for all printers:

```
lpstat -o
```

---

pr   format and print contents of a file

pr [options] [files]

Options

-a
Prints multi-column output across the page.

-d
Double-spaces the output.

-eck
Expands input tabs to character positions k+1, 2*k+1, 3*k+1, etc. If k is 0 or is omitted, default tab settings at every 8th position are assumed. Tab characters in the input are expanded into the appropriate number of spaces. If c (any non-digit character) is given, it is treated as the input tab character (default for c is the tab character).

-f

Uses form feed character for new pages (default is to use a sequence of linefeeds). Pauses before beginning the first page if the standard output is associated with a terminal.

-F

Uses a form feed character for new pages.

-h

Uses the next argument as the header to be printed instead of the filename.

-ick

In output, replaces white space wherever possible by inserting tabs to character positions k+1, 2*k+1, 3*k+1, etc. If k is 0 or is omitted, default tab settings at every 8th position are assumed. If c (any non-digit character) is given, it is treated as the output tab character (default for c is the tab character).

+k

Begins printing with page k (default is 1).

-k

Produces k-column output (default is 1). The options -e and -i are assumed for multi-column output.

-l n

Sets the length of a page to n lines (default is 66).

-m

Merges and prints all files simultaneously, one pcr column (overrides the -k, and -a options).

-nck

Provides k-digit line numbering (default for k is 5). The number occupies the first k+1 character positions of each column of normal output or each line of -m output. If c (any non-digit character) is given, it is appended to the line number to separate it from whatever follows (default for c is a tab).

-o k

Offsets each line by k character positions (default is 0). The number of character positions per line is the sum of the width and offset.

-p

Pauses before beginning each page if the output is directed to a terminal (pr will ring the bell at the terminal and wait for a carriage return).

-r

Prints no diagnostic reports on failure to open files.

-sc

Separates columns by the single character c instead of by the appropriate number of spaces (default for c is a tab).

-t

Prints neither the 5-line identifying header nor the 5-line trailer normally supplied for each page. Quits printing after the last line of each file without spacing to the end of the page.

-w k

Sets the width of a line to k character positions (default is 72 for equal-width multi-column output, no limit otherwise).

Examples

format and print file:

```
pr file
```

replace—overview

Method for substituting or deleting characters

tr   substitute or delete characters

replace

tr   substitute or delete characters

tr [-cs] string1 string2

tr -s [-c] string1

tr -d [-c] string1

tr -ds [-c] string1 string2

Options

-c
Complements the set of characters in string1 with respect to the universe of characters whose ASCII codes are 001 through 377 octal.

-d
Deletes all input characters in string1.

-s
Squeezes all strings of repeated output characters that are in string2 to single characters.

Examples

delete commas for file1 and store result in file.new:

```
tr -d , < file1 > file.new
```

change the lowercase characters in file1 to uppercase characters and output to file2:

```
tr "[:lower:]" "[:upper:]" <file1 >file2
```

search—overview

Methods for searching files

cut	cut selected lines from a file
egrep	find a pattern
fgrep	find a specific string
find	find a file
grep	find a pattern

search

cut   cut selected fields from each line in one or more files, concatenate and output

cut -b list [-n] [file…]

cut -c list [file…]

cut -f list [-d char] [-s] [file…]

Options

-b list
list specifies byte positions. For example, -b 1-100 cuts the first 100 bytes of each line. Each selected byte will be output unless explicitly suppressed by the -n option).

-c list
list specifies character positions. For example, -c 1-72 would keep the first 72 characters of each line.

-f list
list specifies fields assumed to be separated in the file by a delimiter character (see -d). For example, -f 1,7 copies the first and seventh field only. Lines with no field delimiters will be passed through intact (useful for table subheadings), unless -s is specified.

-d char
The character following -d is the field delimiter (-f option only).
Default is Tab. Space or other characters with special meaning to
the shell must be quoted.

-n
Do not split characters. Used in conjunction with the -b option as
in the following example:

 cut -b 1-100 -n file

Here 1 is the low byte and 100 is the high byte. If the low byte is
not the first byte of a character, its value will be decremented by 1
so that the first byte of a character is selected. Similarly, if the
specified high byte is not the last byte of a character, its value will
be decremented by 1 so that the selected byte becomes the last
byte of the character prior to the character selected on the command line.

-s
If the -f option is used, -s suppresses lines with no delimiter characters. Unless specified, lines with no delimiters will be passed
through untouched.

One of the options -b, -c or -f must be specified.

Examples

search file for value "5678" in columns 24-27 returning line
numbers where value found:

```
cut -c24-27 file  | grep -n "5678"
```

---

egrep   find a pattern using full regular expressions in a file (same as grep -E)

egrep [-c | -l | -q] [-bhinsvx] [-e expression] [-f expfile] [expression]
[files]

Options

-E
Each pattern is treated as an extended regular expression. A null extended regular expression matches all lines.

-F
Each pattern is treated as a string instead of a regular expression. A null string matches all lines.

-v
All lines but those matching are displayed.

-x
Displays only exact matches of an entire line.

-c
Only a count of matching lines is displayed.

-l
Only the names of files with matching lines are displayed, separated by newlines.

-h

Prevents the name of the file containing the matching line from being printed before that line. Used when searching multiple files.

-n

Each line is preceded by its relative line number in the file.

-b

Each line is preceded by the block number on which it was found. This is sometimes useful in locating disk block numbers by context.

-s

Suppresses error messages produced for nonexistent or unreadable files. Other error messages are not suppressed.

-i

Turns on matching of letters of either case in the input so that case is insignificant. Conversion between uppercase and lowercase letters is dependent on the locale setting.

-y

Turns on matching of letters of either case in the input so that case is insignificant. Conversion between uppercase and lowercase letters is dependent on the locale setting. Note: -y is not a standard UNIX system option. It is maintained for backwards compatibility with XENIX.

-e expression

Specify patterns to be used during the search. The patterns in the list must be separated by a newline character. Multiple -e and -f options are accepted. Unless the -E or -F options are specified, grep treats the patterns as basic regular expressions.

-f expfile
The regular expression for grep, or extended expression for egrep, or strings list for fgrep is taken from the expfile. Patterns in the file are terminated by a newline character. Unless the -E or -F options are specified, grep treats the patterns as basic regular expressions.

-q
Quiet. Nothing is written to the standard output. grep exits with status 0 if an input line is selected. This provides a quick and easy method of testing if a pattern or string exists in a group of files.

Examples

find value "5678" in file and output line containing expression:

```
egrep "5678" file
```

---

fgrep   find and print line containing specified string

fgrep [-c | -l | -q] [-bhinsvx] [-e expression] [-f expfile] [expression] [files

Options

-E
Each pattern is treated as an extended regular expression. A null extended regular expression matches all lines.

-F
Each pattern is treated as a string instead of a regular expression. A null string matches all lines.

-v
All lines but those matching are displayed.

-x
Displays only exact matches of an entire line.

-c
Only a count of matching lines is displayed.

-l
Only the names of files with matching lines are displayed, separated by newlines.

-h
Prevents the name of the file containing the matching line from being printed before that line. Used when searching multiple files.

-n
Each line is preceded by its relative line number in the file.

-b

Each line is preceded by the block number on which it was found. This is sometimes useful in locating disk block numbers by context.

-s

Suppresses error messages produced for nonexistent or unreadable files. Other error messages are not suppressed.

-i

Turns on matching of letters of either case in the input so that case is insignificant. Conversion between uppercase and lowercase letters is dependent on the locale setting.

-y

Turns on matching of letters of either case in the input so that case is insignificant. Conversion between uppercase and lowercase letters is dependent on the locale setting. Note: -y is not a standard UNIX system option. It is maintained for backwards compatibility with XENIX.

-e expression

Specify patterns to be used during the search. The patterns in the list must be separated by a newline character. Multiple -e and -f options are accepted. Unless the -E or -F options are specified, grep treats the patterns as basic regular expressions.

-f expfile

The regular expression for grep, or extended expression for egrep, or strings list for fgrep is taken from the expfile. Patterns in the file are terminated by a newline character. Unless the -E or -F options are specified, grep treats the patterns as basic regular expressions.

-q
Quiet. Nothing is written to the standard output. grep exits with status 0 if an input line is selected. This provides a quick and easy method of testing if a pattern or string exists in a group of files.

Examples

find lines containing "hello" in file:

```
fgrep "hello" file
```

---

find   find files descending recursively through the directory hierarchy

find pathname-list expression

Options

-atime n
True if the file was last accessed n days ago. The access time refers to the last time that the file's data was read, or the creation of the file. It does not record the time that changes were written to the file's data, or to the information stored in the inode.

-cpio device
Writes the current file on device in cpio(F) format (5120-byte records) by piping output to cpio(C) (equivalent to | /bin/cpio -ocBO device). If -follow is also specified, files referenced by symbolic links are also copied into the archive (equivalent to |

/bin/cpio -ocBLO device). This option sets -depth automatically. Always true.

-ctime n
True if the file was last changed n days ago. The change time refers to modification of the file's data, modification of the information stored in the inode, or creation of the file.

-depth
Causes all entries in a directory to be acted upon before the directory itself. In a depth-first search, find descends the directory hierarchy as far as it can before traversing the filesystem. This option is set automatically by -cpio to stop copied non-writable directories from preventing their contents being copied to them. Always true.

-exec cmd
Executes shell command cmd. A command argument {} is replaced by the current pathname. True if the executed cmd returns a zero value as exit status (most commands return a zero value on successful completion and a non-zero value if an error is encountered). The end of cmd must be followed by a semicolon. The semicolon should be preceded by a shell escape (like "\") because it has a special meaning in the shell.

-follow
Always true; causes symbolic links to be followed. When following symbolic links, find keeps track of the directories visited so that it can detect infinite loops. For example, an infinite loop in a find would occur if a symbolic link pointed to an ancestor. This expression should not be used with the -type l expression.

-group gname
True if the file belongs to the group gname. If gname is numeric and does not appear in the /etc/group file as a group name, it is taken as a group ID.

-inum num
True if the file's inode is num. This is useful for locating files with matching inodes.

-links n
True if the file has n links.

-local
True if the file physically resides on the local system.

-mount
Always true; restricts the search to the filesystem containing the directory specified, or if no directory was specified, the current directory.

-mtime n
True if the file's data was last modified n days ago. The modification time refers only to changes made to the file's data, or the creation of the file. It does not record the time that changes were made to the information stored in the inode.

-name pattern
True if pattern matches the current filename. pattern is a shell regular expression, as described in regexp(M). Because this syntax is interpreted by the shell, care should be taken to escape or quote patterns (to prevent them being evaluated prematurely).

-newer file
True if the current file has been modified more recently than the argument file.

-nogroup
True if the file belongs to a group ID that does not have a group-name associated with it.

-nouser
True if the file belongs to a user ID that does not have a username associated with it.

-ok cmd
Like -exec except that the generated command line is printed with a question mark first, and is executed only if the user responds by typing "y". (The command should be followed by an escaped semicolon.)

-perm [-] mode
The mode argument is used to represent file mode bits. It is identical to the symbolic mode specified by chmod(C). To start with a blank template is created, corresponding to a file's access permissions with no mode bits set. The permissions granted or revoked in the mode string are then applied. If the hyphen is omitted, this primary expression is true when the permissions specified in the resulting template exactly match the file permissions. Otherwise the expression evaluates as true if, at a minimum, all bits in the template that are set are also set in the file permission bits (the other permissions being ignored).

-perm [-]onum
If the dash (-) is omitted, this primary evaluates as true when the file's permission bits exactly match the file permission bits defined by the value of the octal number onum.

If the dash is specified, this primary evaluates as true if all bits that are set in onum are also set in the file's permission bits.

-print
Causes the current pathname to be printed. This option is used to create a list of files matched by the previous primaries. Always true.

-prune
Always true; causes find not to descend the current pathname if it is a directory. If -depth is specified, -prune has no effect.

-size n [c]
True if the file is n blocks long (512 bytes per block), not including indirect blocks. If n is followed by a "c", the size is in characters.

-type x
True if the type of the file is x, where x is b for block special file, c for character special file, d for directory, p for named pipe (first-in-first-out (FIFO)), f for regular file, or l for symbolic link.

-user uname
True if the file belongs to the user uname. If uname is numeric and does not appear as a login name in the /etc/passwd file, it is taken as a user ID.

-xdev Equivalent to the primary -mount.

(expression)
True if the parenthesized expression is true. Usually used with the
-o operator (see below), parentheses are used for grouping.
Parentheses are special to the shell and must be escaped.

The primaries may be combined using the following operators (in
order of decreasing precedence):

! The "!" operator specifies the negation of the next primary (that
is, ! -newer file is true if the current file is not newer than file).
This is the equivalent of the logical "not" operator.

-o
Placing the -o operator between two primaries creates an expression that is true if either of the two primaries is true. It should be
used with parentheses (that is, \(-perm 644 -o -perm 664 \) is true
if the current file has permissions 644 or 664). This is equivalent
to the logical "inclusive or" operator.

Note that placing two primaries next to each other is the equivalent of the logical "and" operation. The precedence of this operation is less than that of the "!" operator but greater than that of
the -o operator.

If no expression is given, -print is assumed. Otherwise, if the given
expression does not contain any of the primaries -exec, -ok, -cpio
or -print, the given expression is assumed to be replaced by:

(given_expression) –print

Examples

find file starting at root directory:

```
find / -name "file" -print
```

---

grep   find and print line containing specified pattern

grep [-E | -F] [-c | -l | -q] [-bhinsvx] [-e expression] [-f expfile] [expression] [files]

Options

-E
Each pattern is treated as an extended regular expression. A null extended regular expression matches all lines.

-F
Each pattern is treated as a string instead of a regular expression. A null string matches all lines.

-v
All lines but those matching are displayed.

-x
Displays only exact matches of an entire line.

-c
Only a count of matching lines is displayed.

-l
Only the names of files with matching lines are displayed, separated by newlines.

-h
Prevents the name of the file containing the matching line from being printed before that line. Used when searching multiple files.

-n
Each line is preceded by its relative line number in the file.

-b
Each line is preceded by the block number on which it was found. This is sometimes useful in locating disk block numbers by context.

-s
Suppresses error messages produced for nonexistent or unreadable files. Other error messages are not suppressed.

-i
Turns on matching of letters of either case in the input so that case is insignificant. Conversion between uppercase and lowercase letters is dependent on the locale setting.

-y
Turns on matching of letters of either case in the input so that case is insignificant. Conversion between uppercase and lowercase letters is dependent on the locale setting. Note: -y is not a standard UNIX system option. It is maintained for backwards compatibility with XENIX.

-e expression
Specify patterns to be used during the search. The patterns in the list must be separated by a newline character. Multiple -e and -f options are accepted. Unless the -E or -F options are specified, grep treats the patterns as basic regular expressions.

-f expfile
The regular expression for grep, or extended expression for egrep, or strings list for fgrep is taken from the expfile. Patterns in the file are terminated by a newline character. Unless the -E or -F options are specified, grep treats the patterns as basic regular expressions.

-q
Quiet. Nothing is written to the standard output. grep exits with status 0 if an input line is selected. This provides a quick and easy method of testing if a pattern or string exists in a group of files.

Examples

find 5% in file:

```
grep "5%" file
```

security—overview

Methods for managing security of files

chgrp	change group on a file
chmod	change permissions on a file
chown	change owner on a file
crypt	encode or decode a file
passwd	change user password

security

chgrp   change group of file or directory

chgrp [-R] group file...

Options

-R
Recursively change file group IDs. For each file that names a directory, chgrp changes the group ID of the directory and all files in the file hierarchy below it.

Examples

change group to mis on file:

```
chgrp mis file
```

chmod   change mode or permissions of a file or directory

Symbolic mode

chmod [-R] [who][+|-|=][mode...] file...

Absolute mode

chmod [-R] mode file...

Options

-R
Recursively change file mode bits. For each specified file that names a directory, chmod will change the file mode bits of the directory and all files in the file hierarchy below it.

Examples

change file permissions to be read/write/executable for owner only:

```
chmod 700 file
```

change file permissions to be read/write/executable for owner, read/write for group, and executable for everyone else:

```
chmod 761 file
```

change file permissions to be read/write/executable for owner, read/executable for group, and read for everyone else:

```
chmod 754 file
```

---

chown   change the owner of a file or directory

chown [-R] owner[:group] file...

Options

-R
Recursively change file user IDs, and if group is specified, group IDs. For each file that names a directory, chown changes the owner and group ID of the directory and all files in the hierarchy below it.

Examples

change owner from root to user on file:

```
chown user file
```

---

crypt   read from standard input and write standard output requiring a key if there is no key

crypt [password]

crypt [-k]

Options

If the -k option is used, crypt will use the key assigned to the environment variable CrYpTkEy.

Examples

encode file1 out to file2:

```
crypt key <file1 >file2
```

decode file out to printer:

```
crypt key <file | pr
```

---

passwd   change user password which the length must be six to eight characters two must be alpha and at least one must be numeric or special character. Login name is not accepted and the new password must differ from the old by three characters

passwd [-m] [-dluf] [-n minimum] [-x expiration]
[-r retries] [name] passwd -s [-a] [name]

Options

-d
Delete the password. A password may be deleted only if the user is authorized to not have a password. System administrators must always specify name; otherwise, the name of the user who logged in is used.

-f
Force user name to change their password the next time they log in. This option may be specified only by system administrators,

and only when the user's password is not being changed or deleted; name must be explicitly given.

-l

Lock user name out of the system by applying an administrative lock; only system administrators may do this and they must specify name.

-u

Remove any administrative lock applied to user name; only system administrators may do this and they must specify name.

-n minimum

Set the amount of time which must elapse between password changes for user name to minimum days. Only system administrators may do this and they must specify name.

-x expiration

Set the amount of time which may elapse before the password of user name expires to expiration days. Only system administrators may do this and they must specify name. Once a password has expired, the user must change it the next time they log in.

-r retries

Up to retries attempts may be made to choose a new password for user name.

-s

Report the password attributes of user name (or, if the -a option is given, of all users). The format of the report is: name status mm/dd/yy minimum expiration where status is "PS" if the user has a password, "LK" if the user is administratively locked, or

"NP" when the user does not have a password. The date of the last successful password change (or deletion) is shown as mm/dd/yy. If neither name nor -a is specified, the name of the user who logged in is assumed. Only system administrators can examine the attributes of users other than themselves.

If no -d, -f, -l, -u, or -s option is specified, the password for user name is changed as described above. If no name is given and no option which requires name is given, then the name of the user who logged in is used. Only the -a option may be specified with the -s option.

Examples

change password:

```
passwd
```

change another users password:

```
passwd user
```

sort—overview

Method for sorting files

sort   sort a file

sort

---

sort   sort a file

sort [-m] [-bdfiMnru] [-o output] [-k keydef]...
[-t x] [-T tmpdir] [-y [kmem]] [-z recsz] [file...]

sort -c [-bdfiMnru] [-k keydef]...[-t x] [-T tmpdir] [-y [kmem]]
[-z recsz] [file]

sort [-mu] [-bdfiMnr] [-o output] [-t x] [-T tmpdir] [-y [kmem]]
[-z recsz] [+pos1 [-pos2]]...[file...]

sort -c [-u] [-bdfiMnr] [-t x] [-T tmpdir] [-y [kmem]] [-z recsz]
[+pos1 [-pos2]]...[file]

Options

-c
Check that the input file is sorted according to the ordering rules.
This option produces no output; it only affects the exit value.

-m
Merge only; the input files should already be sorted.

-o output
The argument output is the name of a file to use instead of the
standard output. This file may be the same as one of the input
files. There may be optional blanks between -o and output.

-T tmpdir

tmpdir is the pathname of a directory to be used for temporary files. The default is to try /usr/tmp and /tmp. If -T is specified then tmpdir and /tmp are tried. There must be a space between -T and tmpdir.

-u

Unique: suppress all but one in each set of lines having equal keys. This option can result in unwanted characters placed at the end of the sorted file.

-y [kmem]

The amount of memory used by sort has a large impact on its performance; for example, sorting a small file in a large amount of memory is inefficient. If the -y option is omitted, sort begins using the default memory size (32KB), and allocates more memory as needed. If kmem is specified, sort starts using that number of kilobytes of memory, unless the administrative minimum (32KB) or maximum (1MB) is violated. In this case, sort uses the corresponding minimum or maximum value.

If kmem is 0, sort uses the minimum memory requirement of 16KB.

By convention, specifying -y with no argument uses the maximum memory requirement of 1MB.

-z recsz

Causes sort to use a buffer size of recsz bytes for the merge phase. Input lines longer than the buffer size will cause sort to terminate abnormally. Normally, the size of the longest line read during the sort phase is recorded and this maximum is used as the record size during the merge phase, eliminating the need for the -z option. However, when the sort phase is omitted (-c or -m options) a system default buffer size is used, and if this is not large enough, the -z option should be used to prevent abnormal termination.

The following options override the default ordering rules.

-d
"Dictionary" order: only letters, digits and blanks (spaces and tabs) are significant in comparisons. Dictionary order is defined by the current setting of LC_CTYPE (see locale(M)).

-f
Fold lowercase letters into uppercase. Conversion between lowercase and uppercase letters are governed by the current setting of LC_CTYPE (see locale(M)).

-i
Ignore non-printable characters in non-numeric comparisons. Non-printable characters are defined by the current setting of LC_CTYPE (see locale(M)).

-M
Compare as months according to the current setting of LC_TIME (see locale(M)). The first month in the year compares low to the second month and so on; for example, in the POSIX locale: "JAN" < "FEB" <...< "DEC" and invalid fields compare low to "JAN". The -M option implies the -b option.

-n
An initial numeric string, consisting of optional blanks, an optional minus sign, and zero or more digits with optional decimal point, is

sorted by arithmetic value. The -n option implies the -b option. Note that the -b option is only effective when restricted sort key specifications are in effect.

-r
Reverse the sense of comparisons.

The treatment of field separators can be altered using the options:

-b
Ignore leading blanks when determining the starting and ending positions of a restricted sort key. If the -b option is specified before the first sort key argument, it will be applied to all sort keys.

-t x
Use x as the field separator character; x is not considered to be part of a field (although it may be included in a sort key). If x is a space, specified as -t " ", all spaces (including those at the beginning of a line) are treated as field separators. Each occurrence of x is significant (for example, xx delimits an empty field).

When ordering options appear before restricted sort key specifications, the requested ordering rules are applied globally to all sort keys. When one or more of the flags b, d, f, i, n, or r is attached to a specific sort key (see "Sort key field definition"). the specified ordering options override all global ordering options for that key.

When there are multiple sort keys, later keys are compared only after all earlier keys compare equal. Lines that otherwise compare equal are ordered with all bytes significant.

Input files are treated as sequences of records (lines), each of which contains one or more fields. By default, the first blank character (space or tab) of a sequence of blank characters acts as the field separator. Remaining blank characters in the sequence are treated as part of the field unless the -b option (ignore leading blanks) is specified. If the -t option is used to specify a field separating character, all occurrences of that character are interpreted as separating fields.

The option -t " " specifies that a space character is to be used as the field separator. In this case, any tab characters are interpreted as being part of a field; any leading tab characters are ignored if the -b option is specified. All space characters are interpreted as field separators and are unaffected by the -b option.

Examples

to sort file in alphabetical order and eliminate duplicates output to standard output:

```
sort -u file1
```

to sort file in numeric order output to file2:

```
sort -n file > file2
```

source code control—overview

Methods for administering source code revisions and maintaining versions. "Check in" completed code or "check out" prior versions (deltas).

admin	create or administer SCCS files
cdc	change delta comments
comb	delete and combine versions
delta	add a version to the SCCS file
get	retrieve the specified delta from the SCCS file
unget	return the retrieved delta to the SCCS file unchanged
help	help with errors or commands
prs	print a delta
rmdel	delete a previous delta
sccsdiff	show difference between two deltas

source code control

---

admin   create or administer SCCS files

admin [[-n] [[-i[name]] [-b] [-rrel]] [-tname] [-m[mrlist]] [-y[comment]]] files

admin [-t[name]] [-fflag[value]] [-dflag[value]] [-alogin] [-elogin] files

admin [-h] [-z] files

Options

-n
Creates a new SCCS file.

-i[name]
Creates a new SCCS file, taking the text from the file name or from standard input if the file name is omitted. (If name is a binary file, then you must specify the -b option.) The text constitutes the first delta of the file (see the -r option for delta numbering scheme). If this option is omitted, then the SCCS file is created empty. Only one SCCS file may be created by an admin command on which the -i option is supplied. Using a single admin command to create two or more SCCS files requires that they be created empty (no -i option). Note that -i implies -n.

-rrel

The release into which the initial delta is inserted; if not specified it is inserted into release 1. This option may be used only if -i is also used. The level of the initial delta is always 1. (Initial deltas are named 1.1 by default.)

-b

Encode the contents of the file specified by -iname. This keyletter must be used if name is a binary file;

-t[name]

Inserts, removes, or replaces descriptive text in an SCCS file. The name argument specifies a file from which the descriptive text is to be taken. When creating a new SCCS file (using -n and/or -i options), the name must be provided. Remove any descriptive text currently in an existing SCCS file, by specifying -t without an argument. Replace any descriptive text currently in an existing SCCS file, by specifying a file name which contains the replacement text.

-fflag

This option specifies a flag, and possibly a value for the flag, to be placed in the SCCS file. The -f option may be supplied several times.

The allowable flags and their values are:

b

Allows use of get -b to create branch deltas.

cceil

The highest release (the "ceiling"), a number greater than 0 but less than or equal to 9999, which may be retrieved by a get(CP) command for editing. The default value for an unspecified c flag is 9999.

ffloor

The lowest release (the "floor"), a number greater than 0 but less than 9999, which may be retrieved by a get(CP) command for editing. The default value for an unspecified f flag is 1.

dSID

The default delta number (SID.1) to be used by a get(CP) command.

i[str]

Causes the No id keywords (ge6) message issued by get(CP) or delta(CP) to be treated as a fatal error. In the absence of this flag, the message is only a warning. The message is issued if no SCCS identification keywords are found in the text retrieved or stored in the SCCS file. If a value is supplied, the keywords must exactly match the given string; however, the string must contain a keyword and no embedded newlines.

j

Allows concurrent get(CP) commands for editing on the same SID of an SCCS file. This allows multiple concurrent updates to the same version of the SCCS file.

llist

A list of releases to which deltas can no longer be made (get -e against one of these "locked" releases fails). The list has the following syntax:

    <list> ::= <range> | <list> , <range>
    <range> ::= RELEASE_NUMBER | a

The character "a" in the list is equivalent to specifying all releases for the named SCCS file.

n
Causes delta(CP) to create a "null" delta in each of those releases (if any) being skipped when a delta is made in a new release (for example, in making delta 5.1 after delta 2.7, releases 3 and 4 are skipped). These null deltas serve as "anchor points" so that branch deltas may later be created from them. The absence of this flag causes skipped releases to be nonexistent in the SCCS file, preventing branch deltas from being created from them in the future.

qtext
User-definable text substituted for all occurrences of the %Q% keyword in SCCS file text retrieved by
    get(CP).

mmod
Module name of the SCCS file substituted for all occurrences of the %M% keyword in SCCS file text retrieved by get(CP). If the m flag is not specified, the value assigned is the name of the SCCS file with the leading s. removed.

ttype
Type of module in the SCCS file substituted for all occurrences of %Y% keyword in SCCS file text retrieved by get(CP).

v[pgm]
Causes delta(CP) to prompt for Modification Request (MR) numbers as the reason for creating a delta. The optional value specifies the name of an MR number validity checking program (see delta(CP)). (If this flag is set when creating an SCCS file, the -m option must also be used even if its value is null.)

x
Causes get to create files with execute permissions.

-dflag
Causes removal (deletion) of the specified flag from an SCCS file. The -d option may be specified only when processing existing SCCS files. The -d option may be specified several times on a single admin command. See the -f keyletter for allowable flag names.

llist
A list of releases to be "unlocked". See the -f keyletter for a description of the l flag and the syntax of a list.

-alogin
A login name or numerical system group ID to be added to the list of users which may make deltas (changes) to the SCCS file. A group ID is equivalent to specifying all login names common to that group ID. Several a keyletters may be used on a single admin command line. As many logins or numerical group IDs as desired may be on the list simultaneously. If the list of users is empty, then anyone may add deltas. If login or group ID is preceded by a "!" it is to be denied permission to make deltas.

-elogin
A login name or numerical group ID to be erased from the list of users allowed to make deltas (changes) to the SCCS file. Specifying a group ID is equivalent to specifying all login names common to that group ID. Several e keyletters may be used on a single admin command line.

-m[mrlist]
The list of Modification Requests (MR) numbers is inserted into the SCCS file as the reason for creating the initial delta in a manner identical to delta(CP). The v flag must be set; the MR numbers are validated if the v flag has a value (the name of an MR number validation program). Diagnostics will occur if the v flag is not set or MR validation fails.

-y[comment]
The comment text is inserted into the SCCS file as a comment for the initial delta in a manner identical to that of delta(CP). Omission of the -y keyletter results in a default comment line being inserted in the form:

date and time created YY/MM/DD HH:MM:SS by login

The -y keyletter is valid only if the -i and/or -n keyletters are specified (that is, a new SCCS file is being created).

-h
Causes admin to check the structure of the SCCS file and to compare a newly computed check-sum (the sum of all the characters in the SCCS file except those in the first line) with the check-sum that is stored in the first line of the SCCS file. Appropriate error diagnostics are produced.

This keyletter inhibits writing on the file, so that it nullifies the effect of any other keyletters supplied, and is, therefore, only meaningful when processing existing files.

-z

The SCCS file check-sum is recomputed and stored in the first line of the SCCS file (see -h, above).

Note that use of this keyletter on a corrupted file may prevent future detection of the corruption.

Examples

create a file named s.ZZZ using the contents of file ZZZ:

```
admin -iZZZ s.ZZZ
```

create an empty file named s.ZZZ:

```
admin -nZZZ
```

---

cdc   change delta comments

cdc -rSID [-m[mrlist]] [-y[comment]] files
cdc -rSID -m[mrlist] -y[comment] -

Options

-rSID
Used to specify the SCCS identification (SID) string of a delta for which the delta commentary is to be changed.

-mmrlist
If the SCCS file has the v flag set (see admin(CP)) then a list of MR numbers to be added and/or deleted in the delta commentary of the SID specified by the -r option may be supplied. A null MR list has no effect.

MR entries are added to the list of MRs in the same manner as that of delta(CP). In order to delete an MR, precede the MR number with the character "!" (see "Examples" below). If the MR to be deleted is currently in the list of MRs, it is removed and changed into a "comment" line. A list of all deleted MRs is placed in the comment section of the delta commentary and preceded by a comment line stating that they were deleted.

If -m is not used and the standard input is a terminal, the prompt "MRs?" is issued on standard output before standard input is read; if the standard input is not a terminal, no prompt is issued. The "MRs?" prompt always precedes the comments? prompt (see -y option).

MRs in a list are separated by blanks and/or tab characters. An unescaped new-line character terminates the MR list.

Note that if the v flag has a value (see admin(CP)), it is taken to be the name of a program (or shell procedure) which validates MR numbers. If a non-zero exit status is returned from the MR number validation program, cdc terminates and the delta commentary remains unchanged.

-y[comment]
Arbitrary text used to replace the comment(s) already existing for the delta specified by the -r option. The previous comments are

kept and preceded by a comment line stating that they were changed. A null comment has no effect.

If -y is not specified and standard input is a terminal, the prompt comments? is issued on standard output before standard input is read; if standard input is not a terminal, no prompt is issued. An unescaped new-line character terminates the comment text.

Simply stated, if you made the delta, or you own the file and directory, you can modify the delta commentary.

Examples

change comments for version 1.2 of SCCS file s.ZZZ:
(prompt displays: comments?)

```
cdc -r1.2 s.ZZZ
```

---

comb   delete and combine versions

comb [-o] [-s] [-pSID] [-clist] files
comb -

Options

-o
For each get -e generated, this argument causes the reconstructed file to be accessed at the release of the delta to be created, otherwise the reconstructed file would be accessed at the

most recent ancestor. Use of the -o may decrease the size of the reconstructed SCCS file. It may also alter the shape of the delta tree of the original file.

-s

This argument causes comb to generate a shell procedure that, when run, produces a report giving the following for each file: the file name, the percentage change in file size after combining, the total file size (in blocks) after combining, and the original file size (also in blocks). The format of the report is as follows:

filename [±]percentage_change newsize/oldsize

A sample command line to use this option would look like this:

comb -s s.filename | sh > report

where report is the name of the file that receives the report information.

It is recommended that before any SCCS files are actually combined, you should use this option to determine exactly how much space can be saved through the combining process.

-pSID

The SID (SCCS identification string) of the oldest delta to be preserved. All older deltas are discarded in the reconstructed file. For example, if you give the command:

comb -p 1.5 s.filename

All deltas from 1.5 to the most recent delta will be preserved. All deltas prior to 1.5 will be removed.

-clist

This command causes the existing deltas in the subject file to be combined. It then overwrites the subject file with the new combined delta. For example, if you give the following command:

    comb -c1.4 s.workfile | sh

all previous deltas to s.workfile will be combined, and the new combined delta will be number 1.4.

If no arguments are specified, comb will preserve only leaf deltas and the minimal number of ancestors needed to preserve the tree.

Examples

delete deltas from s.ZZZ older than version 5.1

```
comb -p5.1 s.ZZZ
```

---

delta   add a version (delta) to the SCCS file by checking in the current version

delta [-rSID] [-s] [-n] [-glist] [-m[mrlist]] [-y[comment]] [-p] files
delta -

Options

-rSID
Uniquely identifies which delta is to be made to the SCCS file. The use of this option is necessary only if two or more outstanding gets for editing (get -e) on the same SCCS file were done by the same person (login name). The SID value specified with the -r option can be either the SID specified on the get command line or the SID to be made as reported by the get command (see get(CP)). A diagnostic results if the specified SID is ambiguous or if a required SID is omitted on the command line.

-s
Suppresses the issue, on the standard output, of the created delta's SID, as well as the number of lines inserted, deleted, and unchanged in the SCCS file.

-n
Specifies retention of the edited g-file (normally removed at completion of delta processing).

-glist
a list (see get(CP) for the definition of list) of deltas which are to be ignored when the file is accessed at the change level (SID) created by this delta.

-m[mrlist]
If the SCCS file has the v flag set (see admin(CP)), then a Modification Request (MR) number must be supplied as the reason for creating the new delta.

If -m is not used and the standard input is a terminal, the prompt MRs? is issued on the standard output before the standard input is read; if the standard input is not a terminal, no prompt is issued. The MRs? prompt always precedes the comments? prompt (see -y option).

MRs in a list are separated by blanks and/or tab characters. An unescaped new-line character terminates the MR list.

Note that if the v flag has a value (see admin(CP)), it is taken to be the name of a program (or shell procedure) which validates MR numbers. If a non-zero exit status is returned from the MR number validation program, delta terminates. (It is assumed that the MR numbers were not all valid.)

-y[comment]
Arbitrary text used to describe the reason for making the delta. A null string is considered a valid comment.

If -y is not specified and the standard input is a terminal, the prompt comments? is issued on standard output before standard input is read; if standard input is not a terminal, no prompt is issued. An unescaped new-line character terminates the comment text.

-p
Causes delta to print (on standard output) the SCCS file differences before and after the delta is applied in a diff(C) format.

Examples

check in ZZZ as the newest version of s.ZZZ and remove write-able ZZZ file:

```
delta s.ZZZ
```

check in ZZZ as the newest version of s.ZZZ and do not remove writeable ZZZ file:

```
delta -ns.ZZZ
```

---

get   retrieve the specified delta from the SCCS file in read-only or writeable mode

get [-rSID] [-ccutoff] [-ilist] [-xlist] [-wstring] [-aseq-no.] [-k] [-e] [-l[p]] [-p] [-m] [-n] [-s] [-b] [-g] [-t] file...

Options

Each of the arguments is explained below as though only one SCCS file is to be processed, but the effects of any argument applies independently to each named file.

-rSID
The SCCS identification string (SID) of the version (delta) of an SCCS file to be retrieved. Table 1 shows what version of an SCCS file is retrieved as a function of the SID specified. Also the SID of the version to be eventually created by delta(CP) if the -e option is used.

-ccutoff
The cutoff date and time, in the form:

YY[MM[DD[HH[MM[SS]]]]]

No changes (deltas) to the SCCS file which were created after the specified cutoff date-time are included in the extracted file. Units omitted from the date-time default to their maximum possible values; that is, -c7502 is equivalent to -c750228235959. Any number of non-numeric characters may separate the various 2-digit pieces of the cutoff date-time. This feature allows you to specify a cutoff date in the form: "-c77/2/2 9:22:25". Note that this implies that you may use the %E% and %U% identification keywords (see below) for nested gets.

get "-c%E% %U%" s.file

-ilist
A list of deltas to be included (forced to be applied) in the creation of the generated file. The list has the following syntax:

<list> ::= <range> | <list> , <range>
<range> ::= SID | SID—SID

SID, the SCCS Identification of a delta, may be in any form shown in the "SID Specified" column of Table 1.

-xlist A list of deltas to be excluded in the creation of the generated file.
See the -i option for the list format.

-e

Indicates that the get is for the purpose of editing or making a change (delta) to the SCCS file via a subsequent use of delta(CP). The -e option used in a get for a particular version (SID) of the SCCS file prevents further gets for editing on the same SID until delta is executed or the j (joint edit) flag is set in the SCCS file (see admin(CP)). Concurrent use of get -e for different SIDs is always allowed.

If the g-file generated by get with an -e option is accidentally ruined in the process of editing it, it may be regenerated by re-executing the get command with the -k option in place of the -e option.

SCCS file protection specified via the ceiling, floor, and authorized user list stored in the SCCS file (see admin(CP)) is enforced when the -e option is used.

-b

Used with the -e option to indicate that the new delta should have an SID in a new branch as shown in Table 1. This option is ignored if the b flag is not present in the file (see admin(CP)) or if the retrieved delta is not a leaf delta. (A leaf delta is one that has no successors on the SCCS file tree.)

Note: A branch delta may always be created from a non-leaf delta. Partial SIDs are interpreted as shown in the "SID Retrieved" column of Table 1.

-k

Suppresses replacement of identification keywords (see below) in the retrieved text by their value. The -k option is implied by the -e option.

-l[p]
Causes a delta summary to be written into an l-file. If -lp is used, then an l-file is not created; the delta summary is written on standard output instead.

-p
Causes the text retrieved from the SCCS file to be written on standard output. No g-file is created. All output which normally goes to the standard output goes to file descriptor 2 instead, unless the -s option is used, in which case it disappears.

-s
Suppresses all output normally written on the standard output. However, fatal error messages (which always go to file descriptor 2) remain unaffected.

-m
Causes each text line retrieved from the SCCS file to be preceded by the SID of the delta that inserted the text line in the SCCS file. The format is: SID, followed by a horizontal tab, followed by the text line.

-n
Causes each generated text line to be preceded with the %M% identification keyword value (see below). The format is: %M% value, followed by a horizontal tab, followed by the text line. When both the -m and -n options are used, the format is: %M% value, followed by a horizontal tab, followed by the -m option generated format.

-g
Suppresses the actual retrieval of text from the SCCS file. It is primarily used to generate an l-file, or to verify the existence of a particular SID.

-t
Used to access the most recently created delta in a given release
(for example, -r1), or release and level (for example, -r1.2).

-w string
Substitute string for all occurrences of %W% when getting the file.

-aseq-no.
The delta sequence number of the SCCS file delta (version) to be
retrieved (see sccsfile(FP)). This option is used by the comb(CP)
command; it is not a generally useful option. If both the -r and -a
options are specified, only the -a option is used. Care should be
taken when using the -a option in conjunction with the -e option,
as the SID of the delta to be created may not be what you expect.
The -r option can be used with the -a and -e options to control the
naming of the SID of the delta to be created.

For each file processed, get responds (on standard output) with
the SID being accessed and with the number of lines retrieved
from the SCCS file.

If the -e option is used, the SID of the delta to be made appears
after the SID accessed and before the number of lines generated. If
there is more than one named file or if a directory or standard
input is named, each file name is printed (preceded by a new-line)
before it is processed. If the -i option is used, included deltas are
listed following the notation "Included"; if the -x option is used,
excluded deltas are listed following the notation "Excluded".

TABLE 1. Determination of SCCS Identification String

SID* Specified	-b Option Used+	Other Conditions	SID Retrieved	SID of Delta to be Created	
none++	no	R defaults to mR		mR.mL	mR.(mL+1)
none++	yes	R defaults to mR		mR.mL	mR.mL.(mB+1).1
R	no	R > mR	mR.mL	R.1***	
R	no	R = mR	mR.mL	mR.(mL+1)	
R	yes	R > mR	mR.mL	mR.mL.(mB+1).1	
R	yes	R = mR	mR.mL	mR.mL.(mB+1).1	
R	—	R < mR and R does not exist	hR.mL**	hR.mL.(mB+1).1	
R	—	Trunk succ.# in release > R and R exists	R.mL	R.mL.(mB+1).1	
R.L	no	No trunk succ.		R.L	R.(L+1)
R.L	yes	No trunk succ.		R.L	R.L.(mB+1).1
R.L	—	Trunk succ. in release >= R		R.L	R.L.(mB+1).1
R.L.B	no	No branch succ.		R.L.B.mS	R.L.B.(mS+1)
R.L.B	yes	No branch succ.		R.L.B.mS	R.L.(mB+1).1
R.L.B.S	no	No branch succ.		R.L.B.S	R.L.B.(S+1)
R.L.B.S	yes	No branch succ.		R.L.B.S	R.L.(mB+1).1
R.L.B.S	—	Branch succ.	R.L.B.S	R.L.(mB+1).1	

* "R", "L", "B", and "S" are the "release", "level", "branch", and "sequence" components of the SID, respectively; "m" means "maximum". Thus, for example, "R.mL" means "the maximum level number within release R"; "R.L.(mB+1).1" means "the first sequence number on the new branch (for example, maximum branch number plus one) of level L within release R". Note that if the SID specified is of the form "R.L", "R.L.B", or "R.L.B.S", each of the specified components must exist.

** "hR" is the highest existing release that is lower than the specified, nonexistent, release R.

*** This is used to force creation of the first delta in a new release.

Successor.

+ The -b option is effective only if the b flag (see admin(CP)) is present in the file. An entry of—means "irrelevant".

++ This case applies if the d (default SID) flag is not present in the file. If the d flag is present in the file, then the SID obtained from the d flag is interpreted as if it had been specified on the command line. Thus, one of the other cases in this table applies.

Examples

retrieve the current delta from s.ZZZ and create a read-only ZZZ file for viewing:

```
get s.ZZZ
```

retrieve the current delta from s.ZZZ and create a writeable ZZZ file for revisions:

```
get -e s.ZZZ
```

---

help   help with errors or commands

help [args]

Options

The arguments may be either message numbers (which normally appear in parentheses following messages) or command names. There are the following types of arguments:

type 1
Begins with non-numerics, ends in numerics. The non-numeric prefix is usually an abbreviation for the program or set of routines which produced the message (for example, ge6, for message 6 from the get command).

type 2
Does not contain numerics (as a command, such as get)

type 3
Is all numeric (for example, 212)

The response of the program will be the explanatory information related to the argument, if there is any.

When all else fails, try "help stuck".

Examples

receive an explanation of error code 1:

```
help 1
```

receive help when unsure:

```
help stuck
```

---

prs   print information on a saved version delta. Specify a version number or default to latest.

prs [-d[dataspec]] [-r[SID]] [-e] [-l] [-c[date-time]] [-a] files
prs -

Options

-d[dataspec]
Used to specify the output data specification. The dataspec is a string consisting of SCCS file data keywords (see "Data Keywords") interspersed with optional user-supplied text.

-r[SID]
Used to specify the SCCS identification (SID) string of a delta for which information is desired. If no SID is specified, the SID of the most recently created delta is assumed.

-e
Requests information for all deltas created earlier than and including the delta designated via the -r option or the date given by the -c option.

-l
Requests information for all deltas created later than and including the delta designated via the -r option or the date given by the -c option.

-c[date-time]
The cutoff [date-time] is in the form:

YY[MM[DD[HH[MM[SS]]]]]

Units omitted from the [date-time] default to their maximum possible values; that is, -c9502 is equivalent to -c950228235959. The -c option must be used with the -e or -l option.

Any number of non-numeric characters may separate the various two-digit pieces of the cutoff date in the form:

-c"94/12/2 9:22:25"

-a
Requests printing of information for both removed (delta type R) and existing (delta type D) deltas (see rmdel(CP). If -a is not specified, information is provided for existing deltas only.

Data keywords

Data keywords specify which parts of an SCCS file are to be retrieved and output. All parts of an SCCS file (see sccsfile(FP)) have an associated data keyword. There is no limit on the number of times a data keyword may appear in a dataspec.

The information printed by prs consists of the user-supplied text and appropriate values (extracted from the SCCS file) substituted for the recognized data keywords in the order of appearance in the dataspec. The format of a data keyword value is either Simple (S), in which keyword substitution is direct, or Multiline (M), in which keyword substitution is followed by a carriage return.

User-supplied text is any text other than recognized data keywords. A tab is specified by \t and new-line is specified by \n. The default data keywords are:

":Dt:\t:DL:\nMRs:\n:MR:COMMENTS:\n:C:"

TABLE 1. SCCS Files Data Keywords

Keyword	Data Item	File Section	Value	Format
:Dt:	Delta information	Delta Table	See below*	S
:DL:	Delta line statistics	"	:Li:/:Ld:/:Lu:	S
:Li:	Lines inserted by Delta	"	nnnnn	S
:Ld:	Lines deleted by Delta	"	nnnnn	S
:Lu:	Lines unchanged by Delta	"	nnnnn	S
:DT:	Delta type	"	D or R	S
:I:	SCCS ID string (SID)	"	:R:.:L:.:B:.:S:	S
:R:	Release number	"	nnnn	S
:L:	Level number	"	nnnn	S
:B:	Branch number	"	nnnn	S
:S:	Sequence number	"	nnnn	S
:D:	Date Delta created	"	:Dy:/:Dm:/:Dd:	S
:Dy:	Year Delta created	"	nn	S
:Dm:	Month Delta created	"	nn	S
:Dd:	Day Delta created	"	nn	S
:T:	Time Delta created	"	:Th:::Tm:::Ts:	S
:Th:	Hour Delta created	"	nn	S
:Tm:	Minutes Delta created	"	nn	S
:Ts:	Seconds Delta created	"	nn	S
:P:	Programmer who created Delta	"	logname	S
:DS:	Delta sequence number	"	nnnn	S
:DP:	Predecessor Delta seq-no.	"	nnnn	S
:DI:	Seq-no. of deltas incl., excl., ignored	"	:Dn:/:Dx:/:Dg:	S
:Dn:	Deltas included (seq #)	"	:DS: :DS:...	S
:Dx:	Deltas excluded (seq #)	"	:DS: :DS:...	S
:Dg:	Deltas ignored (seq #)	"	:DS: :DS:...	S
:MR:	MR numbers for delta	"	text	M
:C:	Comments for delta	"	text	M

:UN:	User names	User Names	text	M
:FL:	Flag list	Flags	text	M
:Y:	Module type flag	"	text	S
:MF:	MR validation flag	"	yes or no	S
:MP:	MR validation pgm name	"	text	S
:KF:	Keyword error/warning flag	"	yes or no	S
:KV:	Keyword validation string	"	text	S
:BF:	Branch flag	"	yes or no	S
:J:	Joint edit flag	"	yes or no	S
:LK:	Locked releases	"	:R:...	S
:Q:	User-defined keyword	"	text	S
:M:	Module name	"	text	S
:FB:	Floor boundary	"	:R:	S
:CB:	Ceiling boundary	"	:R:	S
:Ds:	Default SID	"	:I:	S
:ND:	Null delta flag	"	yes or no	S
:FD:	File descriptive text	Comments	text	M
:BD:	Body	Body	text	M
:GB:	Gotten body	"	text	M
:W:	A form of what(CP) string	N/A	:Z::M:\t:I:	S
:A:	A form of what(CP) string	N/A	:Z::Y: :M: :I::Z:	S
:Z:	what(C) string delimiter	N/A	@(#)	S
:F:	SCCS file name	N/A	text	S
:PN:	SCCS file path name	N/A	text	S

* :Dt: = :DT: :I: :D: :T: :P: :DS: :DP:

Examples

print information on the latest delta of SCCS file s.ZZZ:
prs s.ZZZ

print information on version 1.2 of SCCS file s.ZZZ:

prs -r1.2 s.ZZZ

---

rmdel   delete a previous delta by specifying the version number
to be deleted

rmdel -r SID files
rmdel -

Options

The -r option is used for specifying the SID (SCCS identification)
level of the delta to be removed.

Examples

remove version 1.2 from SCCS file s.ZZZ:

rmdel -r1.2 s.ZZZ

---

sccsdiff   show difference between two deltas

sccsdiff -rSID1 -rSID2 [-p] [-sn] files

Options

-rSID?
SID1 and SID2 specify the deltas of an SCCS file that are to be compared. Versions are passed to bdiff(C) in the order given.

-p
Pipe output for each file through pr(C).

-sn
n is the file segment size that bdiff will pass to diff(C). This is useful when diff fails due to a high system load.

Examples

show difference between s.ZZZ delta 1.2 and delta 1.3:

```
sccsdiff -r1.2 -r1.3 s.ZZZ
```

---

unget　return the retrieved delta to the SCCS file unchanged

unget [-rSID] [-s] [-n] files

Options

-rSID
Uniquely identifies which delta is no longer intended. (This would
have been specified by get as the new delta.) The use of this option
is necessary only if two or more outstanding gets for editing on the
same SCCS file were done by the same person (login name). A
diagnostic results if the specified SID is ambiguous, or if it is necessary and omitted on the command line.

-s
Suppresses printout, on standard output, of the intended delta's
SID.

-n
Causes the retention of the gotten file which would normally be
removed from the current directory.

Examples

remove the writeable ZZZ file and do not check in the revisions as
a new delta to s.ZZZ:

```
unget s.ZZZ
```

do not remove the writeable ZZZ file and do not check in the
revisions as a new delta to s.ZZZ:

```
unget -ns.ZZZ
```

spell check—overview

Method for spell checking files

spell   spell checking

spell check

---

spell   print misspelled words or those not found in the system dictionary to the screen

spell [-bilvx] [+local_file] [file...]

Options

-b
British spelling is checked. Besides preferring centre, colour, labour, programme, speciality, traveled, and so on, this option insists upon the -ise ending for words like standardise.

-i
Ignore all chains of included files.

-l
Follow the chains of all included files. By default, spell follows chains of included files (.so and .nx troff requests), unless the names of such included files begin with /usr/lib.

-v
Print all words not literally in the spelling list, and indicates plausible derivations from the words in the spelling list.

-x
Print every plausible stem with "=" for each word.

+local_file
Remove words found in local_file from spell's output. local_file is the name of a user-provided file that contains a sorted list of words, one per line. With this option, you can specify a set of words that are correct spellings for each job (in addition to spell's own spelling list).

Examples

check spelling of a file:

```
spell file
```

split—overview

Method for splitting files

split   split file

split

split   split file into number of lines to an output file named plus unique suffix

split [-l line_count] [-a suffix_length] [file [name]]

split [-b n[k\m]] [-a suffix_length] [file [name]]

split [-line_count] [-a suffix_length] [file [name]]

Options

-l line_count

-line_count
Specifies the number of lines in the resulting file.

-a suffix_length
Specifies that suffix_length letters are to be used to form the suffix portion of the filenames of the split files.

-b n
Specifies that the file is to be split into n byte pieces.

-b nk
Specifies that the file is to be split into n kilobyte pieces.

-b nm
Specifies that the file is to be split into n megabyte pieces.

If no input file is given, or if a dash (-) is given instead, the standard input file is used.

Examples

split file1 into the default value of 1000 lines per output file called file2:

```
split file1 file2
```

strip—overview

Methods for stripping path names

basename	get base name of path
dirname	get the directory name of the path

strip

---

basename   print the last level of the path name

basename string [suffix]

Options

There are no options for this command.

Examples

set variable FNAME equal to the file of path:

```
FNAME='basename $HOME/personal/file'
```

---

dirname   print all but the last level of the path name

dirname string

Options

There are no options for this command.

Examples

set variable FPATH equal to the directory:

```
FPATH='dirname $HOME/directory/file'
```

system commands—overview

Methods for system management and control

at	schedule commands or jobs to be executed at specific times
batch	run commands sequentially with one running at a time
kill	terminate a process
nohup	continue to execute a command after logging out
ps	list current processes
sleep	wait a certain number of seconds before executing the next command
shutdown	terminate open processes and bring down the system
stty	control settings for terminal devices
tty	display the name of your terminal
umask	remove the read-write-execute permissions using numeric values
uname	display the Unix system name
w	list system and user information
who	list user information

system commands

at   schedule commands or jobs to be executed at specific times

at [-m] [-f file] [-q letter] time [date] [increment]

at [-m] [-f file] [-q letter] -t [[CC]YY]MMDDhhmm.[SS]

at -r job-id...

at -l [job-id...]

at -l -q letter

Options

time
The time can be specified as 1, 2, or 4 digits. One- and two- digit numbers are taken to be hours, four digits to be hours and minutes. The time can alternately be specified as two numbers separated by a colon, meaning hour:minute. A suffix am or pm can be appended; otherwise a 24-hour clock time is understood. The suffix zulu can be used to indicate Greenwich Mean Time (GMT). The special names noon, midnight, and now are also recognized.

date
An optional date can be specified as either a month name followed by a day number (and an optional year number preceded by a comma) or a day of the week (spelt in full or abbreviated to three

characters). Two special "days," today and tomorrow, are recognized. If no date is given, today is assumed if the given hour is greater than the current hour and tomorrow is assumed if it is less. If the given month is less than the current month (and no year is given), next year is assumed.

increment
The time and optional date arguments can be modified with an increment argument of the form +n units, where n is an integer and units is one of the following: minutes, hours, days, weeks, months, or years. The singular form is also accepted, and +1 unit can also be written next unit. Thus, legitimate commands include:

    at 0815am Jan 24, 1995
    at 0815am Jan 24
    at 8:15am Jan 24
    at now + 1 day
    at 5 pm Friday next week

-r job-id...
Removes the specified job or jobs previously scheduled by the at or batch command. job-id is a job identifier returned by at or batch. Unless you are root, you can only remove your own jobs.

-l [job-id...]
Lists schedule times of specified jobs. If no job-ids are specified, lists all jobs currently scheduled for the invoking user. Unless you are root, you can only list your own jobs.

-q letter
Places the specified job in a queue denoted by letter, where letter is any lowercase letter from "a" to "z". The queue letter is

appended to the job identifier. The following letters have special significance:

    a at queue
    b batch queue
    c cron queue

For more information on the use of different queues, see the queuedefs(F) manual page.

-m
Send mail to the invoking user when the at job has run. This is in addition to any unredirected stdin or stderr output.

-f file
Specifies the pathname of a file to use for the source of the at job (instead of stdin).

-t [[CC]YY]MMDDhhmm.[SS]
Alternative format for specifying time in 2 digit codes where:

    CC century
    YY year
    MM month
    DD day
    hh hours
    mm minutes
    SS seconds

Examples

to execute the command at 2:30 pm on November 6:

```
at 2:30pm Nov 6
```

to execute the command 2 hours from now:

```
at now + 2 hours
```

---

batch   run commands sequentially with one running at a time

batch

Options

batch takes no arguments; it submits a job for immediate execution at lower priority than an ordinary at job.

---

kill   terminate a process by specifying the process id

kill -s signame pid...
kill [-signame] pid...
kill -l [exit_status]

Options

-s signame

-signame
Specify signal name signame (see "Signals" below).

Note that the preferred syntax is -s signame; -signame is obsolete and may be dropped from future standards.

-l
List all the signal names recognized by kill.

-l exit_status
If exit_status is the exit status of a previously executed command then kill lists the signal which terminated that process.

When determining the process or processes to send a signal to, kill interprets the value of pid as follows:

>1
Send the signal to the process whose process ID is pid.

0
Send the signal to all processes whose process group ID is equal to the process group ID of the sender (except for processes 0 and 1).

-1
If the effective user ID of the sender is not root, send the signal to all processes (except processes 0 and 1) whose real user ID is equal to the effective user ID of the sender.

If the effective user ID of the sender is root, send the signal to all processes (except processes 0 and 1).

<-1
If the process ID is negative but not -1, send the signal to all processes whose process group ID is equal to the absolute (positive) value of PID.

Examples

to terminate process id 100 without exception:

```
kill -9 100
```

---

nohup   continue to execute a command after logging out

nohup command [arguments]

Options

There are no options for this command.

---

ps   list current processes running on the system

ps [option [arguments]...]

Options

-a

Print information about all processes most frequently requested: all those except session leaders and processes not associated with a terminal.

-A

Print information about all processes (equivalent to -e).

-d

Print information about all processes except session leaders.

-e

Print information about all processes (equivalent to -A).

-f

Generate a full listing (see "Full and long listings").

-g grplist

List only process data whose process group leader ID numbers appear in grplist. (A group leader is a process whose process ID number is identical to its process group ID number. A login shell is a common example of a process group leader.)

-G grplist

List only process data whose real group ID numbers are given in grplist.

-l

Generate a long listing (see "Full and long listings").

-n name
Valid only for users with a real user ID of root or a real group ID of sys. Takes argument signifying an alternate system name in place of /unix. This option is used when the kernel has been relinked and the executable file /unix does not correspond to the kernel loaded into memory. In this case, the argument is the filename of the UNIX executable that was loaded when the machine was last booted; for example, /unix.old.

-o format
List process data in the specified format. Multiple -o options can be specified on the command line.

format is a comma or whitespace separated list of field names; the list must be placed in quotation marks if whitespace separation is used. ps displays the fields in the order specified on the command line.

You can override the default header for a field by appending a "=" and the new header text to the field name:

    -o field=header

If the header text contains whitespace, enclose the entire field=header string in quotation marks and specify it using a separate -o option:

    -o "field=header"

You can prevent a header from being displayed for an individual field by not specifying it after the "=". If all field names have a single "=" appended but no header text, no header line is displayed at all.

ps changes the field width from its default value to match the width of the specified header text.

Allowed field names follow (default headers are shown in parentheses):

pid Process ID as a decimal value. (PID)

ppid Parent process ID as a decimal value. (PPID)

pgid Process group ID as a decimal value. (PGID)

uid Real user ID of the process as a decimal value. (UID)

user The effective user ID of the process. (USER)

ruser Real user ID of the process. (RUSER)

comm Command name; may contain spaces. (COMMAND)

args Command name with its arguments; may contain spaces and may be truncated to fit the width of the field. (COMMAND)

group Effective group ID of the process. (GROUP)

rgroup Real group ID of the process. (RGROUP)

nice nice value of the process; see nice(C) and renice(C). (NI)

pri Priority value of the process. (PRI)

pcpu Percentage of CPU time recently used by the process. (%CPU)

sess Process session leader ID as a decimal value. (SESSION)

size Size of the swappable image of the process (data and stack) in kilobytes. (SZ)

vsz Virtual memory size of the process in kilobytes. (VSZ)

addr Virtual address of the process' entry in the process table. (ADDR)

class Scheduler class of the process. (CLASS)

time Cumulative CPU time used by the process. (TIME)

stime Time when the process started. (STIME)

etime Time elapsed since the process started. (ELAPSED)

tty Name of the controlling terminal for the process. (TTY)

wchan
Address of an event for which a process is sleeping. (WCHAN)

For fields user, ruser, group, and rgroup, ps displays the user or group name if it can be obtained and it will fit in the field. Otherwise it displays the decimal value of the ID.

-p proclist
List only process data whose process ID numbers are given in proclist.

-t termlist
List only process data associated with the terminal given in termlist. Terminal identifiers may be specified in one of two forms: the device's filename (for example, tty04) or, if the device's file-name starts with tty, just the digitidentifier (for example, 04).

-u uidlist
List only process data whose user ID numbers or login names appear in uidlist. In the listing, the numerical user ID will be printed unless you give the -f option, which prints the login name.

-U uidlist
List only process data whose real user ID numbers or login names are given in uidlist.

Full and long listings

Under the -f option, ps tries to determine the command name and arguments given when the process was created by examining the user block. Failing this, the command name is printed, as it would have appeared without the -f option, in square brackets.

The column headings and the meaning of the columns in a ps list-ing are given in the following text; the letters -f and –l indicate the option (full or long, respectively) that causes the corresponding heading to appear; if no option letter is given, the heading always appears. Note that these two options determine only what infor-mation is provided for a process; they do not determine which processes will be listed.

F (-l) Octal flags which are added together to give more information about the current status of a process:

00 If shown on its own, the process has terminated; its process table entry is now available.

01 A system process which is part of the kernel and always resident in primary memory. sched (the swapper), vhand (the pager), and bdflush (the buffer cache manager) are all system processes.

02 Parent is tracing process.

04 Tracing parent's signal has stopped the process; the parent is waiting (ptrace(S)).

10 Process is sleeping at less than or equal to priority 25 and cannot be awakened by a signal; for example, while waiting for an inode to be created.

20 Process is loaded in primary memory; it has not been swapped out to disk.

40 Process is currently locked in primary memory and cannot be swapped out until an event completes; for example, while performing raw I/O.

S (-l) The state of the process:

O Process is running on a processor (SONPROC).

S Sleeping: process is waiting for an event to complete (SSLEEP).

R Runnable: process is on run queue (SRUN).

I Idle: process is being created (SIDL).

Z Zombie state: process terminated and parent not waiting (SZOMB).

T Traced: process stopped by a signal because parent is tracing it (SSTOP).

B Process is waiting for more pages of memory to become available (SXBRK).

UID (-f, -l)
The user ID number of the process owner (the login name is printed under the -f option).

PID The process ID of the process (this number is needed in order to kill a process).

PPID (-f, -l)
The process ID of the parent process.

C (-f, -l)
An estimate of recent CPU usage by the process; the scheduler combines this quantity with the nice value of the process to calculate its priority.

PRI (-l)
The priority of the process (lower numbers mean lower priority). Processes with priorities in the range 0 to 65 are in user mode and

may be selected by the scheduler to run. Processes with priorities between 66 and 95 are sleeping in system mode while waiting for a system resource to become available. If their priority is between 77 and 95, they are also immune to signals while protecting critical data structures. The swapper (sched) sleeps at priority 95. Processes with priorities between 96 and 127 are fixed priority processes.

NI (-l)
The nice value of the process; see nice(C) and renice(C).

ADDR (-l)
The virtual address of the process' entry in the process table.

SZ (-l)
The swappable size (in kilobytes) of the virtual data and stack segments of the process.

WCHAN (-l)
An address that uniquely identifies a process within the process table as sleeping until a particular resource becomes available; for example, until an I/O request has been completed, or in an SXBRK state until more pages of memory are available.

STIME (-f)
The starting time of the process, given in hours, minutes, and seconds. (A process begun more than twenty-four hours before ps is executed is given in months and days.)

TTY
The controlling terminal for the process (the message "?" is printed when there is no controlling terminal).

TIME
The cumulative execution time for the process.

CMD
The name of the command corresponding to the process. The -f option prints the full command name and its arguments.

A process that has exited and has a parent, but has not yet been waited for by the parent, is marked <defunct>.

ps displays a "-" in a field if the process does not have a meaningful value for the field.

Examples

to display a full list of all terminal processes to a page:

```
ps -afe|pg
```

to display a list of processes for user1:

```
ps -fu user1
```

---

sleep   wait a certain number of seconds before executing the next command

sleep time

Options

There are no options for this command.

Examples

sleep for 30 seconds:

```
sleep 30
```

---

shutdown   terminate open processes and bring down the system

*/etc/shutdown [-y] [-g[hh:]mm] [-i[0156sS]] [-f "mesg" | file]
[su]*

Options

-y
Runs the command silently. If this option is not specified, shutdown will prompt for confirmation to shut down the system.

-g[hh:]mm
Specifies the number of hours and minutes before shutdown (maximum: 72 hours). 1 minute is the default. (To shut down the system immediately without a grace period, use /etc/haltsys or /etc/reboot. Note that these commands should not be used if NFS, TCP/IP or certain other services are running.)

-i[0156abcsS]
Specifies the init level to bring the system to (see init(M)). By default, the system is brought to level 0.

-f mesg
mesg is a message enclosed in double quotes ("") to be sent to all terminals warning of the imminent shutdown during the grace period.

-f file
Similar to the -f mesg option, but file is the pathname for a file containing the message.

The optional su argument lets the user go single-user without completely shutting down the system. (This option is identical to -i1 and is present for backwards compatibility with XENIX).

Examples

shutdown the system:

```
/etc/shutdown
```

---

stty   set or print input/output control settings for terminal devices

stty [-a | -g] [—]
stty mode...[—]

Options

With the -a option, stty reports all of the mode settings.

The -g option causes the current stty settings of the terminal to be output as a list of fourteen hexadecimal numbers separated by colons. This output may be used as a command line argument to stty to restore these settings at a later time. It is a more compact form than stty -a. The format of the output depends on the line discipline selected (using the line mode).

stty understands the end-of-options delimiter (—). STTY is a link to stty.

Examples

display current device settings to standard output:

```
stty -g
```

---

tty   display the name of your terminal

tty [-l] [-s]

Options

The -s option inhibits printing of the terminal name, allowing you to test just the exit code.

The -l option tests whether the terminal line is an active synchronous line. An additional message is printed to indicate the status of the line (see "Diagnostics").

Examples

display current device name to standard output:

```
tty
```

---

umask   remove the read-write-execute permissions using numeric values. This command is usually executed within a .profile.

    positions 1—3 are owner-group-other
    numeric values for rwx are 421 (r=4, w=2, x=1)

umask [-S] [mask]

Options

If you omit the mask operand, the shell prints the current value of the mask. By default, the shell prints the mask in octal form; specifying the -S option outputs the mask in symbolic form.

Examples

remove the execute permission for other:

umask 001

remove all permissions for group:

umask 070

remove write permissions for group and other:

umask 022

---

uname   display the Unix system name

uname [-aAmnrsvX]

uname [-S node_name]

Options

The various options to uname return selected information that is available with the uname(S) system call:

-a
Print all the information corresponding to the options -s, -n, -r, -v, and -m.

-A
Print the license field (activation state) information.

-m
Print the machine hardware name.

-n
Print the machine's node name; the name by which it is known to a communications network.

-r
Print the operating system release.

-s
Print the operating system name (the default action of uname).

-S node_name
Change the machine's node name to node_name. Note that only root is allowed to change the node name. This option does not change the operating system name.

The format of node_name is restricted to 8 characters from the set of lowercase letters, numeric digits, dash "-", and underscore "_"; the name may not begin with a digit.

-v
Print the operating system version. (This is the AT&T sub-version number of System V Release 3.2, and always displays "2" under SCO UNIX System V. To determine the SCO version number, examine the line beginning "Release = '" in the output from uname -X.)

-X
Print information about system name, node name, operating system release number, kernel ID, processor type, bus type, serial number, number of users license (2-user, 8-user or unlimited), OEM number, origin number, and number of CPUs.

Examples

display all system information to standard output:

```
uname -a
```

---

w   list system and user information

w [-hlqtwx] [-n namelist] [-s swapdev] [-u utmpfile | -U utmpxfile] [users...]

Options

-h
Do not print the heading or title lines.

-l
Long format (default): for each user, w outputs the user's login name, the terminal or pseudo terminal the user is currently using, when the user logged onto the system, the number of minutes the user has been idle (how much time has expired since the user last typed anything), the CPU time used by all processes and their children attached to the terminal, the CPU time used by the

currently active process, and the name and arguments of the currently active process.

-n namelist
The argument is taken as the name of an alternate namelist (/unix is the default).

-q
Quick format: for each user, w outputs the user's login name, the terminal or pseudo terminal the user is currently using, the number of minutes the user has been idle, and the name of the currently active process.

-s swapdev
Use the file swapdev in place of /dev/swap. This is useful when examining a corefile.

-t
Only the heading line is output (equivalent to uptime(C)).

-u utmpfile
The file utmpfile is used instead of /etc/utmp as a record of who is currently logged in.

-U utmpxfile
The file utmpxfile is used instead of /etc/utmpx.

-w
Both the heading line and the summary of users is output.

-x

Print out the hostname. This option cannot be used with the -u option.

If any users are specified, the user summary is restricted to reporting on these.

---

who   list user information

who [-aAbdfHlmpqrstTux] [-n count] [file]

who am i

who am I

Options

With options, who can list logins, logoffs, reboots, and changes to the system clock, as well as other processes spawned by the init process. These options are:

-a

Process the /etc/utmp file or the named file with all options turned on.

-A

Display UNIX accounting information.

-b

Indicate the time and date of the last reboot.

-d
Display all processes that have expired and have not been respawned by init. The "exit" field appears for dead processes and contains the termination and exit values (as returned by wait(C)), of the dead process. This can be useful in determining why a process terminated.

-f
Suppress pseudo-ttys from who output, except for remote logins.

-H
Display column headings above the regular output.

-l
List only those lines on which the system is waiting for someone to login. The "name" field is LOGIN in such cases. Other fields are the same as for user entries except that the "state" field does not exist.

-m
Equivalent to who am i.

-n count
count specifies the number of columns for the -q option to use when displaying user names.

-p
List any other process which is currently active and has been previously spawned by init. The "name" field is the name of the program executed by init as found in /etc/inittab. The "state", "line", and "idle" fields have no meaning. The "comment" field shows the "id" field of the line from /etc/inittab that spawned this process. See inittab(F).

-q

Quick who; display only the names and the number of users currently logged on. When this option is used, all other options are ignored.

-r

Indicate the current run level of the init process, the date and time at which this run level was entered, the current run level (again), the number of times that the system has been at this run level since last being rebooted, and the previous run level.

-s

List only the "name", "line", and "time" fields. This is the default behavior of who.

-t

Indicate the last change to the system clock (via the date(C) command) by root. See su(C).

-T

Equivalent to the -u option, except that the "state" of the terminal line is printed. The "state" describes whether someone else can write to that terminal. A plus character (+) appears if the terminal is writable by anyone; a minus character (-) appears if it is not. root can write to all lines having a plus character or a minus character in the "state" field. If a bad line is encountered, a question mark (?) is displayed.

-u

List only those users who are currently logged in. The "name" is the user's login name. The "line" is the name of the line as found in the directory /dev. The "time" is the time that the user logged in. The "activity" is the number of hours and minutes since activity last occurred on that particular line. A dot (.) indicates that the terminal has seen activity in the last minute and is therefore "current." If more than twenty-four hours have elapsed or the line has not been used since boot time, the entry is marked "old."

This field is useful when trying to determine whether a person is working at the terminal or not. The "pid" is the process ID of the user's shell. The "comment" is the comment field. It can contain information about where the terminal is located, the telephone number of the dataset, the type of terminal if hard-wired, and so on.

-x
Print the hostname. If file is not used to specify the pathname of a utmpx(F) format file, who reads /etc/utmpx.

Examples

display user information with idle time:

```
who -u
```

system environment—overview

The environment relating to pathnames may be customized by the user by creating variables. The variables may be referenced in Unix by preceding the variable name with a $.

env   list the current environment variable paths

system environment

env list the current environment variable paths that apply for the current login session

env [[-] | [-i]] [name=value]...[command [args]]

Options

The—flag causes the inherited environment to be ignored completely, so that the command is executed with exactly the environment specified by the arguments. The -i flag is equivalent to the—flag, but it conforms to the POSIX utility syntax guidelines.

system files —overview

Files relating to system management and control

crontabs   a file containing commands/shell scripts to be executed at specified times

gettydefs   a file containing device information relating to system ports

inittab   a file containing initialization functions performed at system startup

profile   a file containing commands and/or environments to be invoked at login

rc   a file containing commands to be executed during the boot process

termcap   a file containing terminal map definitions

terminfo   a compiled database which provides terminal compatibility for Unix

ttytypes   a file containing device types and associated ttys

system files

---

crontabs   a file containing commands/shell scripts to be executed at specified times which may be customized by the system administrator

Examples

to execute the script USRSTAT.sh every ten seconds with the environment defined in.profile, add the following line to crontabs:

```
0,10,20,30,40,50 * * * *   .profile;.USRSTAT.sh
```

---

gettydefs   a file containing device information relating to system ports

```
19200# B19200 HUPCL OPOST ONLCR TAB3 BRKINT IGNPAR
IXON IXANY PARENB ISTRIP ECHO
ECHOE ECHOK ICANON ISIG CS7 CREAD # B19200 HUPCL
OPOST ONLCR TAB3 BRKINT IGNPAR
IXON IXANY PARENB ISTRIP ECHO ECHOE ECHOK ICANON
ISIG CS7 CREAD #login: #9600

9600# B9600 HUPCL OPOST ONLCR TAB3 BRKINT IGNPAR
IXON IXANY PARENB ISTRIP ECHO E
CHOE ECHOK ICANON ISIG CS7 CREAD # B9600 HUPCL OPOST
ONLCR TAB3 BRKINT IGNPAR IX
ON IXANY PARENB ISTRIP ECHO ECHOE ECHOK ICANON ISIG
CS7 CREAD #login: #4800
```

```
4800# B4800 HUPCL OPOST ONLCR TAB3 BRKINT IGNPAR
IXON IXANY PARENB ISTRIP ECHO E
CHOE ECHOK ICANON ISIG CS7 CREAD # B4800 HUPCL OPOST
ONLCR TAB3 BRKINT IGNPAR IX
ON IXANY PARENB ISTRIP ECHO ECHOE ECHOK ICANON ISIG
CS7 CREAD #login: #2400
```

---

inittab   a file containing initialization functions performed at system startup

```
r5:5:wait:/sbin/rc5   reboot  1>  /dev/sysmsg  2>&1
</dev/console
r7:7:wait:/sbin/rc7   reboot  1>  /dev/sysmsg  2>&1
</dev/console
xd::boot:/sbin/rm -rf /dev/X/* >/dev/sysmsg 2>&1
c0:0:respawn:/sbin/vtgetty vt00 9600NP
c1:1:respawn:/sbin/vtgetty vt00 9600NP
```

---

profile   a file containing commands and/or environments to be invoked at login which can be customized with additional environment variable paths, terminal settings, and executable scripts

```
PATH=:$HOME/bin:/bin:/usr/bin:/etc; export PATH

MAIL=/usr/spool/mail/`logname`                        ;
export MAIL

eval `tset -m ansi:${TERM:-ansi} -m :\?${TERM:-ansi}
-r -s -Q`
```

Examples

to automatically execute the command file startupscript at user login, the following line would be added to the user .profile:

```
startupscript
```

to alias the l command with the ls-ltr command, the following line would be added to the user .profile:

```
alias l='ls -ltr'
```

---

rc   a file containing commands to be executed during the boot process which may be customized to include additional system processes to be executed

---

termcap   a file containing terminal map definitions which may be customized by adding new terminal definitions or changing key mapping in current definitions; some software packages use their own termcap definitions file due to special key mapping requirements

```
dn|vt100nam|vt-100|pt100|pt-100|DEC   VT100   without
automargins:\
```

```
:co#80:li#24:cl=50\E[;H\E[2J:bs:cm=5\E[%i%d;%dH:nd=
2\E[C:up=2\E[A:\
```

```
:ce=3\E[K:cd=50\E[J:so=2\E[7m:se=2\E[m:us=2\E[4m:ue
=2\E[m:\
```

```
:is=\E>\E[?1l\E[?3l\E[?4l\E[?5l\E[?7h\E[?8h:\

:if=/usr/share/lib/tabset/vt100:ku=\E[A:kd=\E[B:kr=
\E[C:kl=\E[D:\

:kh=\E[H:k1=\EOP:k2=\EOQ:k3=\EOR:k4=\EOS:pt:xn:sr=5
\EM:\
        :ks=\E\075:ke=\E\076:\

:GS=\E(0:GE=\E(B:GV=x:GH=q:G1=k:G2=l:G3=m:G4=j:GU=v
:\
        :GD=w:GC=n:GL=t:GR=u:\
        :CL=\EOP:CR=\EOQ:WL=\EOR:WR=\EOS:\
        :UK=\E[A:DK=\E[B:LK=\E[D:RK=\E[C:\
        :cs=%i\E[%2;%2r:
```

terminfo   a compiled database which provides terminal compatibility for Unix

---

ttytypes   a file containing device types and associated ttys which may be customized to associate specific terminal definitions with a tty

```
unknown console
AT386-M vt00
AT386-M vt01
AT386-M vt06
AT386-M vt07
```

```
ansi     tty00
ansi     tty01
ansi     tty02
ansi     tty03
ansi     tty04
ansi     tty05
ansi     tty06
```

Examples

to customize tty06 to use the vt100 terminal definition, modify the file as follows:

```
vt100   tty06
```

system—overview

Methods for gathering information about the system

disk usage:
df	disk space used
du	blocks used

shells:
csh	C Shell
ksh	Korne Shell
sh	Bourne Shell

system-disk usage

---

df   print amount of disk space used by mounted file systems including used space, available space, and total capacity usage

df [-B | -P] [-k] [filesystem...]
df [-iv] [-flt] [-k] [filesystem...]
df [-I] [filesystem...]

Options

-B
Use portable XPG4/POSIX2 output formatting (as for option -P) but do not truncate the filesystem device name.

-f
Report only an actual count of the blocks in the free list (free inodes are not reported). With this option, df reports on raw devices.

-i
Report the percent of inodes used as well as the number of inodes used and free. Use the -i option with the -v option to display counts of blocks and inodes free as well as the percentage of inodes and blocks used.

-I
Report inode information using the same format as the -B option.

-k

Report blocks as 1024-byte logical blocks instead of default 512-byte physical blocks.

-l

Report local resources only.

-P

Use portable XPG4/POSIX2 output formatting. The first line of the output is a header that includes the block size. Lines following the header show the following information for each filesystem: device name, total space, space used, free space, percentage of space used, and mount point.

-t

Report the total number of allocated blocks as well as the number of free blocks.

-v

Report the percent of used blocks as well as the numbers of used and free blocks.

The -B and -P options cannot be used with any other options except -k. The -I option cannot be combined with any other.

Examples

results of df command:

```
filesystem  kybtes  used   avail   capacity  mounted
/usr        42277   35291  2758    93%       /usr
/u          137681  86350  20532   80%       /u
```

du   report the number of blocks of files and recursive directories

du [-afkrsuVx] [names]

Options

-a
causes an entry to be generated for each file. Without the -a option, the default behavior is to output the block count for directories and those files explicitly named by the names argument.

-f
has the same effect as the -x option.

-k
causes du to report in units of 1024 bytes. The default is to report in units of 512 bytes.

-r
causes du to report directories that cannot be read, files that cannot be opened, and so on. This option is obsolete since this is now the default behavior of du.

-s
causes only the grand total (for each of the specified names) to be given.

-u
causes du to ignore files that have more than one link.

-V

causes du to display a three-column output reporting the space usage for versioned files. The first column displays the current space taken up by files in the directory. The second shows the space taken up by previous files, that is, files which have been deleted and the space shown is that used by the hidden versioned file(s). The third is the total of the first and second columns, providing usage information for versioned files.

-x

causes du to display the usage of files in the current filesystem only. Directories containing mounted filesystems will be ignored.

Examples

results of du command:

```
4544  ./sqls
1440  ./4gls
6080  .
```

system shells

---

csh   allows user to interact with operating system through a shell command interpeter with syntax similar to the C programming language that uses commands not available in the standard shell

csh [-cefinstv VxX] [arg...]

See Appendix A

---

ksh   allows user to interact with the operating system through a shell programming language that is based on the Bourne Shell with some C Shell capabilities

ksh [±aefhikmnoprstuvx] [±o option]...[-c string] [arg...]

See Appendix A

---

sh   allows the user to interact with the operating system through a standard shell command interpreter where each command is a separate process and is waited upon for termination

sh [-aceikLnrstuvx] [args]

See Appendix A

view—overview

Methods for viewing files

view contents of a file:

bfs	big file scan
cat	display contents of a file on the screen
grep	display lines containing pattern
head	display contents at the top of file
more	display contents of a file one screen at a time
pg	display a file one screen at a time
tail	display contents at the bottom of file
tr	translate characters
vi	text editor
view	vi read-only mode

view file list:

l	list
lc	list columnar
ls	list

view – contents

---

bfs   view contents of a file similar to ed in read-only mode—
accepts large files

bfs [—] name

Options

The optional dash (-) suppresses printing of sizes

Examples

view contents of file:

```
bfs file
```

---

cat   display file on terminal screen and if file is more than what
fits on the screen it will scroll off the top until the end of file is displayed

cat [-suvte] file

Options

-s

Suppresses warnings about nonexistent files.

-u

Causes the output to be unbuffered.

-v

Causes non-printing characters (with the exception of tabs, new-lines, and form feeds) to be displayed. Control characters are displayed as ^X (<Ctrl>x), where X is the key pressed with the <Ctrl> key (for example, <Ctrl>m is displayed as ^M). The <Del> character (octal 0177) is printed as ^?. Non-ASCII characters (with the high bit set) are printed as M -x, where x is the character specified by the seven low order bits.

-t

Causes tabs to be printed as ^I and form feeds as ^L. This option is ignored if the -v option is not
specified.

-e

Causes a "$" character to be printed at the end of each line (prior to the new-line). This option is ignored if the -v option is not set.

Examples

view contents of file:

```
cat file
```

grep find and print line containing specified pattern

grep [-E | -F] [-c | -l | -q] [-bhinsvx] [-e expression] [-f expfile]
[expression] [files]

Options

-E
Each pattern is treated as an extended regular expression. A null
extended regular expression matches all lines.

-F
Each pattern is treated as a string instead of a regular expression.
A null string matches all lines.

-v
All lines but those matching are displayed.

-x
Displays only exact matches of an entire line.

-c
Only a count of matching lines is displayed.

-l
Only the names of files with matching lines are displayed, separated by newlines.

-h

Prevents the name of the file containing the matching line from being printed before that line. Used when searching multiple files.

-n

Each line is preceded by its relative line number in the file.

-b

Each line is preceded by the block number on which it was found. This is sometimes useful in locating disk block numbers by context.

-s

Suppresses error messages produced for nonexistent or unreadable files. Other error messages are not suppressed.

-i

Turns on matching of letters of either case in the input so that case is insignificant. Conversion between uppercase and lowercase letters is dependent on the locale setting.

-y

Turns on matching of letters of either case in the input so that case is insignificant. Conversion between uppercase and lowercase letters is dependent on the locale setting. Note: -y is not a standard UNIX system option. It is maintained for backwards compatibility with XENIX.

-e expression

Specify patterns to be used during the search. The patterns in the list must be separated by a newline character. Multiple -e and -f options are accepted. Unless the -E or -F options are specified, grep treats the patterns as basic regular expressions.

-f expfile

The regular expression for grep, or extended expression for egrep, or strings list for fgrep is taken from the expfile. Patterns in the file are terminated by a newline character. Unless the -E or -F options are specified, grep treats the patterns as basic regular expressions.

-q

Quiet. Nothing is written to the standard output. grep exits with status 0 if an input line is selected. This provides a quick and easy method of testing if a pattern or string exists in a group of files.

Examples

find 5% in file:

```
grep "5%" file
```

---

head   display the first ten lines of a file unless more lines are specified

head [-count] [file...]

head [-n number] [file...]

Options

The head filter prints the first count lines of each of the specified files. If no files are specified, head reads from the standard input. If no count is specified, then 10 lines are printed.

The -n number option is equivalent to the -count option, but, in addition, it conforms to the POSIX utility syntax guidelines.

head understands—as the option delimiter.

Examples

view contents of first 15 lines of file:

```
head -15 file
```

---

more   display file on standard output if more lines than the screen allows, hold screen until spacebar pressed giving next set of lines, the enter key is pressed giving the next line, or q is pressed quitting

more [-cdeilrsuv] [-n number] [-p command] [-t tag] [-/ pattern] [file...]

more [-cdeilrsuv] [-number] [+command] [-t tag] [-/ pattern] [file...]

Options

-/ pattern
Start listing at the first occurrence of the regular expression given by pattern.

-c
Draw each page by beginning at the top of the screen and erasing each line just before it draws on it. This avoids scrolling the screen, making it easier to read while more is writing. This option is ignored if the terminal does not have the ability to clear to the end of a line.

-d
Prompt with the message "Hit space to continue, Rubout to abort" at the end of each full screen. This is useful if more is being used as a filter in some setting, such as a class, where many users may be inexperienced.

-e
Exit immediately on writing the last line of the last file.

-i
Perform pattern matching that is insensitive to case.

-l
Do not treat <Ctrl>l (form feed) specially. If this option is not given, more pauses after any line that contains a <Ctrl>l, as if the end of a full screen has been reached. Also, if a file begins with a form feed, the screen is cleared before the file is printed.

-number
Specify a whole number of lines which more will use instead of the
default. The second form of the option is obsolescent.

-p command

+command
Specify the more command to be executed initially for each file
examined. The second form of the option is obsolescent. See the
"Commands" section for details of the commands that are supported.

-r
Cause carriage returns to be printed as "^M".

-s
Squeeze multiple blank lines from the output, producing only one
blank line. Especially helpful when viewing nroff output, this
option maximizes the useful information present on the screen.

-t tag
Display one screenful of the file containing the string tag. This is
equivalent to using the more command :t. For more information
about tags, see ctags(C).

-u
Normally, more handles underlining, such as that produced by
nroff, in a manner appropriate to the particular terminal: if the
terminal can perform underlining or has a stand-out mode, more
outputs appropriate escape sequences to enable underlining or
stand-out mode for underlined information in the source file. The
-u option suppresses this processing.

-v
Normally, more ignores control characters that it does not interpret in some way. The -v option causes these to be displayed as ^C where C is the corresponding printable ASCII character. Non-printing non-ASCII characters (with the high bit set) are displayed in the format M-C, where C is the corresponding character without the high bit set. If output is not going to a terminal, more does not interpret control characters.

Examples

view contents of file:

```
more file
```

pg   display file on standard output if more than 23 lines hold screen until enter is pressed giving next 23 lines, a number is entered taking you to that number screen, or q is pressed quitting (scrolls differently than the more command by one line and space bar has no effect)

pg [-number] [-p string] [-cefns]
[+linenumber] [+/pattern/] [file...]

Options

-number
Specifies the size (in lines) of the window that pg is to use instead
of the default. (On a terminal containing 24 lines, the default window size is 23.)

-p string
Causes pg to use string as the prompt. If the prompt string contains a "%d", the first occurrence of "%d" in the prompt will be
replaced by the current page number when the prompt is issued.
The default prompt string is a colon (:).

-c
Homes the cursor and clears the screen before displaying each
page. This option is ignored if cl (clear screen) is not defined for
this terminal type in the termcap(F) database.

-e
Causes pg not to pause at the end of each file.

-f
Inhibits pg from splitting lines. In the absence of the -f option, pg
splits lines longer than the screen width, but some sequences of
characters in the displayed text (for example, escape sequences for
underlining) give undesirable results.

-n
Normally, commands must be terminated by pressing the <Return>
key (ASCII newline character). This option causes an automatic end
of command as soon as a command letter is entered.

-s
Causes pg to display all messages and prompts in standout mode (usually inverse video).

+linenumber
Starts up at linenumber.

+/pattern/
Starts up at the first line containing the regular expression pattern.

Examples

view contents of a file:

```
pg file
```

---

tail   display the last 10 lines of a file unless more lines are specified

tail [±[number] [lbc] [-f]] [file]

tail [-f] [-c number] [-n number] [file]

Options

Copying begins at distance +number from the beginning, or -number from the end of the input (if number is null, the alue 10 is assumed). number is counted in units of lines, blocks, or characters, according to the appended option l, b, or c. When no units are specified, counting is by lines.

With the -f ("follow") option, if the input file is not a pipe, the program will not terminate after the last line of the input file has been copied, but will enter an endless loop, in which it sleeps for a second and then attempts to read and copy further records from the input file. Thus it may be used to monitor the growth of a file that is being written by some other process. For example, the command tail -f file will print the last ten lines of file, followed by any lines that are appended to file between the time tail is initiated and killed.

Examples

view contents of the last 20 lines of file:

```
tail -20 file
```

---

vi   use full screen text editor

vi [-option...] [command...] [filename...]

See Appendix B

Options

-x
Encryption option; when used, the file is encrypted as it is being written and requires an encryption key to be read. vi makes an educated guess to determine if a file is encrypted or not.

Refer to the crypt(C) page for information about restrictions on the availability of encryption options.

-C
Encryption option; the same as -x except that vi assumes files are encrypted.

Refer to the crypt(C) page for information about restrictions on the availability of encryption options.

-c command
Begins editing by executing the specified editor command (usually a search or positioning command).

-t tag
Equivalent to an initial tag command; edits the file containing tag and positions the editor at its definition.

-r file
Used in recovering after an editor or system crash; retrieves the last saved version of the named file.

-l
Specific to editing LISP; sets the showmatch and lisp options.

-L
Lists the names of all files saved as a result of an editor or system crash. Files may be recovered with the -r option.

-wn
Sets the default window size to n; useful on dialups to start in small windows.

-R
Sets a read-only option so that files can be viewed but not edited.

Examples

view contents of file in edit mode:

```
vi file
```

---

view   invoke vi in read only mode

view [-option...] [command...] [filename...]

Options

see vi

Examples

view contents of a file:

```
view file
```

view file lists

l   list files and directories that are in current directory showing permissions, links, owner, group, size, date and time of last access, file name. Not available under HP or ATT equivalent is ls -l

l [-ACFLRabcdfginopqrstu] [-Ws | -Wv] [directory | file...]

Options

-1
Forces an output format with one entry per line, for lc, lf, lr, and lx.

-a
Lists all entries; "." and ".." are not suppressed.

-A
Lists all entries. Entries whose name begin with a dot (.) are listed. This option does not list current directory "." and directory above "..".

-b
Forces printing of non-graphic characters in the \ddd notation, in octal.

-c Uses the last time that the file was changed for sorting. The change time refers to modification of the file's data, modification of the information stored in the inode, or creation of the file.

This option is used with -t option.

-C

Lists in columns with entries sorted down the columns. If the argument(s) are filename(s), output is across the page, rather than down the page in columns.

-d

If an argument is a directory, lists only its name (not its contents); often used with -l to get the status of a directory.

-f

Forces each argument to be interpreted as a directory and lists the name found in each slot. This option turns off -l, -t, -s, and -r, and turns on -a. The order is the order in which entries appear in the directory.

-F

Causes directories to be marked with a trailing "/", executable files to be marked with a trailing "*", symbolic links to be marked with a trailing "@", and named pipes (or FIFOs) to be marked with a "|".

-g

The same as -l, except that the owner is not printed.

-i

For each file, prints the inode number in the first column of the report.

-l

Lists in long format, giving mode, number of links, owner, group, size in bytes, and the time that each file was last modified.

Unless one of the -c or -u options is specified, the modification time refers only to changes made to the file's data, or the creation of the file. It does not record the time that changes were made to the information stored in the inode.

If the file is a symbolic link, the filename is printed followed by "->" and the pathname of the referenced file.

If the file is a special file, the size field will contain the major and minor device numbers, rather than a size. A total count of blocks in the directory, including indirect blocks, is printed at the top of long format listings.

A description of the mode listing is given in "File modes".

-L
If an argument is a symbolic link, lists the information for the file or directory the link references.

-m
Forces stream output format; files are listed across the page, separated by commas.

-n
The same as -l, except that the user ID (UID) and group ID (GID) numbers are printed, rather than the owner name and the group name.

-o
The same as -l, except that the group is not printed.

-p
Puts a slash (/) after each directory.

-q
Forces printing of non-graphic characters in filenames as the character "?".

-r
Reverses the order of sort to get reverse alphabetic or oldest first, as appropriate.

-R
Recursively lists arbitrarily deep subdirectories.

-s
Gives size in 512-byte blocks, including indirect blocks, for each entry.

-t
Sorts by time modified (latest first) instead of by name. Files with equivalent modification times are then sorted alphabetically. The modification time sorted on depends on whether the -c, or -u option is also specified.

-u
Uses the time that the file was accessed for sorting. The access time refers to the last time that the file's data was read, or the creation of the file. It does not record the time that changes were written to the file's data, or to the information stored in the inode.

This option is used with the -t option.

-Ws

Prints a long listing similar to that obtained using the -l option. If the file is a symbolic link, this option displays the inode details of the file at the end of the symbolic link chain, and appends an "@" to the name of the symbolic link.

-Wv

Prints a long listing similar to that obtained using the -l option. If the file is the start of a chain of symbolic links, this option displays the inode details of the file at the end of the chain, and prints the pathnames of all files in the chain separated by "->" symbols.

-x

Lists in columns with entries sorted across, rather than down, the page. If the argument(s) are filename(s), output is across the page, rather than down the page in columns.

Examples

get directory listing in order of date and time:

```
l -t
```

---

lc   list only the filename of files and/or directories in current directory in columnar format

lc [-1AFLRabcdfgilmnopqrstux] [-Ws | -Wv] [directory | file...]

Options

see l

Examples

list all files in directory in column format:

```
lc
```

```
file1              file2              file3
```

---

ls   list only the filename of files and/or directories in current directory in a single list format

ls [-ACFLRabcdfgilmnopqrstux] [-Ws | -Wv] [directory | file...]

Options

see l

Examples

list all files in directory:

```
ls
file1
file2
```

```
file3
```

list all files in directory in long format:

```
ls -al
```

-rwxrwx—links owner	group	bytes	datetime	file1
-rw-rw-r—links owner	group	bytes	datetime	file2
-rw-r—r—links owner	group	bytes	datetime	file3

update—overview

Methods for updating files

| make | update program files |
| touch | update access and modification date and time |

update

make execute commands in a makefile to update one or more computer programs allowing a programmer to maintain and regenerate groups of programs

make [-f makefile] [-eiknpPqrstuw] [-b | -B] [names] [macro definitions]

Options

-f makefile
Description file name. makefile is assumed to be the name of a description file.

-e
Environment variables override assignments within makefiles.

-i
Ignore error codes returned by invoked commands. This mode is entered if the fake target name .IGNORE appears in the description file.

-k
Abandon work on the current entry if it fails, but continue on other branches that do not depend on that entry.

-n
No execute mode. Print commands, but do not execute them. Even lines beginning with an @ are printed.

-p
Print out the complete set of macro definitions and target descriptions.

-P
Update in parallel more than one target at a time. The number of targets updated concurrently is determined by the environment variable PARALLEL and the presence of .MUTEX directives in makefiles.

-q Question.
The make command returns a zero or non-zero status code depending on whether the target file is or is not up-to-date.

-r
Do not use the built-in rules.

-s
Silent mode. Do not print command lines before executing. This mode is also entered if the fake target name .SILENT appears in the description file.

-t
Touch the target files (causing them to be up-to-date) rather than issue the usual commands.

-u
Unconditionally make the target, ignoring all timestamps.

-w

Suppress warning messages. Fatal messages will not be affected.

-b

Compatibility mode for old makefiles; this is the default mode.

-B

Turn off compatibility mode for old makefiles.

Examples

lines from a sample makefile:

```
ARFILES = armast.o artrx.o
TXFILES = txmast.o txtrx.o
AR_MAIN.4ge: ARMAIN.4gl $(ARFILES)  $(TXFILES)
c4gl   -o  AR_MAIN.4ge:  $(ARFILES)   $(TXFILES)
$(SRC)/library/lib.a
strip AR_MAIN.4ge
INSTALL:
mv AR_MAIN.4ge  /ar/executables
```

---

touch   update the date and time of access and modifications of a file

touch [-acm] [-r ref_file] [-t [[CC]YY]MMDDhhmm[.ss]] file…
touch [-acm] [MMDDhhmm[yy]] file…

Options

-a

Update the access time only. The modification time is not changed unless the -m option is also specified.

-c

Silently prevent touch from creating a file if it does not already exist.

-m

Update the modification time only. The access time is not changed unless the -a option is also specified.

-r

Use the access and modification times of the file ref_file instead of the current time.

-t

Use the specified time instead of the current time. The form of the specified time is [[CC]YY]MMDDhhmm[.ss]:

CC first two digits of the year (the century minus one) [19-20];

YY last two digits of the year [00-99]

MM month [01-12]

DD day [01-31]

hh hour [00-23]

mm minute [00-59]

ss second [00-61]; the values 60 and 61 are used for leap seconds

If neither -a nor -m is given, touch updates both the access and modification times (equivalent to specifying -am).

Examples

change date and time on file:

```
touch file
```

width—overview

Method for modifying width of a file

fold   break lines of a file

width

fold   break lines of file at maximum width and insert a newline character, however line is not broken in middle of character

fold [-bs] [-w width] [file...]

Options

-b
Turn off the special treatment of backspace, carriage return and tab characters (as described above).

-s
If a line contains blank characters within the first width positions, break the line after the last such blank character. (If there is no such blank character, the -s has no effect.) This option is useful for readable text files; it ensures that lines are broken on word boundaries rather than in the middle of a word.

-w width
width is the column width in column positions. The default value is 80.

Examples

print file that is 132 characters wide, down to 80 characters :

```
fold -w 80 file | lp
```

ABOUT THE AUTHOR

Georgia Faulkner owns Business Software Services, Inc., a software development and training company, which she founded in 1994. Georgia has 12 years of experience in the Unix environment. She lives in Suffolk, Virginia, with her husband of 20 years, Darwin.

Karen Morris has a Computer Management Bachelor of Science Degree and 12 years of programming experience in the Unix environment. She has owned and operated her own software consulting business, Morris Integrated Systems, Inc., since 1997. Karen Morris has been a resident in Suffolk, VA since 1991. She has been married to her husband Rob for twelve years. She has two children: Jordan and Joshua.

APPENDIX A

system shells

---

csh allows user to interact with operating system through a shell command interpeter with syntax similar to the C programming language that uses commands not available in the standard shell

csh [-cefinstv VxX] [arg...]

Options

Description

csh is a command language interpreter. When it is first invoked, csh executes commands from the file .cshrc, located in the home directory of the user. If it is a login shell, it then executes commands from the file .login (in the same directory). Subsequently, if it is running in interactive mode, csh reads commands from the terminal, prompting the user for each new line by printing a "%". Arguments to the shell, and the use of the shell to process files containing command scripts, are described later.

The shell repeatedly performs the following actions: a line of command input is read and broken into words. This sequence of words is placed on the command history list and then parsed. Finally, each command in the current line is executed.

When a login shell terminates, it executes commands from the file .logout in the user's home directory.

Lexical structure

The shell splits input lines into words at blanks and tabs with the following exceptions. The characters & | ; < > (and) are treated as separate words. Some of these characters can be paired up; the pairs &&, ||, <<, >> are treated as single words. In order to use these metacharacters within other words, their special meaning must be suppressed by preceding them with a backslash (\). A newline preceded by a "\" is equivalent to a blank.

In addition, strings enclosed in matched pairs of quotations, (`, ´ or "), form parts of a word; metacharacters in these strings, including blanks and tabs, are not treated as separate words. The semantics of quoted strings are described below. Within quoted strings delimited by pairs of (´) or (") characters, a newline preceded by a "\" gives a true newline character.

If the shell reads the character "#" in its input, it treats the rest of the current line (that is, all the text to the right of the "#") as a comment, and ignores it. The "#" character loses this special meaning if it is preceded by a backslash character (\) or placed inside quotation marks (`, ´, or ").

Commands

A simple command is a sequence of words, the first of which specifies the command to be executed. A simple command or a sequence of simple commands separated by "|" characters (pipes) forms a pipeline. The output from each command in a pipeline is used as the input to the next command. Sequences of pipelines may be separated by semi-colons (;); the elements of such a sequence are executed sequentially. A sequence of pipelines may be executed without waiting for it to terminate by ending the command line with an ampersand character (&). Such a sequence is protected from termination by hangup signals sent by the shell; the nohup command need not be used.

Any of the above commands may be placed in parentheses to form a new simple command (which in turn may be used as a component of a pipeline or some other more complex command). It is also possible to separate pipelines with the "&&" or "||" expressions: these stand for logical-OR and logical-AND respectively. (Due to an historical bug, csh assigns these symbols the opposite meaning to that assumed by the C programming language and other UNIX® utilities.) Use of these
expressions makes the execution of the second pipeline conditional upon the success (logical-AND) or failure (logical-OR) of the first. (See "Expressions" for more information.)

Substitutions

The following sections describe the various transformations the shell performs on the input in the order in which they are carried out.

History substitutions

History substitutions can be used to reintroduce sequences of words from previous commands, possibly altering them in the process. Thus, history substitutions provide a general redo facility.

History substitutions begin with the character "!" and may begin anywhere in the input stream unless a history substitution is already in progress. A "!" preceded by a backslash (\), or followed by a space, tab, newline, "=" or "(", is treated as a literal "!" and its special meaning is suppressed. History substitutions may also occur when an input line begins with "^". This special abbreviation is described later.

The text of any input line containing a history substitution is echoed on the terminal after the substitution has been carried out, so that the user can see the literal command that is being executed.

Commands entered at the terminal and consisting of one or more words are saved on the history list, the size of which is controlled by the history variable. The previous command is always retained. Commands are assigned numbers incrementally, starting with 1 (the first command executed under the current csh).

For example, enter the command:

history

This internal command causes csh to print a list of the commands stored on the history list, along with their event numbers. Now, consider the following (sample) output from the history command:

    9 write michael
    10 ex write.c
    11 cat oldwrite.c
    12 diff *write.c

It is not usually necessary to use event numbers, but the current event number can be made part of the prompt by placing a "!" in the prompt string.

If the current event (the current command line) is 13, we can refer to previous command lines in several ways:

By event number:

!11

to re-run cat oldwrite.c

By relative event number:

!-2

to go back two events; this will also re-run cat oldwrite.c

By part of a command:

!d

to re-run the most recent command starting with a "d", in this case diff *write.c, or:

!?mic?

to re-run the most recent command containing the string "mic", write michael

These forms simply reproduce the words of the specified event, each separated by a single blank. The special case "!!" refers to the previous command; thus the history substitution "!!" means "repeat the last command." The form "!#" references the current command (the one being entered on the current line). It allows a word to be selected from further left in the line, for example to avoid retyping a long name, as in "!#:1".

To select words from an event, we can follow the event specification by a colon (:) and a designator for the desired words. The words of an input line are numbered from 0, the first (usually command) word being 0, the second word (first argument) being 1, and so on. The basic word designators are:

0 first (command) word

n nth argument

^ first argument, that is, 1

$ last argument

% word matched by (immediately preceding) ?s? search

x-y range of words

-y abbreviates 0-y

* abbreviates ^-$, or nothing if only 1 word in the event

x* abbreviates x-$

x- like x* but omitting word $

The ":" separating the event specification from the word designator can be omitted if the argument selector begins with a ^, $, *,— or %. After the optional word designator, a sequence of modifiers can be placed, each preceded by a colon. The following modifiers are defined:

h removes a trailing pathname component

r removes a trailing .xxx component

e returns the trailing .xxx pathname component

s/l/r/ substitutes r for l

t removes all leading pathname components

& repeats the previous substitution

g applies the change globally, prefixing the above

p prints the new command but does not execute it

q quotes the substituted words, preventing substitutions

x like q, but breaks into words at blanks, tabs, and newlines

Unless preceded by g, the modification is applied only to the first modifiable word. In any case it is an error for no word to be applicable.

The left sides of substitutions are not regular expressions like those recognized by the editors, but rather strings. Any character

may be used as the delimiter instead of "/"; if it is necessary to include an instance of the delimiter character within one of the substitution strings, its special meaning may be removed by preceding it with a "\". An ampersand character (&) in the right side of a substitution is replaced by the text from the left side of the substitution. An ampersand preceded by a backslash (\&) is treated as a literal ampersand (&) with no special meaning. A null l uses the previous string
either from an l or from a contextual scan string s in "!?s?". The trailing delimiter in the substitution may be omitted if a newline follows immediately, as may the trailing "?" in a contextual scan.

A history reference may be given without an event specification (for example, !$). It is assumed that the reference is to the previous command unless a history substitution precedes it on the same line, in which case it is assumed to refer to the last event substitution. Thus !?foo?^!$ gives the first and last arguments from the command matching ?foo?.

A special abbreviation of a history reference occurs when the first nonblank character of an input line is a "^". This is equivalent to !:s^, providing a convenient shorthand for substitutions on the text of the previous line. Thus ^lb^lib fixes the spelling of lib in the previous command.

Finally, a history substitution may be surrounded with "{" and "}" if necessary to insulate it from the characters that follow. Thus, after ls -ld ~paul, the command !{l}a performs ls -ld ~paula, while the command !la looks for a command starting la.

Quotations with ' and ''

Quoted (´) or double quoted (") strings are exempt from some or all of the substitutions. Strings enclosed in single quotes are not subject to interpretation. Strings enclosed in double quotes are subject to variable and command expansion. Since history (!) substitution occurs within all quotes, you must escape "!" with a backslash (\), even within quotes, if you want to prevent history substitution.

In both cases, the resulting text becomes all or part of a single word; only in one special case (see "Command substitution" below) does a double quoted string yield parts of more than one word; single quoted strings never do.

Alias substitution

The shell maintains a list of aliases which can be established, displayed and modified by the alias and unalias commands. After a command line is scanned, it is parsed into distinct commands and the first word of each command, left-to-right, is checked to see if it has an alias. If it has, then the text of the alias for that command is reread, and the history mechanism is applied to it as though that command were the previous input line. The resulting words replace the command and argument list. If no reference is made to the history list, then the argument list is left unchanged.

Thus, if the alias for ls is ls -l, the command ls /usr maps to ls -l /usr. Similarly if the alias for lookup is grep \!^ /etc/passwd, then lookup bill maps to grep bill /etc/passwd.

If an alias is found, the word transformation of the input text is performed and the aliasing process begins again on the newly generated input line. Looping is prevented by flagging the first word of the old text; if the first word of the new text is the same, further aliasing is prevented. Other loops are detected and cause an error.

Note that the mechanism allows aliases to introduce parser metasyntax. Thus:

alias print 'pr :* | lpr'

makes a command that paginates its arguments to the lineprinter.

There are four csh aliases distributed. These are pushd, popd, swapd, and flipd. These aliases maintain a directory stack.

pushd dir
Pushes the current directory onto the top of the directory stack, then changes to the directory dir.

popd
Changes to the directory at the top of the stack, then removes (pops) the top directory from the stack, and announces the current directory.

swapd
Swaps the top two directories on the stack. The directory on the top becomes the second to the top, and the second to the top directory becomes the top directory.

flipd

Flips between two directories, the current directory and the top directory on the stack. If you are currently in dir1, and dir2 is on the top of the stack, when flipd is invoked you change to dir2, and dir1 is replaced as the top directory on the stack. When flipd is again invoked, you change to dir1, and dir2 is again the top directory on the stack.

Variable substitution

The shell maintains a set of variables, each of which has a list of zero or more words as its value. Some of these variables are set by the shell or referred to by it. For instance, the argv variable is an image of the shell's argument list, and words of this variable's value are referred to in special ways.

The values of variables may be displayed and changed by using the set and unset commands. Of the variables referred to by the shell a number are toggles; the shell does not care what their value is, only whether they are set or not. For instance, the verbose variable is a toggle which causes command input to be echoed. The setting of this variable results from the –v command line option.

Other operations treat variables numerically. The @ command permits numeric calculations to be performed and the result to be assigned to a variable. However, variable values are always represented as zero or more strings. For the purposes of numeric operations, the null string is considered to be 0, and the second and subsequent words of multiword values are ignored.

After the input line is aliased and parsed, and before each command is executed, variable substitution is performed, keyed by dollar sign ($) characters. This expansion can be prevented by preceding the dollar sign with a backslash (\) except within double quotation marks (") where it always occurs, and within single quotation marks (´) where it never occurs. Strings quoted by back quotation marks (`) are interpreted later (see "Command substitution" below) so dollar sign substitution does not occur there until later, if at all. A dollar sign is passed unchanged if followed by a blank, tab, or end-of-line.

Input and output redirections are recognized before variable expansion, and are expanded separately. Otherwise, the command name and entire argument list are expanded together. It is thus possible for the first (command) word to generate more than one word, the first of which becomes the command name, and the rest of which become arguments.

Unless enclosed in double quotation marks or given the :q modifier, the results of variable substitution may eventually be subject to command and filename substitution. Within double quotation marks ("), a variable whose value consists of multiple words expands to a portion of a single word, with the words of the variable's value separated by blanks. When the :q modifier is applied to a substitution, the variable expands to multiple words with each word separated by a blank and quoted to prevent later command or filename substitution.

The following sequences are provided for introducing variable values into the shell input. Except as noted, it is an error to reference a variable which is not set.

$name

${name}
Are replaced by the words of the value of variable name, each separated by a blank. Braces insulate name from following characters which would otherwise be part of it. Shell variables have names consisting of up to 20 letters, digits, and underscores. If name is not a shell variable, but is set in the environment, then that value is returned (but ":" modifiers and the other forms given below are not available in this case).

$name[selector]

${name[selector]}
May be used to select only some of the words from the value of name. The selector is subjected to $ substitution and may consist of a single number or two numbers separated by a "-". The first word of a variable's value is numbered 1. If the first number of a range is omitted it defaults to 1. If the last member of a range is omitted it defaults to $#name. The selector "*" selects all words. It is not an error for a range to be empty if the second argument is omitted or in range.

$#name

${#name}
Give the number of words in the variable. This is useful for later use in a [selector].

$0 Substitutes the name of the file from which command input is being read. An error occurs if the name is not known.

$number

${number}
Are equivalent to $argv[number].

$* Is equivalent to $argv[*].

The modifiers :h, :t, :r, :q and :x may be applied to the substitutions above, as may :gh, :gt and :gr. If braces ({ and }) appear in the command form then the modifiers must appear within the braces. Only one ":" modifier is allowed on each $ expansion.

The following substitutions may not be modified with ":" modifiers.

$?name

${?name}
Substitutes the string 1 if name is set, 0 if it is not.

$?0 Substitutes 1 if the current input filename is known, 0 if it is not.

$$ Substitutes the decimal process number of the parent shell.

Command and filename substitution

Command and filename substitution are applied selectively to the arguments of built-in commands. This means that portions of expressions which are not evaluated are not subjected to these expansions. For commands which are not internal to the shell, the command name is substituted separately from the argument list.

This occurs very late, after input-output redirection is performed, and in a child of the main shell.

Command substitution

Command substitution is indicated by a command enclosed in back quotation marks (`). The output from such a command is normally broken into separate words at blanks, tabs and new-lines, with null words being discarded. This text then replaces the original string. Within double quotation marks, only newlines force new words; blanks and tabs are preserved.

In any case, the single final newline does not force a new word. Note that it is possible for a command substitution to yield only part of a word, even if the command outputs a complete line.

Filename substitution

If a word contains any of the characters * ? [{ or begins with the character "~", then that word is a candidate for filename substitution, also known as globbing. This word is then regarded as a pattern, and is replaced with an alphabetically sorted list of filenames which match the pattern.

The character "~" at the beginning of a filename is used to refer to home directories. Standing alone, it expands to the invoker's home directory contained in the variable HOME. When "~" is followed by a name consisting of letters, digits, and underscore characters (like_this), the shell searches for a user with that name and substitutes the user's home directory; thus ~ken might expand to /usr/ken and ~ken/chmach to /usr/ken/chmach. If the character

"~" is followed by a character other than a letter or "/", or if it does not appear at the beginning of a word, it is left unchanged.

The file patterns (shell regular expressions) matched by the C shell are described in regexp(M).

Spelling checker

If the local variable cdspell has been set, the shell checks spelling whenever cd is used to change directories. For example, if you change to a different directory using cd and misspell the directory name, the shell responds with an alternative spelling of an existing directory. Enter "y" and press <Enter> (or just press <Enter>) to change to the offered directory. If the offered spelling is incorrect, enter "n", then retype the command line. In this example the csh response is in light type:

% cd /usr/spool/uucp

  /usr/spool/uucp?y
  ok

Input/output

The standard input and standard output of a command may be redirected with the following syntax:

< name
  Opens file name (after variable, command and filename expansion) as the standard input.

<< word

Reads the shell input up to a line which is identical to word. word is not subjected to variable, filename or command substitution, and each input line is compared to word before any substitutions are done on this input line. Unless a quoting backslash, double, or single quotation mark, or a back quotation mark appears in word, variable and command substitution is performed on the intervening lines, allowing "\" to quote "$", "\" and "`". Commands which are substituted have all blanks, tabs, and newlines preserved, except for the final newline which is dropped. The resulting text is placed in an anonymous temporary file which is given to the command as standard input.

> name

>! name

>& name

>&! name
Opens the file name as the standard output. If the file does not exist, then it is created; if the file exists, it is overwritten.

If the variable noclobber is set, then an error results if the file already exists or if it is not a character special file (for example, a terminal or /dev/null). This helps prevent accidental destruction of files. In this case, the "!" forms can be used to suppress this check.

The forms involving "&" route the standard error into the specified file as well as the standard output. name is expanded in the same way as "<" input filenames are.

>> name

>>& name

>>! name

>>&! name
Uses file name as the standard output. This is like ">" but places output at the end of the file. If the variable noclobber is set, then it is an error for the file not to exist unless one of the "!" forms is given. Otherwise it is similar to ">".

If a command is run in the background (followed by "&") then the default standard input for the command is the empty file /dev/null. Otherwise, the command receives the input and output parameters from its parent shell. Thus, unlike some previous shells, commands run from a file of shell commands have no access to the text of the commands by default; rather they receive the original standard input of the shell. The << mechanism should be used to present inline data. This permits shell command scripts to function as components of pipelines and allows the shell to block read its input.

The standard error may be directed through a pipe with the standard output. Simply use the form "|&" rather than "|".

Expressions

A number of the built-in commands (to be described later) take expressions, in which the operators are similar to those of C, with the same precedence. These expressions appear in the @, exit, if, and while commands. The following operators are available:

```
|| && | ^ & == != <= >= < > << >>
+—* / % ! ~ ( )
```

Here the precedence increases to the right, == and !=, <=, >=, <, and >, << and >>, + and -, * / and % being, in groups, at the same level. The == and != operators compare their arguments as strings, all others operate on numbers. Strings which begin with 0 are considered octal numbers. Null or missing arguments are considered 0. The results of all expressions are strings, which represent decimal numbers. Note that no two components of an expression can appear in the same word unless the word is adjacent to components of expressions that are syntactically significant to the parser (& | < > ( )). These components should be surrounded by spaces.

Also available in expressions as primitive operands are command executions enclosed in "{" and "}" and file enquiries of the form -l name where l is one of:

r Read access

w Write access

x Execute access

e Existence

o Ownership

z Zero size

f Plain file

d Directory

Command and filename expansion is applied to the specified name, then the result is tested to see if it has the specified relationship to the real user. If the file does not exist or is inaccessible then all enquiries return false, that is 0. Command executions succeed, returning true, that is 1, if the command exits with status 0, otherwise they fail, returning false, that is 0.

If more detailed status information is required then the command should be executed outside of an expression and the variable status examined.

Control flow

The shell contains a number of commands which can be used to regulate the flow of control in command files (shell scripts) and (in limited but useful ways) from terminal input. Due to the implementation, some restrictions are placed on the word placement for the foreach, switch, and while statements, as well as the if-then-else form of the if statement. Please pay careful attention to these restrictions in the descriptions in the next section.

If the shell's input is not seekable, the shell buffers up input whenever a loop is being read and performs seeks in this internal buffer to accomplish the rereading implied by the loop. (To the extent that this allows, backward goto commands will succeed on non-seekable inputs.)

Built-in commands

Built-in commands are executed within the shell. If a built-in command occurs as any component of a pipeline except the last, then it is executed in a subshell.

alias

alias name

alias name wordlist
The first form prints all aliases. The second form prints the alias for name. The final form assigns the specified wordlist as the alias of name. wordlist is the command; filename substitution may be applied to wordlist. name is not allowed to be alias or unalias.

break
This causes execution to resume after the end of the nearest enclosing foreach or while statement. The remaining commands on the current line are executed. Multilevel breaks are thus possible by writing them all on one line.

breaksw
This causes a break from a switch, resuming after the endsw.

case label:
This is part of the switch statement discussed below.

cd [-L | -P] [name]

chdir [-L | -P] [name]

These commands change the shell's working directory to directory name. If no argument is given, the new directory is the home directory of the user. If name is not found as a subdirectory of the current directory (and does not begin with "/", "./", or "../"), then each component of the variable cdpath is checked to see if it has a subdirectory name.
Finally, if all else fails but name is a shell variable whose value begins with "/", then this is tried to see if it is a directory.

If cdspell has been set, the shell runs a spelling check as follows. If the shell is reading its commands from a terminal, and the specified directory does not exist (or some component cannot be searched), spelling correction is applied to each component of directory in a search for the "correct" name. The shell then asks whether or not to try and change the directory to the corrected directory name; an answer of n means "no", and anything else is taken as "yes."

The -L and -P flags are relevant to systems with symbolic links:

-L
reserve logical pathnames so that cd -L .. moves up one component towards the root along the current logical path.

-P
Use a physical model for pathnames so that cd -L .. moves up one component towards the root by following the link to the parent of the current directory. This is the default behavior.

For example, if /usr/include/sys/h is a symbolic link to the directory /sys/h, then cd /usr/include/sys/h; cd -L .. would make

/usr/include/sys the current directory; cd /usr/include/sys/h; cd -P ..
would make /sys the current directory.

If the variable cdlogical is set, the default behavior of cd and chdir
is to use logical pathnames when changing directories.

continue
This continues execution of the nearest enclosing while or foreach. The rest of the commands on the current line are executed.

default:
This labels the default case in a switch statement. The default
should come after all case labels.

echo wordlist
The specified words are written to the shell's standard output. A
"\c" causes the echo to complete without printing a newline. A
"\n" in wordlist causes a newline to be printed. Otherwise the
words are echoed, separated by spaces.

else

end

endif

endsw
See the description of the foreach, if, switch, and while statements
below.

exec command
The specified command is executed in place of the current shell.

exit

exit (expr)
The shell exits either with the value of the status variable (first form) or with the value of the specified expr (second form).

foreach name (wordlist)

end The variable name is successively set to each member of wordlist and the sequence of commands between this command and the matching end are executed. (Both foreach name (wordlist) and end must appear alone on separate lines.)

The built-in command continue may be used to continue the loop prematurely and the built-in command break to terminate it prematurely. When this command is read from the terminal, the contents of the loop are read by prompting with "?" until end is typed before any statements in the loop are executed.

glob wordlist
This is like echo but no "\" escapes are recognized and words are delimited by null characters in the output. This is useful for programs which wish to use the shell to apply filename expansion to a list of words.

goto word
Filename and command expansion is applied to the specified word to yield a string of the form label:. The shell rewinds its input as much as possible and searches for a line of the form label: possibly preceded by blanks or tabs. Execution continues after the specified line.

history
This displays the history event list.

if (expr) command
If the specified expression evaluates true, then the single command with arguments is executed. Variable substitution on command happens early, at the same time as for the rest of the if command. command must be a simple command, not a pipeline, a command list, or a parenthesized command list. Input/output redirection occurs even if expr is false, and command is not executed.

if (expr) then

...

else if (expr2) then

...

else

...

endif If the specified expr is true then the commands before the first else are executed; else if expr2 is true then the commands after the second then and before the second else are executed, etc. Any number of else-if pairs are possible; only one endif is needed. The else part is likewise optional. (The words else and endif must appear at the beginning of input lines; the if (expr) then must appear alone on its input line or after an else.)

logout
This terminates a login shell. Use this if ignoreeof is set.

nice

nice +number

nice command

nice +number command
The first form sets the nice for this shell to 4. By default, commands run under C-Shell have a "nice value" of 0. The second form sets the nice to the given number. The final two forms run command at priority 4 and number respectively. root may specify negative niceness by using nice -number.... The command is always executed in a subshell, and the restrictions placed on commands in simple if statements apply.

nohup

nohup command
The first form can be used in shell scripts to cause hangups to be ignored for the remainder of the script. The second form causes the specified command to be run with hangups ignored. Unless the shell is running in the background, nohup has no effect. All processes running in the background with "&" are automatically nohuped.

onintr

onintr -

onintr label
This controls the action of the shell on interrupts. The first form restores the default action of the shell on interrupts, which is to terminate shell scripts or to return to the terminal command input level. The second form, onintr -, causes all interrupts to be ignored. The final form causes the shell to execute a goto label when an interrupt is received or a child process terminates because it was interrupted. In any case, if the shell is running in the background, interrupts are ignored whether any form of onintr is present or not.

pwd [-L | -P]
Prints the current working directory. The -L and -P flags are useful with symbolic links:

-L Show the logical pathname to the directory preserving the route taken to get there.

-P Show the physical pathname to the directory. This is the default behavior.

For example, if /usr/include/sys/h is a symbolic link to the directory /sys/h, then cd /usr/include/sys/h; pwd –L prints /usr/include/sys/h as the current working directory; cd/usr/include/sys/h; pwd -P prints /sys/h as the current working directory.

If the variable cdlogical is set, the default behavior of pwd is to report logical pathnames.

rehash
This causes the internal hash table of the contents of the directories in the path variable to be recomputed. This is needed if new commands are added to directories in the path while you are logged in.

repeat count command
The specified command, which is subject to the same restrictions as the command in the simple if statement above, is executed count times. I/O redirection occurs exactly once, even if count is 0.

set

set name

set name=word

set name[index]=word

set name=(wordlist)
The first form of the command shows the value of all shell variables. Variables which have other than a single word as value print as a parenthesized word list. The second form sets name to the null string. The third form sets name to the single word. The fourth form sets the indexth component of name to word; this component must already exist.
The final form sets name to the list of words in wordlist. Command and filename expansion is applied in all cases. These arguments may be repeated to set multiple values in a single set command. Note however, that variable expansion happens for all arguments before any setting occurs.

setenv name value
This sets the value of the environment variable name to be value, which must be a single string. Two useful environment variables are TERM, the type of your terminal and SHELL, the shell you are using.

shift

shift variable
In the first form, the members of argv are shifted to the left, discarding argv[1]. It is an error for argv not to be set or to have less than one word as a value. The second form performs the same function on the specified variable.

source name
The shell reads commands from name. source commands may be nested, but if they are nested too deeply, the shell may run out of file descriptors. An error in a source at any level terminates all nested source commands, including the csh process from which source was called. If source is called from the login shell, it is logged out. Input during source commands is never placed on the history list.

switch (string)

case str1:

...

breaksw

...

default:

...

breaksw

endsw
Command and filename substitution is applied to string; each case
label is then successively matched against the result. Variable
expansion is also applied to the case labels, so the file metacharacters "*", "?", and "[...]" can be used. If none of the labels match
before a default label is found, then the execution begins after the
default label. Each case label and the default label must appear at
the beginning of a line. The command breaksw causes execution
to continue after the endsw. Otherwise control may fall through
case labels and default labels, as in C. If no label matches and
there is no default, execution continues after the endsw.

time

time command
With no argument, a summary of CPU time used by this shell and
its children is printed. If arguments are given, the specified simple
command is timed and a time summary as described under the
time variable is printed. If necessary, an extra shell is created to
print the time statistic when the command completes. command
has the same restrictions as the simple if statement described
above.

umask

umask -S

umask mask
The file creation mask is displayed if no arguments are given. Alternatively, the file creation mask is set to the value specified by mask. If mask is an octal integer, the specified bits will be set in the umask. Otherwise mask should be a symbolic mode (see chmod(C)), the new value of the file creation mask being the logical complement of the file permission bits specified.

If no umask is specified, the current file mode creation mask is printed. The default format is an octal integer. If the -S argument is given the symbolic form is printed. Common values for the mask are 002, giving all access to the group and read and execute access to others, and 022, giving read and execute access to users in the group and all other users. See also umask(C).

unalias pattern
All aliases whose names match the specified pattern are discarded. Thus, all aliases are removed by unalias *. It is not an error for nothing to be unaliased.

unhash
Use of the internal hash table to speed location of executed programs is disabled.

unset pattern
All variables whose names match the specified pattern are removed. Thus, all variables are removed by unset *; use this with care. It is not an error for nothing to be unset.

unsetenv pattern
All environment variables whose names match the specified pattern are removed.

wait All child processes are waited for. If the shell is interactive, then an interrupt can disrupt the wait, at which time the shell prints names and process numbers of all children known to be outstanding.

while (expr)

...

end While the specified expression evaluates non-zero, the commands between the while and the matching end are evaluated. break and continue may be used to terminate or continue the loop prematurely. (The while (expr) and end must appear alone on their input lines.) Prompting occurs here the first time through the loop as for the foreach statement if the input is a terminal.

@

@ name = expr

@ name[index] = expr
The first form prints the values of all the shell variables. The second form sets the specified name to the value of expr. If the expression contains <, >, & or | then at least this part of the expression must be placed within ( ). The third form assigns the value of expr to the indexth argument of name. Both name and its indexth component must already exist.

The operators *=, +=, etc. are available as in C. The space separating the name from the assignment operator is optional. Spaces are mandatory in separating components of expr which would otherwise be single words. The space between @ and name is also mandatory.

Special postfix ++ and—operators increment and decrement name respectively, that is @ i++.

Predefined variables

The following variables have special meaning to the shell. Of these, ARGV, CHILD, HOME, PATH, PROMPT, SHELL and STATUS are always set by the shell. Except for CHILD and STA-TUS this setting occurs only at initialization; these variables will not be modified unless done explicitly by the user.

The shell copies the environment variable PATH into the variable PATH, and copies the value back into the environment whenever PATH is set. Thus it is not necessary to worry about its setting other than in the file .login, since inferior csh processes will import the definition of PATH from the environment.

ARGV
Set to the arguments to the shell, it is from this variable that positional parameters are substituted, that is, $1 is replaced by argv[1], and so on. argv[0] is not defined, but $0 is.

CDPATH
This gives a list of alternate directories searched to find subdirectories in cd commands.

CHILD
This is the process number of the last command forked with "&". This variable is unset when this process terminates.

ECHO

This is set when the -x command line option is given. It causes each command and its arguments to be echoed just before it is executed. For non-built-in commands all expansions occur before echoing. Built-in commands are echoed before command and file-name substitution, since these substitutions are then done selectively.

HISTCHARS

This can be assigned a two-character string. The first character is used as a history character in place of "!", the second character is used in place of the "^" substitution mechanism. For example, set histchars=",;" will cause the history characters to be comma and semicolon.

HISTORY

This can be given a numeric value to control the size of the history list. Any command which has been referenced in this many events will not be discarded. A history that is too large may run the shell out of memory. The last executed command is always saved on the history list.

HOME

This is the home directory of the invoker, initialized from the environment. The filename expansion of "~" refers to this variable.

IGNOREEOF

If this is set, the shell ignores end-of-file from input devices that are terminals. This prevents a shell from accidentally being terminated by pressing <Ctrl>d.

MAIL

These are files where the shell checks for mail. This check is executed after each command completion. The shell responds with, "You have new mail" if the file exists with an access time not greater than its modify time.

If the first word of the value of MAIL is numeric, it specifies a different mail checking interval: in seconds, rather than the default, which is 10 minutes.

f multiple mail files are specified, then the shell responds with "New mail in name", when there is mail in the file name.

NOCLOBBER

As described in the section "Input/output", restrictions are placed on output redirection to insure that files are not accidentally destroyed, and that >> redirections refer to existing files.

NOGLOB

If this is set, filename expansion is inhibited. This is most useful in shell scripts which are not dealing with filenames, or after a list of filenames has been obtained and further expansions are not desirable.

NONOMATCH

If this is set, it is not an error for a filename expansion not to match any existing files; rather, the primitive pattern is returned. It is still an error for the primitive pattern to be malformed, that is, echo [still gives an error.

PATH

Each word of the PATH variable specifies a directory in which commands are to be sought for execution. A null word specifies the current directory. If there is no path variable, then only full pathnames execute. The usual search path is /bin, /usr/bin, and ., but this may vary from system to system. For root, the default search path is /etc, /bin and /usr/bin. A shell which is given neither the -c nor the -t option will normally hash the contents of the directories in the path variable after reading .cshrc, and each time the path variable is reset. If new commands are added to these directories while the shell is active, it may be necessary to give the rehash command, or the commands may not be found.

PROMPT

This is the string which is printed before reading each command from an interactive terminal input. If a "!" appears in the string, it will be replaced by the current event number unless a preceding "\" is given. The default is "%", or "#"
for root.

SHELL

This is the file in which the shell resides. This is used in forking shells to interpret files which have execute bits set, but which are not executable by the system. (See the description of "Non-built-in command execution" below.) It is initialized to the home of the shell.

STATUS

This is the status returned by the last command. If it terminated abnormally, then 0200 is added to the status. Built-in commands which fail return exit status 1, otherwise these commands set status to 0.

TIME
This controls automatic timing of commands. If it is set, then any command which takes more than this many cpu seconds will cause a line to be sent to the screen displaying user time, system time, real time, and a utilization percentage which is the ratio of user plus system times to real time.

VERBOSE
Set by the -v command line option, this causes the words of each command to be printed after history substitution.

Non-built-in command execution

When a command to be executed is found not to be a built-in csh command, the shell attempts to execute the command via exec(S). Each word in the variable PATH names a directory from which the shell will attempt to execute the command. If it is given neither a -c nor a -t option, the shell will hash the names in these directories into an internal table so that it will only try an exec in a directory if there is a possibility that the command resides there. This greatly speeds command location when a large number of directories are present in the search path.

The shell concatenates each directory component of PATH with the given command name to form a pathname of a file which it then attempts to execute. This concatenation occurs if any of the following is true:

the non-built-in command execution mechanism is turned off via unhash

the shell is given a -c or -t argument

the directory component of PATH does not begin with a "/"

Parenthesized commands are always executed in a subshell. Thus:

(cd; pwd); pwd

prints the home directory but leaves you in the original directory, while:

cd; pwd

moves you to the home directory.

If the file has execute permissions but is not an executable binary to the system, then it is assumed to be a file containing shell commands and a new shell is spawned to read it.

If there is an alias for SHELL then the words of the alias are prefixed to the argument list to form the shell command. The first word of the alias should be the full pathname of the shell (for example, $shell). Note that this is a special, late occurring, case of alias substitution, and only allows words to be prefixed to the argument list without modification.

Argument list processing

If argument 0 to the shell is "-" then this is a login shell. The flag arguments are interpreted as follows:

-c
Commands are read from the (single) following argument which must be present. Any remaining arguments are placed in argv.

-e

The shell exits if any invoked command terminates abnormally or yields a non-zero exit status.

-f

The shell starts faster, because it neither searches for nor executes commands from the file .cshrc in the invoker's home directory.

-i

The shell is interactive and prompts for its top-level input, even if it appears not to be a terminal. Shells are interactive without this option if their input and output are terminals.

-n

Commands are parsed, but not executed. This may aid in syntactic checking of shell scripts.

-s

Command input is taken from the standard input.

-t

A single line of input is read and executed. A "\" may be used to escape the newline at the end of this line and continue onto another line.

-v

This causes the VERBOSE variable to be set, with the effect that command input is echoed after history substitution.

-x

This causes the ECHO variable to be set, so that commands are echoed immediately before execution.

-V

This causes the VERBOSE variable to be set even before .cshrc is executed.

-X

This causes the ECHO variable to be set even before .cshrc is executed.

After processing the flag arguments, if arguments remain but none of the -c, -i, -s, or -t options were given, the first argument is taken as the name of a file of commands to be executed. The shell opens this file, and saves its name for possible resubstitution by $0. On a typical system, most shell scripts are written for the standard shell (see sh(C)). The C shell will execute such a standard shell if the first character of the script is not a "#" (that is, if the script does not start with a comment). Remaining arguments initialize the variable ARGV.

Signal handling

The shell normally ignores quit signals. The interrupt and quit signals are ignored for an invoked command if the command is followed by "&"; otherwise the signals have the values which the shell inherited from its parent. The shell's handling of interrupts can be controlled by onintr. By default, login shells catch the terminate signal; otherwise this signal is passed on to children from the state in the shell's parent. In no case are interrupts allowed when a login shell is reading the file .logout.

Limitations

Built-in control structure commands like foreach and while cannot be used with "|", "&" or ";".

Commands within loops, prompted for by "?", are not placed in the history list.

It is not possible to use the colon (:) modifiers on the output of command substitutions.

The C shell has many built-in commands with the same name and functionality as Bourne shell commands. However, the syntax of these C shell and Bourne shell commands often differs. Two examples are the nice and echo commands. Be sure to use the correct syntax when working with these built-in C shell commands.

When a C-shell user logs in, the system reads and executes commands in /etc/cshrc before executing commands in the user's $HOME/.cshrc and $HOME/.login. You can, therefore, modify the default C shell environment for all users on the system by editing /etc/cshrc.

During intervals of heavy system load, pressing the delete key while at a C shell prompt (%) may cause the shell to exit. Ifcsh is the login shell, the user is logged out.

csh attempts to import and export the PATH environment variable for use with regular shell scripts. This only works forsimple cases, where the PATH contains no command characters.

The || and && operators are reversed in this implementation.

Words can be no longer than 512 characters. The number of arguments to a command which involves filename expansion is limited to 1/6th the number of characters allowed in an argument list, which is 5120, less the characters in the environment. The length of any argument of a command after filename expansion cannot exceed 159 characters. Also, command substitutions may substitute no more characters than are allowed in an argument list.

To detect looping, the shell restricts the number of alias substitutions on a single line to 20.

Files

~/.cshrc
    read by each shell at the beginning of execution

/etc/cshrc
    systemwide default .cshrc file for login C shells

~/.login
    read by login shell, after .cshrc at login

~/.logout
    read by login shell, at logout

/bin/sh
    shell for scripts not starting with a "#"

/tmp/sh*
    temporary file for <<

/dev/null
   source of empty file

/etc/passwd
   source of home directories for username

---

ksh   allows user to interact with the operating system through a shell programming language that is based on the Bourne Shell with some C Shell capabilities

ksh [±aefhikmnoprstuvx] [±o option]...[-c string] [arg...]

Options

Description

rksh- invoke a restricted Korn shell

The Korn shell ksh is a command interpreter; it reads input typed at a terminal (or saved in a file) and interprets the commands it encounters on each line. In addition to executing named programs, the Korn shell incorporates a high-level programming language that can be used to automate the execution of other programs. The Korn shell language is a superset of that defined by the Bourne shell sh; see sh(C) for details.

NOTE: /bin/posix/sh, linked to ksh, supplies the functionality for sh(C) and echo(C), as defined by ISO/IEC DIS 9945-2:1992, Information technology—Portable Operating System Interface (POSIX)—Part 2: Shell and Utilities (IEEE Std 1003.2-1992) and X/Open CAE Specification, Commands and Utilities, Issue 4, 1992.

The Korn shell incorporates interactive command editing facilities, which make it easier to work with than the Bourne shell;see "In-line editing options".

rksh is a restricted version of the command interpreter ksh; it is used to set up login names and execution environments with capabilities more restricted than those of the standard shell.

See "Invocation" for the meaning of arguments to the shell.

Definitions

The following terms are used throughout this reference, and require a formal definition.

A metacharacter is one of the following characters:

; & ( ) | < > newline space tab

A blank is a space or a tab.

An identifier is a sequence of letters, digits, or underscores starting with a letter or underscore. Identifiers are used as names for functions and named parameters.

A word is a sequence of characters separated by one or more non-quoted metacharacters.

In-line editing options

Normally, each command line entered from a terminal device is simply typed followed by a newline (<Enter> or linefeed). If the emacs, gmacs, or vi option is active, the user can edit the command line. To be in one of these edit modes, use set for the corresponding option. An editing option is automatically selected each time the VISUAL or EDITOR variable is assigned a value ending in either of these option names.

When in an editing mode, the shell behaves like a text editor with a window one line high (that line being the current shell prompt line). It is possible to scroll the window up or down through a history file containing all the previously issued commands, and to edit or execute any of those commands. It is also possible to type and issue a new command, which is then appended to the history file.

The window width in characters is the value of COLUMNS if it is defined, otherwise 80. If the line is longer than the window width minus two, a mark is displayed at the end of the window to notify the user. As the cursor moves and reaches the window boundaries the window will be centered about the cursor. The mark is a ">" if the line extends on the right side of the window; < if it extends on the left; * if it extends on both.

The search commands in each edit mode provide access to the history file. Only strings are matched, not patterns, although a leading "^" in the string restricts the match to begin at the first character in the line.

The editing features require that the user's terminal accept <Enter> as a carriage return without line feed and that a space " '' must overwrite the current character on the screen. ADM terminal users should set the "space—advance" switch to `space'. Hewlett-Packard® Series 2621 terminal users should set the straps to `bcGHxZ etX'.

vi editing mode

To enter vi editing mode, enter the command set -o vi:

There are two typing modes. Initially, when you enter a command you are in the input mode. To edit, enter the control mode by typing <Esc> (ASCII 033) and move the cursor to the point needing correction and then insert or delete characters or words as needed. Most control commands accept an optional repeat count prior to the command.

When in vi mode on most systems, canonical processing is initially enabled and the command is echoed again if it contains any control characters and the speed is 1200 baud or greater, or if less than one second has elapsed since the prompt was printed. The <Esc> character terminates canonical processing for the remainder of the command and the user can then modify the command line. This scheme has the advantages of canonical processing with the type-ahead echoing of raw mode.

If the option viraw is also set, the terminal always has canonical processing disabled. This may be helpful for certain terminals.

Input edit commands

By default the editor is in input mode. These commands edit user input:

erase
Delete the previous character. This is the user-defined erase character as defined by the stty(C) command, usually ^H or #.

^W
Delete the previous blank-separated word.

^D
End of file, if it is the first character on a line. The shell interprets this as indicating that there is no more input to read from the terminal. This terminates the shell unless ignoreeof is set.

^V
Escape the next character. Editing characters and the user's erase and kill characters may be entered in a command line or in a search string if preceded by a ^V. ^V removes the next character's editing features (if any).

\
Escape the next erase or kill character.

Motion edit commands

These commands move the cursor:

[count]l
Move the cursor forward (right) one character.

[count]w
Move the cursor forward one alpha-numeric word.

[count]W
Move the cursor to the beginning of the next word that follows a blank.

[count]e
Move the cursor to the end of the word.

[count]E
Move the cursor to the end of the current blank delimited word.

[count]h
Move the cursor backward (left) one character.

[count]b
Move the cursor backward one word.

[count]B
Move the cursor to the preceding blank-separated word.

[count]|
  Move the cursor to the column count.

[count]fc
Find the next character c in the current line.

[count]Fc
Find the previous character c in the current line.

[count]tc

Equivalent to f followed by h.

[count]Tc
Equivalent to F followed by l.

[count];
Repeat count times, the last single-character find command, f, F, t, or T.

[count],
Reverse the last single-character find command count times.

0 Move the cursor to the start of the line.

^ Move the cursor to the first non-blank character in the line.

$ Move the cursor to the end of the line.

Search edit commands

These commands access the command history:

[count]k
Fetch the previous command.

[count]-
Equivalent to k.

[count]j
Fetch the next command.

[count]+

Equivalent to j.

[count]G
Fetch the command number count. The default is the least recent command.

/string
Search backward for a command containing string. string is terminated by a <Enter> or a linefeed character (/n). If string is preceded by a "^", the matched line must begin with string. If string is null the previous string is used.

?string
Same as "/" except that the search is in the forward direction.

n
Search for the next match of the last "/" or "?" command.

N
Search for the next match of the last "/" or "?" commands, but in the reverse direction. Search the history for the string entered by the previous "/" command.

Text modification edit commands

These commands modify the line:

a
Enter input mode and enter text after the current character.

A
Append text to the end of the line. Equivalent to $a.

[count]cmotion

c[count]motion
Delete from the current character through the character to which motion moves the cursor and enter input mode. If motion is "c", the entire line is deleted.

C
Delete from the current character through the end of the line and enter input mode. Equivalent to c$.

S
Equivalent to cc.

D
Delete from the current character through the end of the line. Equivalent to d$.

[count]dmotion

d[count]motion
Delete the current character through the character to which motion moves. If motion is "d", the entire line is deleted.

i
Enter input mode and insert text before the current character.

I
Insert text before the beginning of the line. Equivalent to 0i.

[count]P
Place the previous text modification before the cursor.

[count]p
Place the previous text modification after the cursor.

R
Enter input mode and replace characters on the screen with characters typed overlay fashion.

[count]rc
Replace the count character(s) starting at the current cursor position with c, and advance the cursor.

[count]x
Delete the current character.

[count]X
Delete the preceding character.

[count].
Repeat the previous text modification command.

[count]~
Invert the case of the count character(s) starting at the current cursor position and advance the cursor.

[count]_
Append the count word of the previous command and enter input
mode. The last word is used if count is omitted.

* Append an "*" to the current word and attempt filename generation. If no match is found, it rings the system bell. Otherwise, the
word is replaced by the matching pattern and input mode is
entered.

\ Complete filename. The current word is replaced by the longest common prefix of all filenames matching the current word with an " * " appended. If the match is unique, a "/" is appended if the file is a directory and a space is appended if the file is not a directory.

Other edit commands

[count]ymotion

y[count]motion
Yank from the current character through the character to which motion moves the cursor and put them into the delete buffer. The text and cursor are unchanged.

Y
Yank from the current position to the end of the line. Equivalent to y$.

u
Undo the last text modifying command.

U
Undo all the text modifying commands performed on the line.

[count]v
Return the command fc -e ${VISUAL:-${EDITOR:-vi}} count in the input buffer. If count is omitted, then the current line is used.

^L
Line feed and print the current line. This has effect only in control mode.

^J
New line and execute the current line, regardless of mode.

^M
Return and execute the current line, regardless of mode.

\# Send the line after inserting a "\#" in front of the line. This is useful for causing the current line to be inserted in the history without being executed.

= List the filenames that match the current word if an "*" were appended to it.

@letter
Search the alias list for an alias by the name _letter and if an alias of this name is defined, insert its value in the input queue for processing.

emacs editing mode

This mode is entered by enabling either the emacs or gmacs option. The only difference between these two modes is the way they handle ^T. To edit, the user moves the cursor to the point needing correction and then inserts or deletes characters or words as needed. All the editing commands are control characters or escape sequences. The notation for control characters is caret (^) followed by the character. For example, ^F is the notation for control F. This is entered by depressing the F key while holding down the <Ctrl> (control) key. The <Shift> key is not depressed. (The notation ^? indicates the <Del> (delete) key.)

The notation for escape sequences is M- followed by a character. For example, M-f (pronounced Meta f) is entered by depressing <Esc> (ASCII 033) followed by the F key. (M-F would be the notation for <Esc> followed by <Shift> (capital) F.)

All edit commands operate from any place on the line (not just at the beginning). Neither <Enter> nor <Line Feed> is entered after edit commands except when noted.

^F Move the cursor forward (right) one character.

M-f Move the cursor forward one word. (In emacs mode, a word is a string of characters consisting only of letters, digits and underscores.)

^B Move the cursor backward (left) one character.

M-b Move the cursor backward one word.

^A Move the cursor to the start of the line.

^E Move the cursor to the end of the line.

^]char
Move the cursor forward to the character char on the current line.

M-^]char
Move the cursor back to the character char on the current line.

^X^X Interchange the cursor and mark.

erase (This is the user-defined erase character as defined by the stty(C) command, usually ^H or #.) Delete the previous character.

^D Delete the current character.

M-d Delete the current word.

M-^H
(Meta-backspace) Delete the previous word.

M-h Delete the previous word.

M-^? (Meta-<Del>) Delete the previous word (if your interrupt character is ^? (<Del>, the default) then this command will not work).

^T In emacs mode transpose the current character with the next character. In gmacs mode transpose the two previous characters.

^C Capitalize the current character.

M-c Capitalize the current word.

M-l Change the current word to lowercase.

^K Delete from the cursor to the end of the line. If it is preceded by a numerical parameter whose value is less than the current cursor position, then delete from the given position up to the cursor. If it is preceded by a numerical parameter whose value is greater than the current cursor position, then delete from the cursor up to the given cursor position.

^W Kill from the cursor to the mark.

M-p Push the region from the cursor to the mark onto the stack.

kill (This is the user-defined kill character as defined by the stty command, usually ^U or @.) Kill the entire current line. If two kill characters are entered in succession, all kill characters from then on cause a line feed (useful when using paper terminals).

^Y Restore the last item removed from the line. (Yank the item back to the line.)

^L Line feed and print the current line.

^@ (Null character) Set the mark.

M-space
(Meta space) Set the mark.

^J (New line) Execute the current line.

^M (Return) Execute the current line.

eof The end-of-file character, normally ^D, is processed as an End-of-file only if the current line is null.

^P Fetch the previous command. It moves back one line when not on the first line of a multi-line command.

M-< Fetch the least recent (oldest) history line.

M-> Fetch the most recent (youngest) history line.

^N Fetch the next command line.

^Rstring
Reverse the search history for a previous command line containing string. If a parameter of 0 is given, the search is forward. string is terminated by a <Enter> or /n. If string is preceded by a "^", the matched line must begin with string. If string is omitted, then the next command line containing the most recent string is accessed. In this case a parameter of 0 reverses the direction of the search.

^O Execute the current line and fetch the next line from the history file.

M-digits
Define a numeric parameter. The digits are taken as a parameter to the next command. The commands that accept a parameter are ^F, ^B, erase, ^C, ^D, ^K, ^R, ^P, ^N, ^], M-., M-^], M-_, M-b, M-c, M-d, M-f, M-h, M-l and M-^H.

M-letter
Search alias list for an alias by the name _letter and if an alias of this name is defined, insert its value on the input queue. The letter must not be one of the above meta-functions.

M-]letter
Search alias list for an alias by the name __letter (two underscores precede letter) and if an alias of this name is defined, insert its value on the input queue. This can be used to program function keys on many terminals.

M-. Insert the last word of the previous command on the line. If preceded by a numeric parameter, the value of this parameter determines which word to insert rather than the last word.

M-_ Same as M-..

M-* Attempt filename generation on the current word. An "*" is appended if the word does not match any file or contain any special pattern characters.

M-ESC
Perform filename-completion on the current word. The current word is treated as a root to which an "*" is appended. A search is conducted for files matching the current word. The first match found then replaces the current word. Subsequent matches are obtained by repeating M-ESC. If the match is both unique and a directory, a "/" is appended to it. If it is unique but not a directory, a space is appended to it.

M-= List the files matching the current word pattern if an "*" were appended.

^U Multiply the parameter of the next command by 4.

\ Escape the next character. Editing characters and the user's erase, kill and interrupt (normally ^?) characters may be entered in a command line or in a search string if preceded by a "\". The "\" removes the next character's editing features (if any).

^V Display the version of the shell.

M-\# Insert a "\#" at the beginning of the line and execute it. This causes a comment to be inserted in the history file.

History file

The text of the last HISTSIZE (default 128) commands entered from a terminal device is saved in a history file. The file $HOME/.sh_history is used if the HISTFILE parameter is not set or is not writable. A shell can access the commands of all interactive shells which use the same named HISTFILE. The special command fc is used to list or edit a portion of this file. The portion of the file to be edited or listed can be selected by number or by giving the first character or characters of the command. A single command or range of commands can be specified. If an editor program is not specified as an argument to fc then the value of the parameter FCEDIT is used. If FCEDIT is not defined then /bin/ed is used. The edited command(s) is printed and re-executed upon leaving the editor. The editor name "-" is used to skip the editing phase and to re-execute the command. In this case a substitution parameter of the form old=new can be used to modify the command before execution. For example, if r is aliased to 'fc -e -' then:

r bad=good c

re-executes the most recent command which starts with the letter "c", replacing the first occurrence of the string bad with the string good.

Commands

A command is a sequence of characters in the syntax of the shell language. The shell reads each command and carries out the desired action either directly or by invoking separate programs. For example, when the name of a program to execute is typed, the shell searches for the program and runs it; if the program is a script of shell commands, it creates a subshell which interprets the commands.

The following sections constitute a detailed definition of the Korn shell language.

A special command is a command that is carried out by the shell without creating a separate process. Except for documented side effects, most special commands can be implemented as separate utilities.

A simple command is a sequence of blank-separated words which may be preceded by a parameter assignment list (see "Environment"). The first word specifies the name of the command to be executed. Except as specified below, the remaining words are passed as arguments to the invoked command. The command name is passed as argument 0 (see exec(S)). The value of a simple-command is its exit status if it terminates normally, or (octal) 200+status if it terminates abnormally (see signal(S) for a list of status values).

A pipeline is a sequence of one or more commands separated by "|". The standard output of each command but the last is connected by a pipe(S) to the standard input of the next command. Each command is run in a separate subshell environment except for the last command in the pipeline; the shell waits for the last command to terminate. The exit status of a pipeline is the exit status of the last command.

A list is a sequence of one or more pipelines separated by ; & &&
or || and optionally terminated by ; & or |&. Of these five sym-
bols, && and || have highest precedence. The following three
symbols, ; & and |& are of equal precedence, as are && and ||. A
semicolon (;) causes sequential execution of the preceding
pipeline; an ampersand (&) causes asynchronous execution of the
preceding pipeline (that is, the shell does not wait for that pipeline
to finish). The symbol |& causes asynchronous execution of the
preceding command or pipeline with a two-way pipe established
to the parent shell. The parent shell can write to and read from the
standard input and standard output of the spawned command
using the -p option of the special commands read and print
(described later). The symbol && (||) causes the list following it to
be executed only if the preceding pipeline returns a zero (non-
zero) value. An arbitrary number of new-lines may appear in a
list, instead of a semicolon, to delimit a command.

A command is either a simple-command or one of the following
compound-commands. A compound-command is a command
that results in the execution of one or more simple-commands,
depending upon the state of its input. Unless otherwise stated, the
value returned by a command is that of the last simple-command
executed in the command.

for identifier [in word...] ;do list ;done
Each time a for command is executed, identifier is set to the next
word taken from the in word list. If in word...is omitted, then the
for command executes the do list once for each positional parameter that is set (see "Parameter substitution"). Execution ends
when there are no more words in the list.

select identifier [in word...] ;do list ;done

A select command prints on standard error (file descriptor 2), the set of words, each preceded by a number. If in word…is omitted, then the positional parameters are used instead (see "Parameter substitution"). The PS3 prompt is printed and a line is read from the standard input. If this line consists of the number of one of the listed words, then the value of the parameter identifier is set to the word corresponding to this number. If this line is empty the selection list is printed again. Otherwise the value of the parameter identifier is set to null. The contents of the line read from standard input is saved in the parameter REPLY. The list is executed for each selection until a break or an end-of-file is encountered.

case word in [[(] pattern [| pattern]…) list ;;]…esac
A case command executes the list associated with the first pattern that matches word. The form of the patterns is the same as that used for filename generation (see regexp(M) for details).

if list ;then list [elif list ;then list]…[;else list] ;fi
The list following if is executed and, if it returns a 0 exit status, the list following the first then is executed. Otherwise, the list following elif is executed and, if its value is 0, the list following the next then is executed. Failing that, the else list is executed. If no else list or then list is executed, the if command returns a 0 exit status.

while list ;do list ;done

until list ;do list ;done
A while command repeatedly executes the while list and, if the exit status of the last command in the list is 0, executes the do list; otherwise the loop terminates. If no commands in the do list are

executed, then the while command returns a 0 exit status; until may be used in place of while to negate the loop termination test.

(list) This executes list in a separate environment. Note that if two adjacent open parentheses are needed for nesting, a space must be inserted to avoid arithmetic evaluation as described below.

{ list ;}
This simply executes list. Note that unlike the metacharacters "(" and ")", "{" and "}" are reserved words and must be at the beginning of a line or after a ";" in order to be recognized.

[[expression]]
This evaluates expression and returns a 0 exit status when expression is true. See "Conditional expressions" for a description of expression.

function identifier { list ;}

identifier () { list ;}
This defines a function which is referenced by identifier. The body of the function is the list of commands between "{" and "}". (See "Functions".)

time pipeline
The pipeline is executed and the elapsed time as well as the user and system time are printed on standard error.

The following words are only reserved when they are the first word of a command and when they are not quoted:

if then else elif fi case
esac for while until do done
{ } function select time [[ ]]

Comments

A word beginning with "#" causes that word and all the following characters up to a new-line to be ignored.

Aliasing

The first word of each command is replaced by the text of an alias if an alias for this word has been defined. An alias name consists of any number of characters excluding metacharacters, quoting characters, file expansion characters, command substitution characters, and the equals sign (=). The replacement string can contain any valid shell script including the metacharacters listed above. The first word of each command in the replaced text, other than any that are in the process of being replaced, is tested for aliases. If the last character of the alias value is a blank then the word following the alias is also checked for alias substitution. Aliases can be used to redefine special built-in commands but cannot be used to redefine the reserved words listed above. Aliases can be created, listed, and exported with the alias command and can be removed with the unalias command. Exported aliases remain in effect for scripts invoked by name, but must be reinitialized for separate invocations of the shell (see "Invocation".)

Aliasing is performed when scripts are read, not while they are executed. Therefore, for an alias to take effect the alias definition command has to be executed before the command which references the alias is read.

Aliases are frequently used as an abbreviation for full pathnames. An option to the aliasing facility allows the value of the alias to be automatically set to the full pathname of the corresponding command. These aliases are called tracked aliases. The value of a tracked alias is defined the first time the corresponding command is looked up and becomes undefined each time the PATH variable is reset. These aliases remain tracked so that the next reference redefines the value. Several tracked aliases are compiled into the shell. The -h option of the set command makes each referenced command name into a tracked alias.

The following exported aliases are compiled into the shell but can be unset or redefined:

autoload='typeset -fu'
functions='typeset -f'
history='fc -l'
integer='typeset -i'
nohup='nohup '
r='fc -e -'

(The alias of nohup with a trailing space allows nohup to be used with aliased commands.)

Tilde substitution

After alias substitution is performed, each word is checked to see if it begins with an unquoted "~". If it does, then the word up to a "/" is checked to see if it matches a user name in the /etc/passwd file. If a match is found, the "~" and the matchedlogin name are replaced by the login directory of the matched user. This is called a tilde substitution. If no match is found, the original text is left unchanged. A "~" by itself, or in front of a "/", is replaced by the value of the HOME parameter. A "~" followed by a "+" or "-" is replaced by $PWD and $OLDPWD respectively.

In addition, tilde substitution is attempted when the value of a variable assignment parameter begins with a "~".

Command substitution

The standard output from a command enclosed in parentheses preceded by a dollar sign ($) or a pair of grave accents (") may be used as part or all of a word; trailing new-lines are removed. In the second (archaic) form, the string between the quotes is processed for special quoting characters before the command is executed. (See "Quoting".) The command substitution $(cat file) can be replaced by the equivalent $(<file). Command substitution of most special commands that do not perform input/output redirection is carried out without creating a separate process.

An arithmetic expression enclosed in double parentheses preceded by a dollar sign ($((expr))) is replaced by the value of the arithmetic expression within the double parentheses.

Process Substitution

A command of the form <(list) or >(list) executes process list, connected asynchronously to some file in /dev/fd. The name of this file will become the argument to the command. If the form with > is selected, then writing on this file provides input for list. If < is used, then the file passed as an argument contains the output of the list process. For example:

paste <(cut -f1 file1) <(cut -f3 file2) | tee >(process1) >(process2)

cuts fields 1 and 3 from the files file1 and file2 respectively, pastes them together, and sends the result to the processes process1 and process2, as well as putting it onto the standard output. Note that the file, which is passed as an argument to the command, is a UNIX system pipe(S), so programs that expect to lseek(S) on the file will not work.

NOTE: This feature is available on SCO OpenServer[tm] systems and other versions of the UNIX operating system that support the /dev/fd directory for naming open files. Programs which make use of this feature may not be portable to UNIX systems which do not support the /dev/fd feature.

Parameter substitution

A parameter is an identifier, one or more digits, or any of the characters *, @, #, ?, -, $, and !. A named parameter (a parameter denoted by an identifier) has a value and zero or more attributes. Named parameters can be assigned values and attributes by using the typeset special command. The attributes supported by the shell are described later with the typeset special command. Exported parameters pass values and attributes to the environment.

The shell supports a one-dimensional array facility. An element of an array parameter is referenced by a subscript. A subscript is denoted by a "[", followed by an arithmetic expression (see "Arithmetic evaluation") followed by a "]". To assign values to an array, use set -A name value.... The value of all subscripts must be in the range 0 through 1023. Arrays need not be declared. Any reference to a named parameter with a valid subscript is legal and an array will becreated if necessary. Referencing an array without a subscript is equivalent to referencing the element 0.

The value of a named parameter may also be assigned by writing:

name = value [name\1 = value\1]...

If the integer attribute, -i, is set for a given name the corresponding value is subject to arithmetic evaluation as described below.

Positional parameters, that is parameters denoted by a number, may be assigned values with the set special command.
Parameter $0 is set from argument zero when the shell is invoked.

The character "$" is used to introduce substitutable parameters.

${parameter}
The shell reads all the characters from "${" to the matching "}" as part of the same word even if it contains braces or metacharacters. The value, if any, of the parameter is substituted. The braces are required when parameter is followed by a letter, digit, or underscore that is not to be interpreted as part of its name or when a named parameter is subscripted. If parameter is one or more digits then it is a positional parameter. A positional parameter of more than one digit must be enclosed in braces. If parameter is "*" or "@", then all the positional parameters, starting with $1, are substituted (separated by a field separator character). If an array identifier with subscript "*" or "@" is used, then the value for each of the elements is substituted (separated by a field separator character).

${#parameter}
If parameter is "*" or "@", the number of positional parameters is substituted. Otherwise, the length of the value of the parameter is substituted.

${#identifier[*]}
The number of elements in the array identifier is substituted.

${parameter:-word}
If parameter is set and is non-null then its value is substituted; otherwise word is substituted.

${parameter:=word}
If parameter is not set or is null then it is set to word; the value of the parameter is then substituted. Positional parameters may not be assigned to in this way.

${parameter:?word}
If parameter is set and is non-null then its value is substituted; otherwise, word is printed and the shell is exited. If word is omitted then a standard message is printed.

${parameter:+word}
If parameter is set and is non-null then word is substituted; otherwise nothing is substituted.

${parameter#pattern}

${parameter##pattern}
If the shell pattern matches the beginning of the value of parameter, then the value of this substitution is the value of the parameter with the matched portion deleted; otherwise the value of this

parameter is substituted. In the first form the smallest matching pattern is deleted and in the second form the largest matching pattern is deleted.

${parameter%pattern}

${parameter%%pattern}
If the shell pattern matches the end of the value of parameter, then the value of this substitution is the value of the parameter with the matched part deleted; otherwise the value of parameter is substituted. In the first form the smallest matching pattern is deleted and in the second form the largest matching pattern is deleted.

In the above, word is not evaluated unless it is to be used as the substituted string, so that, in the following example, pwd is executed only if d is not set or is null:

echo ${d:-$(pwd)}

If the colon (:) is omitted from the above expressions, then the shell only checks whether parameter is set or not.

The following parameters are automatically set by the shell:

The number of positional parameters in decimal.

- Flags supplied to the shell on invocation or by the set command.

? The decimal value returned by the last executed command.

$ The process number of this shell.

_ Initially, the absolute pathname of the shell or script being executed as passed in the environment. Subsequently it is assigned the last argument of the previous command. This parameter is not set for commands which are asynchronous. This parameter is also used to hold the name of the matching MAIL file when checking for mail.

! The process number of the last background command invoked.

ERRNO
The value of errno as set by the most recent failed system call. This value is system dependent and is intended for debugging purposes.

LINENO
The line number of the current line within the script or function being executed.

OLDPWD
The previous working directory set by the cd special command.

OPTARG
The value of the last option argument processed by the getopts special command.

OPTIND
The index of the last option argument processed by the getopts special command.

PPID The process number of the parent of the shell.

PWD The present working directory set by the cd command.

RANDOM

Each time this parameter is referenced, a random integer, uniformly distributed between 0 and 32767, is generated. The sequence of random numbers can be initialized by assigning a numeric value to RANDOM.

REPLY

This parameter is set by the select statement and by the read special command when no arguments are supplied.

SECONDS

Each time this parameter is referenced, the number of seconds since shell invocation is returned. If this parameter is assigned a value, then the value returned upon reference is the value that was assigned plus the number of seconds since the assignment.

The following parameters are used by the shell:

CDPATH

The search path for the cd special command.

COLUMNS

If this variable is set, the value is used to define the width of the edit window for the shell edit modes and for printing select lists.

EDITOR

If the value of this variable ends in emacs, gmacs, or vi and the VISUAL variable is not set, then the corresponding option (see "Special commands")—set is turned on.

ENV If this parameter is set, then parameter substitution is performed on the value to generate the pathname of the script that is executed when the shell is invoked (see "Invocation"). This file is typically used for alias and function definitions.

FCEDIT
The default editor name for the fc special command.

FPATH
The search path for function definitions. This path is searched when a function with the -u attribute is referenced but has not yet been defined. The shell searches for an executable file of the same name. If the file is found, it is sourced in: it should define the function, which is then executed. If the function is already defined, the function definition file is not searched for.

HISTFILE
If this parameter is set when the shell is invoked, then the value is the pathname of the file used to store the command history (see "History file").

HISTSIZE
If this parameter is set when the shell is invoked, then the number of previously entered commands that are accessible by this shell is greater than or equal to this number. The default is 128.

HOME
The default argument (home directory) for the cd special command.

IFS Internal field separators, normally space, tab, and newline, that are used to separate command words which result from command or parameter substitution, and for separating words with the special command read. The first character of the IFS parameter is used to separate arguments for the $* substitution. (See "Quoting".)

LINES
If this variable is set, the value is used to determine the column length for printing select lists. select lists print vertically until about two-thirds of LINES lines are filled.

MAIL
If this parameter is set to the name of a mail file and the MAIL-PATH parameter is not set, then the shell informs the user of arrival of mail in the specified file.

MAILCHECK
This variable specifies how often (in seconds) the shell checks for changes in the modification time of any of the files specified by the MAILPATH or MAIL parameters. The default value is 600 seconds. When the time has elapsed the shell checks before issuing the next prompt.

MAILPATH
A colon (:) separated list of filenames. If this parameter is set, then the shell informs the user of any modifications to the specified files that have occurred within the last MAILCHECK seconds. Each filename can be followed by a "?" and a message to be printed. The message undergoes parameter substitution with the parameter $_ defined as the name of the file that has changed. The default message is

    you have mail in $_.

PATH
The search path for commands (see "Execution"). The user may not change PATH if executing under rksh (except in .profile).

PS1
The value of this parameter is expanded for parameter substitution to define the primary prompt string which by default is "$ " (dollar-space). The character "!" in the primary prompt string is replaced by the command number (see "History file").

PS2
The secondary prompt string, by default "> ".

PS3
The selection prompt string used within a select loop, by default "#? ".

PS4
The value of this parameter is expanded for parameter substitution and precedes each line of an execution trace. If omitted, the execution trace prompt is "+ ".

SHELL
The pathname of the shell is kept in the environment. At invocation, if the basename of this variable matches the pattern *r*sh, then the shell becomes restricted.

TMOUT
If TMOUT is set to a value greater than 0, the shell terminates if a command is not entered within the prescribed number of seconds after issuing the PS1 prompt. (Note that the shell can be compiled with a maximum bound for this value which cannot be exceeded.)

VISUAL

If the value of this variable ends in emacs, gmacs, or vi, then the corresponding option (see "Special commands") is turned on.

The shell gives default values to PATH, PS1, PS2, MAILCHECK, TMOUT and IFS, while HOME, SHELL, ENV, and MAIL are not set at all by the shell (although HOME, MAIL, and SHELL are set by login(M)).

Blank interpretation

After parameter and command substitution, the results of substitutions are scanned for field separator characters (those found in IFS) and split into distinct arguments where such characters are found.

Explicit null arguments ("" or '') are retained. Implicit null arguments (those resulting from parameters that have no values) are removed.

Filename generation

Following substitution, each command word is scanned for the characters *, ?, and [unless the -f option has been set. If one of these characters appears then the word is regarded as a pattern. The word is replaced with lexicographically sorted filenames that match the pattern. If no filename is found that matches the pattern, then the word is left unchanged. For details of patterns (shell regular expressions) matched by ksh, see regexp(M).

Quoting

Each of the specified metacharacters (see "Definitions") has a special meaning to the shell and causes termination of a word unless quoted. A character may be quoted (that is, made to stand for itself) by preceding it with a backslash (\). The pair "\<Enter>" is ignored. All characters enclosed between a pair of single quote marks (' ') are quoted. A single quote cannot appear within single quotes. Inside double quote marks (""), parameter and command substitution occurs, and "" quotes the characters \, ', " and $. The meaning of $* and $@ is identical when not quoted or when used as a parameter assignment value or as a filename. However, when used as a command argument, $* is equivalent to "$1d$2d...", where d is the first character of the IFS parameter, whereas $@ is equivalent to "$1" "$2".... Inside grave quote marks (` `) \ quotes the characters \, `, and $. If the grave quotes occur within double quotes then \ also quotes the character ".

The special meaning of reserved words or aliases can be removed by quoting any character of the reserved word. The recognition of function names or special command names listed below cannot be altered by quoting them.

Arithmetic evaluation

An ability to perform integer arithmetic is provided with the special command let. Evaluations are performed using long arithmetic. Constants are of the form [base#]n where base is a decimal number between two and thirty-six representing the arithmetic base and n is a number in that base. If base is omitted then base 10 is used.

An arithmetic expression uses the syntax, precedence, and associativity of expression of the C language. All the integral operators, other than ++, —, ?:, and comma (,) are supported. Named parameters can be referenced by name within an arithmetic expression without using the parameter substitution syntax. When a named parameter is referenced, its value is evaluated as an arithmetic expression.

An internal integer representation of a named parameter can be specified with the -i option of the typeset special command. Arithmetic evaluation is performed on the value of each assignment to a named parameter with the -i attribute. If an arithmetic base is not specified, the first assignment to the parameter determines the arithmetic base. This base is used when parameter substitution occurs.

Since many of the arithmetic operators require quoting, an alternative form of the let command is provided. For any command which begins with a ((, all the characters until a matching)) are treated as a quoted expression. More precisely, ((...)) is equivalent to let "...".

Prompting

When used interactively, the shell prompts with the value of PS1 before reading a command. If at any time a newline is typed and further input is needed to complete a command, then the secondary prompt (that is, the value of PS2) is issued.

Conditional expressions

A conditional expression is used with the [[compound command to test attributes of files and to compare strings. Word splitting and filename generation are not performed on the words between [[and]]. Each expression can be constructed from one or more of the following unary or binary expressions:

-a file True, if file exists.

-b file True, if file exists and is a block special file.

-c file True, if file exists and is a character special file.

-d file True, if file exists and is a directory.

-e file True, if file exists.

-f file True, if file exists and is an ordinary file.

-g file True, if file exists and has its setgid bit set.

-G file
True, if file exists and its group matches the effective group ID of this process.

-H file
True, if file exists and is a semaphore.

-k file True, if file exists and has its sticky bit set.

-L file True, if file exists and is a symbolic link.

-M file
True, if file exists and is shared memory.

-n string
True, if the length of string is non-zero.

-o option
True, if the option named option is on.

-O file
True, if file exists and is owned by the effective user ID of this process.

-p file True, if file exists and is a fifo special file or a pipe.

-r file True, if file exists and is readable by the current process.

-s file True, if file exists and has a size greater than zero.

-S file True, if file exists and is a socket.

-t fildes
True, if file descriptor number fildes is open and associated with a terminal device.

-u file True, if file exists and has its setuid bit set.

-w file True, if file exists and is writable by the current process.

-x file True, if file exists and is executable by the current process. If file exists and is a directory, then the current process has permission to search in the directory.

-z string
True, if the length of string is 0.

file1 -nt file2
True, if file1 exists and is newer than file2.

file1 -ot file2
True, if file1 exists and is older than file2.

file1 -ef file2
True, if file1 and file2 exist and refer to the same file.

string = pattern
True, if string matches pattern.

string != pattern
True, if string does not match pattern.

string1 < string2
True, if string1 comes before string2 based on the ASCII value of
their characters.

string1 > string2
True, if string1 comes after string2 based on the ASCII value of
their characters.

exp1 -eq exp2
True, if exp1 is equal to exp2.

exp1 -ne exp2
True, if exp1 is not equal to exp2.

exp1 -lt exp2
True, if exp1 is less than exp2.

exp1 -gt exp2
True, if exp1 is greater than exp2.

exp1 -le exp2
True, if exp1 is less than or equal to exp2.

exp1 -ge exp2
True, if exp1 is greater than or equal to exp2.

In each of the above expressions, if file is of the form /dev/fd/n, where n is an integer, then the test is applied to the open file whose descriptor number is n.

A compound expression can be constructed from these primitives by using any of the following, listed in decreasing order of precedence.

(expression)
True, if expression is true. This is used to group expressions.

! expression
True if expression is false.

expression1 && expression2
True, if expression1 and expression2 are both true.

expression1 || expression2
True, if either expression1 or expression2 is true.

Spelling checker

By default, the shell checks spelling whenever cd is used to change directories. For example, if you change to a different directory using cd and misspell the directory name, the shell responds with an alternative spelling of an existing directory. Enter y and press <Enter> (or just press <Enter>) to change to the offered directory. If the offered spelling is incorrect, enter n, then retype the command line. In this example the user input is boldfaced:

\# cd /usr/spool/uucp

> /usr/spool/uucp? y
> ok

The spell check feature is controlled by the CDSPELL environment variable. The default value of CDSPELL is set to the string "cdspell" whenever a ksh session is run. A user can change it to any value, including the null string, but the value is immaterial: if CDSPELL is set to any value, the spell check feature is engaged.

To disable the spelling checker, enter the following at the ksh prompt :

unset CDSPELL

When the user does a set at the ksh prompt, CDSPELL is not listed if the unset was successful.

Input/output

Before a command is executed, its input and output may be redirected using a special notation interpreted by the shell. The following may appear anywhere in a simple-command or may precede or follow a command, and are not passed on to the invoked command. Command and parameter substitution occurs before word or digit is used, except as noted below. Filename generation occurs only if the pattern matches a single file and blank interpretation is not performed.

<word
Use file word as standard input (file descriptor 0).

>word
Use file word as standard output (file descriptor 1). If the file does not exist then it is created. If the file exists, and the noclobber option is on, this causes an error; otherwise, it is truncated to zero length.

>|word
Same as >, except that it overrides the noclobber option.

>>word
Use file word as standard output. If the file exists then output is appended to it (by first seeking the end-of-file); otherwise, the file is created.

<>word
Open file word for reading and writing as standard input.

<<[-]word
Read the shell input up to a line that is the same as word, or to an end-of-file. No parameter substitution, command substitution or

filename generation is performed on word. The resulting document, called a here-document, becomes the standard input. If any character of word is quoted, then no interpretation is placed upon the characters of the document; otherwise, parameter and command substitution occurs, \newline is ignored, and "\" must be used to quote the characters \, $, `, and the first character of word. If "-" is appended to <<, then all leading tabs are stripped from word and from the document.

<&digit
Duplicate the standard input from file descriptor digit (see dup(S)); similarly for the standard output using >&digit.

<&- Close the standard input; similarly for the standard output using >&-.

<&p Move the input from the co-process to standard input.

>&p Move the output to the co-process to standard output.

If one of the above is preceded by a digit, then the file descriptor number referred to is that specified by the digit (instead of the default 0 or 1). For example:

...2>&1

means file descriptor 2 is to be opened for writing as a duplicate of file descriptor 1.

File descriptor 0 is standard input; 1 is standard output; 2 is standard error.

The order in which redirections are specified is significant. The shell evaluates each redirection in terms of the file descriptor, file association at the time of evaluation. For example:

...1>fname 2>&1

first associates file descriptor 1 with file fname. It then associates file descriptor 2 with the file associated with file descriptor 1 (that is, fname). If the order of redirections were reversed, file descriptor 2 would be associated with the terminal
(assuming this was the initial state of file descriptor 1) and then file descriptor 1 would be associated with file fname.

If a command is followed by "&" and job control is not active, then the default standard input for the command is the empty file /dev/null. Otherwise, the environment for the execution of a command contains the file descriptors of the invoking shell as modified by input/output specifications.

Environment

The environment (see environ(M)) is a list of name-value pairs that is passed to an executing process in the same way as a normal argument list. The names must be identifiers and the values are character strings. The shell interacts with theenvironment in several ways. On invocation, the shell scans the environment and creates a parameter for each name found, giving it the corresponding value and marking it export. Executed commands inherit the environment. If the user modifies the values of these parameters or creates new ones, using the export or typeset-x commands causes them to become part of the environment. The environment seen by any executed command is thus composed of any name-value pairs originally inherited by the shell, whose values may be modified by the current shell, plus any additions which must be noted in export or typeset-x commands.

The environment for any simple-command or function may be augmented by prefixing it with one or more parameter assignments. A parameter assignment argument is a word of the form identifier=value. Thus:

TERM=wy60 cmd args

and

(export TERM; TERM=wy60; cmd args)

are equivalent (as far as the above execution of cmd is concerned, except for commands listed with one or two daggers (+)in "Special commands").

If the -k flag is set, all parameter assignment arguments are placed in the environment, even if they occur after the command name. The following first prints a=b c and then c:

```
echo a=b  c
set  -k
echo a=b  c
```

This feature is intended for use with scripts written for early versions of the shell and its use in new scripts is strongly discouraged. It is likely to disappear in the future.

Functions

The function reserved word, described in "Commands", is used to define shell functions. Shell functions are read in and the function is read. Functions are executed like commands with thearguments passed as positional parameters (see "Execution").

Functions execute in the same process as the caller and share all files and the present working directory with the caller. Traps caught by the caller are reset to their default action inside the function. A trap condition that is not caught or ignored by the function causes the function to terminate and the condition to be passed on to the caller. A trap on EXIT set inside a function is executed after the function completes in the environment of the caller. Ordinarily, variables are shared between the calling program and the function. However, the typeset special command used within a function defines local variables whose scope includes the current function and all functions it calls.

The special command return is used to return from function calls. Errors within functions return control to the caller.

Function identifiers can be listed with the -f or +f option of the typeset special command. The text of functions are also listed with -f. Functions can be undefined with the -f option of the unset special command.

Ordinarily, functions are unset when the shell executes a shell script. The -xf option of the typeset command allows a function to be exported to scripts that are executed without a separate invocation of the shell. Functions that need to be defined across separate invocations of the shell should be specified in the ENV file with the -xf option of typeset.

Jobs

If the monitor option of the set command is turned on, an interactive shell associates a job with each pipeline. It keeps a table of current jobs, printed by the jobs command, and assigns them small integer numbers. When a job is started asynchronously with "&", the shell prints a line which looks like:

[1] 1234

indicating that the job which was started asynchronously was job number 1 and had one (top-level) process, whose process ID was 1234.

If you are running a job and wish to do something else you may hit the key ^Z (<Ctrl>Z) which sends a STOP signal to the current job. (This is known as the suspend character, and is ^Z by default; this can be changed in the stty susp line in a user's .profile file.) The shell then normally indicates that the job has been `Stopped', and prints another prompt. You can then manipulate the state of this job, putting it in the background with the bg command, or run some other commands and then eventually bring the job back into the foreground with the foreground command fg. A ^Z takes effect immediately and is like an interrupt in that pending output and unread input are discarded when it is typed.

A job being run in the background stops if it tries to read from the terminal. Background jobs are normally allowed to produce output, but this can be disabled by giving the command stty tostop. If you set this tty option, then background jobs stop when they try to produce output.

There are several ways to refer to jobs in the shell. A job can be referred to by the process ID of any process of the job orby one of the following:

%number
The job with the given number.

%string
Any job whose command line begins with string.

%?string
Any job whose command line contains string.

%%

%+ The current job.

%- The previous job.

The shell learns immediately whenever a process changes state. It normally informs you whenever a job becomes blocked so that no further progress is possible, but only just before it prints a prompt. This is done so that it does not otherwise disturb your work.

When the monitor mode is on, each background job that completes triggers any trap set for CHLD.

When you try to leave the shell while jobs are running or stopped, you will be warned that "You have stopped(running) jobs." You may use the jobs command to see what they are. If you do this or immediately try to exit again, the shell will not warn you a second time, and the stopped jobs will be terminated.

Signals

The INT and QUIT signals for an invoked command are ignored if the command is followed by "&" and the job monitor option is not active. Otherwise, signals have the values inherited by the shell from its parent (but see also the trap command below).

Execution

Each time a command is executed, the substitutions described in the previous sections are carried out. If the command name matches one of the "Special commands", it is executed within the current shell process. Next, the command name is checked to see if it matches one of the user-defined functions. If it does, the positional parameters are saved and then reset to the arguments of the function call. When the function completes or issues a return, the positional parameter list is restored and any trap set on EXIT within the function is executed. The value of a function is the value of the last command executed. A function is also executed in the current shell process. If a command name is neither a special command nor a user-defined function, a process is created and an attempt is made to execute the command via exec(S).

The shell parameter PATH defines the search path for the directory containing the command. Alternative directory names are separated by a colon (:). The default path is /bin:/usr/bin: (specifying /bin, /usr/bin, and the current directory in that order). The current directory can be specified by two or more adjacent colons, or by a colon at the beginning or end of the path list. If the command name contains a "/" then the search path is not used. Otherwise, each directory in the path is searched for an executable file. If the file has execute permission but is not a directory or an a.out file, it is assumed to be a

file containing shell commands. A sub-shell is spawned to read it. In this case, all non-exported aliases, functions, and named parameters are removed. If the shell command file does not have read permission, or if the setuid and/or setgid bits are set on the file, then the shell executes an agent whose job is to set up the permissions and execute the shell with the shell command file passed down as an open file. A parenthesized command is executed in a sub-shell without removing non-exported quantities.

Special commands

The following simple-commands are executed in the shell process. Input/output redirection is permitted. Unless otherwise indicated, the output is written on file descriptor 1 and the exit status, when there is no syntax error, is 0. Commands that are preceded by one or two daggers (+) are treated specially in the following ways:

1.Parameter assignment lists preceding the command remain in effect when the command completes.

2.I/O redirections are processed after parameter assignments.

3.Errors cause a script that contains them to abort.

4.Words, following a command preceded by ++ that are in the format of a parameter assignment, are expanded with the same rules as a parameter assignment. This means that tilde substitution is performed after the "=" sign and that word splitting and filename generation are not performed.

+ : [arg...]
Expand parameters.

+ . file [arg...]
Read the complete file then execute the commands. The syntax for this is dot-space-file followed by optional arguments. The commands are executed in the current shell environment. The search path specified by PATH is used to find the directory containing file. If any arguments arg are given, they become the positional parameters. Otherwise the positional parameters are unchanged. The exit status is the exit status of the last command executed.

++ alias [-tx] [name [= value]]...
   With no arguments, print the list of aliases in the form name=value on standard output. An alias is defined for each name whose value is given. A trailing space in value causes the next word to be checked for alias substitution.

The -t flag is used to set and list tracked aliases. The value of a tracked alias is the full pathname corresponding to the given name. The value becomes undefined when the value of PATH is reset but the aliases remained tracked. Without the -t flag, for each name in the argument list for which no value is given, the name and value of the alias is printed.

The -x flag is used to set or print exported aliases. An exported alias is defined for scripts invoked by name. The exit status is non-zero if a name is given, but no value, for which no alias has been defined.

See also alias(C).

bg [job...]
Run jobs in the background. This command only works if job control is enabled. It puts each specified job into the background. The current job is put in the background if job is not specified. See "Jobs" for a description of the format of job.

See also bg(C).

+ break [n]
Exit from the enclosing for, while, until, or select loop, if any. If n is specified then break n levels.

+ continue [n]
Resume the next iteration of the enclosing for, while, until, or select loop. If n is specified then resume at the nth   enclosing loop.

cd [-L | -P] [arg]

cd [-L | -P] old new
If the first form, change the current directory to arg and set the parameter PWD to the current directory.

If arg is "-", the directory is changed to the previous directory (taken from the value of the shell parameter OLDPWD).

If no arg is specified, the shell parameter HOME is used as a default arg.

The shell parameter CDPATH defines the search path for the directory containing arg. Alternative directory names are separated by a colon ":". The default path is <null> (specifying the current directory). Note that the current directory is specified by a null pathname, which can appear immediately after the equal sign or between the colon delimiters anywhere else in the path list. If arg begins with a "/" then the search path is not used. Otherwise, each directory in the path is searched for arg.

The second form of cd substitutes the string new for the string old in the current directory name, PWD, and tries to change to the new directory formed.

The -L and -P flags are relevant to systems with symbolic links:

-L Preserve logical pathnames so that cd -L .. moves up one component towards the root along the current logical path. This is the default behavior.

-P Use a physical model for pathnames so that cd -L .. moves up one component towards the root by following the link to the parent of the current directory.

For example, if /usr/include/sys/h is a symbolic link to the directory /sys/h, then cd /usr/include/sys/h; cd .. or cd/usr/include/sys/h; cd -L .. would make /usr/include/sys the current directory; cd /usr/include/sys/h; cd -P ..would make /sys the current directory.

The cd command may not be executed by rksh.

See also cd(C).

command [-p] name [argument...]

command [-v | -V] name
Execute a command without invoking a user-defined function, or prevent an error in a built-in command aborting the shell. See command(C) for usage and description.

echo [arg...]
Write arguments to the standard output.

NOTE: /bin/posix/sh, linked to ksh, supplies the functionality for echo as defined by ISO/IEC DIS 9945-2:1992, Information technology—Portable Operating System Interface (POSIX)—Part 2: Shell and Utilities (IEEE Std 1003.2-1992) and X/Open CAE Specification, Commands and Utilities, Issue 4, 1992.

See echo(C) for usage and description.

+ eval [arg...]
Read the arguments as input to the shell and execute the resulting command(s).

+ exec [arg...]
If arg is given, execute the command specified by the arguments in place of this shell without creating a new process. Input/output arguments may appear and affect the current process. If no arguments are given, the effect of this command is to modify file descriptors as prescribed by the input/output redirection list. In this case, any file descriptor numbers greater than 2 that are opened with this mechanism are closed when invoking another program.

+ exit [n]

Cause the shell to exit with the exit status specified by n. If n is omitted then the exit status is that of the last command executed. An end-of-file will also cause the shell to exit except for a shell which has the ignoreeof option (see "set" below) turned on.

++ export [-p] [name [= value]]...

Mark the given names for automatic export to the environment of subsequently executed commands. The -p flag, if present, causes currently exported names to be listed on the standard output.

false Always return a non-zero value. See also false(C).

fc [-e ename] [-nlr] [first [last]]

fc -s [old\=new] [command]

fc -e—[old\=new] [command]

In the first form, select a range of commands from first to last from the last HISTSIZE commands that were typed at the terminal. The arguments first and last may be specified as a number or as a string. A string is used to locate the most recent command that starts with that string. A negative number is used as an offset to the current command number.

-l lists commands on standard output. Otherwise, the editor program ename is invoked on a file containing these keyboard commands. If ename is not supplied, then the value of the parameter FCEDIT (default /bin/ed) is used as the editor. When editing is complete, the edited command(s) is executed. If last is not specified then it is set to first. If first is not specified the default is the previous command for editing and -16 for listing.

-n suppresses command numbers when listing.

-r reverses the order of the commands when listing.

In the second and third forms, the command is re-executed after the substitution old=new is performed.

See also fc(C).

fg [job...]
Run jobs in the foreground. This command only works if job control is enabled. Each job specified is brought to the foreground. Otherwise, the current job is brought into the foreground. See "Jobs" for a description of the format of job.

See also fg(C).

getopts optstring name [arg...]
Check arg for legal options. If arg is omitted, the positional parameters are used. An option argument begins with a "+" or a "-". An option not beginning with "+" or "-" or the special argument "—" ends the options. optstring contains the letters that getopts recognizes. If a letter is followed by a ":", that option is expected to have an argument. The options can be separated from the argument by blanks.

getopts places the next option letter it finds inside variable name each time it is invoked with a "+" prefixed when arg begins with a "+". The index of the next arg is stored in OPTIND. The option argument, if any, is stored in OPTARG.

A leading ":" in optstring causes getopts to store the letter of an invalid option in OPTARG, and to set name to "?" for an unknown option and to ":" when a required option is missing. Otherwise, getopts prints an error message. The exit status is non-zero when there are no more options. See also getopts(C).

hash [utility...]

hash -r
Remember, report, or forget locations of commands. See hash(C) for usage and description.

jobs [-l | -p] [-n] [job...]
List information about each given job, or all active jobs if job is omitted. See "Jobs" for a description of the format of job.

jobs accepts the following options:

   -l List process IDs in addition to the normal information.

   -n List only jobs that have stopped or exited since last notified.

   -p List only the process group.

   See also jobs(C).

kill [-sig] [-s signame] job...

kill -l [exit_status]
Send either the TERM (terminate) signal or the specified signal to the specified jobs or processes. Signals are either given by number or by names (as given in /usr/include/signal.h, stripped

of the prefix SIG). If the signal being sent is TERM (terminate) or HUP (hangup), then the job or process will be sent a CONT (continue) signal if it is stopped.

The argument job can specify the process ID of a process that is not a member of one of the active jobs. See "Jobs" for a description of the format of job.

In the second form, kill -l, the signal names are listed. If an exit_status is given, the signal name corresponding to the status is output.

See kill(C) for a full description of this command.

let arg...
Each arg is a separate arithmetic expression to be evaluated. See "Arithmetic evaluation" for a description of arithmetic expression evaluation.

The exit status is 0 if the value of the last expression is non-zero, and 1 otherwise.

newgrp [—| -l] [group...]
Set a new real and effective group ID. This is equivalent to exec /bin/newgrp. See newgrp(C) for a full description of this command.

print [-Rnprs] [-u [n]] [arg...]
The shell output mechanism. With no flags or with flag "-" or """ the arguments are printed on standard output as described in echo(C). In raw mode, -R or -r, the escape conventions of echo are ignored. The -R option prints all subsequent arguments and options other than -n. The -p option causes the arguments to be

written onto the pipe of the process spawned with |& instead of standard output. The -s option causes the arguments to be written onto the history file instead of standard output. The -u flag can be used to specify a one-digit file descriptor unit number n on which the output is placed. The default is 1. If the flag -n is used, no new-line is added to the output.

pwd [-L | -P]
Print the pathname of the current working directory. This is equiv-alent to print -r—$PWD .

The -L and -P flags are relevant only on systems with symbolic links:

-L Show the logical pathname to the directory preserving the route taken to get there. This is the default behavior.

-P Show the physical pathname to the directory.

For example, if /usr/include/sys/h is a symbolic link to the direc-tory   /sys/h,   then   cd   /usr/include/sys/h;   pwd   or   cd /usr/include/sys/h; pwd -L prints /usr/include/sys/h as the current working directory; cd/usr/include/sys/h; pwd -P prints /sys/h as the current working directory.

See also pwd(C).

read [-prs] [-u [n]] [name?prompt] [name...]
The shell input mechanism. One line is read and is broken up into fields using the characters in IFS as separators.

The first field is assigned to the first name, the second field to the second name, and so on, with leftover fields assigned to the last name.

read accepts the following options:

-p Take the input line from the input pipe of a process spawned by the shell using |&. An end-of-file with this option causes cleanup for this process so that another can be spawned.

-r A "\" at the end of a line does not signify line continuation.

-s Save the input as a command in the history file.

-u n Specify a one-digit file descriptor n to read from. The file descriptor can be opened with the exec special
    command. The default value of n is 0.

If name is omitted then REPLY is used as the default name. If the first name argument contains a "?", the remainder of this word (beyond "?") is used as a prompt on standard error when the shell is interactive.

The exit status is 0 unless an end-of-file is encountered.

++ readonly [-p] [name [= value]]...
Mark the given names read-only; these names cannot be changed by subsequent assignment. If the -p option is specified, current read-only names are listed on the standard output.

+ return [n]

Return a shell function to the invoking script with the return status specified by n. If n is omitted then the return status is that of the last command executed. If return is invoked while not in a function or a "." script, then it is the same as an exit.

set [±aefhkmnopstuvx] [±o option]...[±A name] [arg...]
Perform the following functions:

With no options or arguments, list the variables set in the current shell together with their values.

Override the positional parameters for the current shell. For example, set $(date) sets the positional parameters $1, $2,...to the output from the date command.

Redefine the behavior of the current shell.
set takes the following options:

-A Array assignment. Unset the variable name and assign values sequentially from the list arg. If +A is used, the variable name is not unset first.

-a Automatically export all subsequent parameters that are defined.

-e If a command has a non-zero exit status, execute the ERR trap, if set, and exit. This mode is disabled while reading profiles.

-f Disable filename generation.

-h Cause each command to become a tracked alias when first encountered.

-k Place all parameter assignment arguments in the environment for a command, not just those that precede the command name.

-m Run background jobs in a separate process group and print a line upon completion. The exit status of background jobs is reported in a completion message. This flag is turned on automatically for interactive shells.

-n Read commands and check them for syntax errors, but do not execute them. This is ignored for interactive shells.

-o List all option settings.

The argument following -o can be one of the following option names:

allexport
Same as -a.

errexit
Same as -e.

bgnice
Run all background jobs at a lower priority. This is the default mode.

emacs
Switch to an emacs style in-line editor for command entry.

gmacs
Switch to a gmacs style in-line editor for command entry.

ignoreeof
Do not exit the shell on end-of-file. The command exit must be used.

keyword
Same as -k.

markdirs
Append all directory names resulting from filename generation with a trailing "/".

monitor
Same as -m.

noclobber
Prevent output redirection (>) from truncating existing files. Enforce >| to truncate a file when turned on.

noexec
Same as -n.

noglob
Same as -f.

nolog Do not save function definitions in the history file.

nounset
Same as -u.

privileged
Same as -p.

trackall
Same as -h.

verbose
Same as -v.

vi Switch to insert mode of a vi style in-line editor escape character until 033 is entered. This switches to move mode.
    <Enter> sends the line.

viraw Process each character as it is typed in vi mode.

xtrace
Same as -x.

If no option name is supplied then the current option settings are printed.

-p Disable processing of the $HOME/.profile file and use the file /etc/suid_profile instead of the ENV file. This mode is on whenever the effective user ID (group ID) is not equal to the real user ID (group ID). Turning this off causes the effective user ID and group ID to be set to the real user ID and group ID.

-s Sort the positional parameters lexicographically.

-t Exit after reading and executing one command.

-u Treat unset parameters as an error when substituting.

-v Print shell input lines as they are read.

-x Print commands and their arguments as they are executed.

- Turn off -x and -v flags and stop examining arguments for flags.

—Do not change any of the flags; this is useful in setting $1 to a value beginning with "-". If no arguments follow this flag then the positional parameters are unset.

Using "+" rather than "-" causes these flags to be turned off. These flags can also be used upon invocation of the shell. The current set of flags may be found in $-. Unless -A is specified, the remaining arguments are positional parameters and are assigned, in order, to $1 $2…. If no arguments are given then the names and values of all named parameters are printed on the standard output. If the only argument is "+", the names of all named parameters are printed.

+ shift [n]
   Rename the positional parameters from $n+1…to 1…, where the default n is 1. The parameter n can be any arithmetic expression that evaluates to a non-negative number less than or equal to $#.

test expr

[expr]
Evaluate an expression as being true or false. This built-in command is equivalent to /bin/test. It differs slightly from conditional expressions of the form [[expr]].

See the section "Conditional expressions" and test(C).

+ times
Print the accumulated user and system times for the shell and for processes run from the shell.

+ trap [arg] [sig]...
arg is a command to be read and executed when the shell receives signal(s) sig. (Note that arg is scanned once when the trap is set and once when the trap is taken.) Each sig can be given as a number or as the name of the signal(see the description of kill or kill(C)). Trap commands are executed in order of signal number. Any attempt to set a trap on a signal that was ignored on entry to the current shell is ineffective.

If arg is omitted or is "-", then all trap signals are reset to their original values.

If arg is the null string then this signal is ignored by the shell and by the commands it invokes.

If sig is ERR then arg is executed whenever a command has a non-zero exit status.

If sig is DEBUG then arg is executed after each command.

If sig is 0 or EXIT and the trap statement is executed inside the body of a function, then the command arg is executed after the function completes.

If sig is 0 or EXIT for a trap set outside any function, then the command arg is executed on exit from the shell.

Entering trap with no arguments prints a list of commands associated with each signal number.

true Always return 0. See also true(C).

type command...
Determine command type. See type(C) for usage and description.

++ typeset [±HLRZfilrtux[n]] [name[=value]]...
Set attributes and values for shell parameters. When invoked inside a function, a new instance of the parameter name is created. The parameter value and type are restored when the function completes. The following list of attributes may be specified:

-H Provide UNIX system to host-name file mapping on non-UNIX system machines.

-L Left justify and remove leading blanks from value. If n is non-zero it defines the width of the field; otherwise it is determined by the width of the value of first assignment. When the parameter is assigned to, it is filled on the right with blanks or truncated, if necessary, to fit into the field. Leading zeros are removed if the -Z flag is also set. The -R flag is turned off.

-R Right justify and fill with leading blanks. If n is non-zero it defines the width of the field; otherwise it is determined by the width of the value of first assignment. The field is left-filled with blanks or truncated from the end if the parameter is reassigned. The -L flag is turned off.

-Z Right justify and fill with leading zeros if the first non-blank character is a digit and the -L flag has not been set. If n is non-zero it defines the width of the field; otherwise it is determined by the width of the value of first assignment.

-f Cause names to refer to function names rather than parameter names. No assignments can be made and the only other valid flags are -t, -u and -x. The flag -t turns on execution tracing for this function. The flag -u causes this function to be marked as undefined. The FPATH variable is searched to find the function definition when the function is referenced. The flag -x allows the function definition to remain in effect across shell procedures invoked by name.

-i Declare the parameter to be an integer. This makes arithmetic faster. If n is non-zero it defines the output arithmetic base; otherwise the first assignment determines the output base.

-l Convert all uppercase characters to lowercase. The uppercase flag, -u, is turned off.

-r Mark the given names read-only; these names cannot be changed by subsequent assignment.

-t Tag the named parameters. Tags are user definable and have no special meaning to the shell.

-u Convert all lowercase characters to uppercase characters. The lowercase flag, -l, is turned off.

-x Mark the given names for automatic export to the environment of subsequently-executed commands.

Using "+" rather than "-" causes these flags to be turned off. If no name arguments are given but flags are specified, a list of names (and optionally the values) of the parameters which have these flags set is printed. (Using "+" rather than "-" keeps the values from being printed.) If no names and flags are given, the names and attributes of all parameters are printed.

ulimit [-acdfnstvHS] [limit]
Set or display a resource limit. If a limit is provided, then the resource limit is set. The list of available resources is given below. The limit argument should be either a number or the word "unlimited". The -H flag sets the hard limit and the -S flag sets the soft limit. If neither -H nor -S is specified, both the hard and soft limits will be set. The hard limit cannot be raised, but the soft limit can be set to any value up to the hard limit.

If no limit is provided, the current limit is printed. The soft limit is printed unless the -H flag is specified. If more than one resource limit is printed, a description of each resource is printed before the limit.

If no resource is specified when setting or displaying limits, the -f flag is assumed.

The following flags are recognized:

  -a List all the current resource limits.

  -c Size of core files (in 512-byte blocks).

  -d Size of data region (in KB).

-f Size of files created (in 512-byte blocks).

-n Number of open file descriptors.

-s Size of process's stack (in KB).

-t Number of seconds used by each process.

-v Size of a process's virtual address space (in KB).
See also ulimit(C).

umask [-S] [mask]
Get or set the file-creation mode mask. See umask(C) for usage and description.

unalias name...

unalias -a
In the first form of the command, remove the parameters given by the list of names from the alias list. The secondform removes all aliases from the list. See also the description of unalias on the alias(C) manual page.

unset [-f] name...
Unassign the parameters given by the list of names, that is, erase their values and attributes. readonly variables cannot be unset. If the flag -f is set, then the names refer to function names. Unsetting ERRNO, LINENO, MAILCHECK, OPTARG, OPTIND, RANDOM, SECONDS, TMOUT, and "_" removes their special meaning even if they are subsequently assigned to.

+ wait [job]
Wait for the specified job and report its termination status. If job is not given then all currently active child processes are waited for. The exit status from this command is that of the process waited for. See "Jobs" for a description of the format of job.

See also wait(C).

whence [-pv] name…
For each name, indicate how it would be interpreted if used as a command name.

whence accepts the following options:

-v Produce a more verbose report.

-p Do a path search for name even if name is an alias, a function, or a reserved word.

Invocation

If the shell is invoked by exec(S), and the first character of argument zero ($0) is "-", then the shell is assumed to be a login shell and commands are read from /etc/profile and then from either .profile in the current directory or $HOME/.profile, if either file exists. Next, commands are read from the file named by performing parameter substitution on the value of the environment parameter ENV, if the file exists. If the -s flag is not present and arg is, then a path search is performed on the first arg to determine the name of the script to execute. The script arg must have read permission and any setuid and setgid settings are ignored.

Commands are then read as described below; the following flags are interpreted by the shell when it is invoked:

-c string
If the -c flag is present then commands are read from string.

-s If the -s flag is present or if no arguments remain then commands are read from the standard input. Shell output, except for the output of the special commands listed above, is written to file descriptor 2.

-i If the -i flag is present or if the shell input and output are attached to a terminal (as told by ioctl(S)) then this shell is interactive. In this case TERM is ignored (so that kill 0 does not kill an interactive shell) and INTR is caught and ignored (so that wait is interruptible). In all cases, QUIT is ignored by the shell.

-r If the -r flag is present the shell is a restricted shell.

The remaining flags and arguments are described under the set command above.

rksh only

rksh is used to set up login names and execution environments whose capabilities are more controlled than those of the standard shell. The actions of rksh are identical to those of ksh, except that the following are disallowed:

changing directory (see cd(C))

setting the value of SHELL, ENV, or PATH

specifying path or command names containing "/"

redirecting output (>, >l, <>, and >>)

The restrictions above are enforced after .profile and the ENV files are interpreted.

When a command to be executed is found to be a shell procedure, rksh invokes ksh to execute it. Thus, it is possible to provide shell procedures to the end-user that have access to the full power of the standard shell, while imposing a limited menu of commands; this scheme assumes that the end-user does not have write and execute permissions in the same directory.

The net effect of these rules is that the writer of the .profile has complete control over user actions, by performingguaranteed setup actions and leaving the user in an appropriate directory (probably not the login directory).

The system administrator often sets up a directory of commands (for example, /usr/rbin) that can be safely invoked by rksh. There is also a restricted editor, red.

Note that simply setting a user's login shell to rksh does not make their account "safe". Some thought and care must be put into creating a properly restricted environment.

Diagnostics

Errors detected by the shell, such as syntax errors, cause the shell to return a non-zero exit status. Otherwise, the shell returns the exit status of the last command executed (see also the exit command above). If the shell is being used non-interactively then execution of the shell file is abandoned. Run-time errors detected by the shell are reported by printing the command or function name and the error condition. If the line number that the error occurred on is greater than 1, then the line number is also printed in square brackets ([ ]) after the command or function name.

Examples

For numerous examples, see Chapter 11, "Automating frequent tasks" in the Operating System User's Guide, which contains a brief tutorial in the shell programming language, with explicit reference to the Korn shell.

Limitations

If a command which is a tracked alias is executed, and then a command with the same name is installed in a directory in the search path before the directory where the original command was found, the shell continues to exec the original command. Use the -t option of the alias command to correct this situation.

Some very old shell scripts contain a "^" as a synonym for the pipe character "|".

Using the fc built-in command within a compound command causes the whole command to disappear from the history file.

The built-in command . file reads the whole file before any commands are executed. Therefore, alias and unalias commands in the file do not apply to any functions defined in the file.

Traps are not processed while a job is waiting for a foreground process. Thus, a trap on CHLD is not executed until the foreground job terminates.

Files

/etc/passwd
/etc/profile
/etc/suid_profile
$HOME/.profile
/tmp/sh*
/dev/null

Examples

recall command and use vi type commands to edit the command line:

ESC k

---

sh   allows the user to interact with the operating system through a standard shell command interpreter where each command is a separate process and is waited upon for termination

sh [-aceikLnrstuvx] [args]

Options

Description

The shell is the standard command programming language that executes commands read from a terminal or a file. The shell reads lines and either executes them (if they are an external program), or interprets them as statements in the shell programming language. Each input line is scanned and split into tokens; parameters are substituted (subject to quoting), filenames are generated, input and output are (optionally) redirected, then the commands are executed. See "Invocation" for the meaning of arguments to the shell.

NOTE: If you require the functionality supplied by sh as defined by ISO/IEC DIS 9945-2:1992, Information technology - Portable Operating System Interface (POSIX)—Part 2: Shell and Utilities (IEEE Std 1003.2-1992) and X/Open CAE Specification, Commands and Utilities, Issue 4, 1992, refer to ksh(C), which documents /bin/posix/sh.

Commands

A simple-command is a sequence of non-blank words separated by blanks (a blank is a tab or a space). The first word specifies the name of the command to be executed. Except as specified below, the remaining words are passed as arguments to the invoked command. The command name is passed as argument 0 (see exec(S)). The value of a simple-command is its exit status if it terminates normally. If it terminates abnormally, it returns the value of the exit signal number + SIGFLG, where SIGFLG is (octal) 0200. See signal(S) for a list of signal numbers.

A pipeline is a sequence of one or more commands separated by a vertical bar (|). (The caret (^), is an obsolete synonym for the vertical bar and should not be used in a pipeline. Scripts that use "^" for pipelines are incompatible with the Korn shell.) The standard output of each command but the last is connected by a pipe(S) to the standard input of the next command. Each command is run as a separate process; the shell waits for the last command to terminate.

A list is a sequence of one or more pipelines separated by ;, &, &&, or ||, and optionally terminated by ; or &. Of these four symbols, ; and & have equal precedence, which is lower than that of && and ||. The symbols && and || also have equal precedence. A semicolon (;) causes sequential execution of the preceding pipeline; an ampersand (&) causes asynchronous execution of the preceding pipeline (that is, the shell does not wait for that pipeline to finish). The symbol && causes the list following it to be executed if the preceding pipeline succeeded (returned a 0 exit status). The symbol || causes the list following it to be executed only if the preceding pipeline failed (returned a non-zero exit status). An arbitrary number of newlines may appear in a list, instead of semicolons, to delimit commands.

A command is either a simple-command or one of the following commands. Unless otherwise stated, the value returned by a command is that of the last simple-command executed in the command:

for name [in word...]
do

list
done

Each time a for command is executed, name is set to the next word taken from the in word list. If in word is omitted, then the for command executes the do list once for each positional parameter that is set (see "Parameter substitution"). Execution ends when there are no more words in the list.

case word in
[pattern [| pattern]...) list
;;]
esac

A case command executes the list associated with the first pattern that matches word. The form of the patterns is thesame as that used for filename generation (see regexp(M) for details).

if list
then
list
[elif list
then
list]
...
[else list]
fi

The list following if is executed and, if it returns a 0 exit status, the list following the first then is executed. Otherwise, the list following elif is executed and, if its value is 0, the list following the next then is executed. Failing that, the else list isexecuted. If no else list or then list is executed, then the if command returns a 0 exit status. Note that the then keyword must fall on a new line.

```
while list
do
list
done
```

A while command repeatedly executes the while list and, if the exit status of the last command in the list is 0, executes the do list; otherwise the loop terminates. If no commands in the do list are executed, then the while command returns a 0 exit status; until may be used in place of while to negate the loop termination test.

```
until list
do
list
done
```

until is similar to while, except that until continues execution until the first list returns a 0 exit status. In other words, untilworks until the test condition succeeds (it works the whole time the command is failing); while works until the test condition fails. until is useful when you are waiting for a particular event to occur.

(list)

This executes list in a subshell.

{list;}

This simply executes list.

name ( ) {list;}

This defines a function which is referenced by name. The body of functions is the list of commands between { and }.
Execution of functions is described later (see "Execution").

The following words are reserved only when they are the first word of a command and when they are not quoted:

if then else elif fi case esac
for while until do done { }

Comments

A word beginning with # causes that word and all the following characters up to a newline to be ignored.

Command substitution

The standard output from a command enclosed between grave accents (``) may be used as part or all of a word; trailing newlines are removed.

No interpretation is done on the command string before the string is read, except to remove backslashes (\) used to escape other characters. Backslashes may be used to escape grave accents (`) or other backslashes and are removed before the command string is read. Escaping grave accents allows nested command substitution. If the command substitution lies within a pair of double quotes ( " `...` "), backslashes used to escape a double quote (\") are removed; otherwise, they are left intact.

If a backslash is used to escape a newline character, both the backslash and the newline are removed (see the section on "Quoting"). In addition, backslashes used to escape dollar signs (\$) are removed. Since no interpretation is done on the command string before it is read, inserting a backslash to escape a dollar sign has no effect. Backslashes that precede characters other than \, `, ", newline, and $ are left intact.

Parameter substitution

The character $ is used to introduce substitutable parameters. There are two types of parameters, positional and keyword. If a parameter is a digit, it is a positional parameter. Positional parameters may be assigned values by set. Keyword parameters, (also known as variables) may be assigned values by writing:

name = value [name = value]…

Pattern-matching is not performed on value. There cannot be a function and a variable with the same name.

${parameter}
A parameter is a sequence of letters, digits, or underscores (a name), a digit, or any of the characters *, @, #, ?, -, $, and !. The value, if any, of the parameter is substituted. The braces are required only when parameter is followed by a letter, digit, or underscore that is not to be interpreted as part of its name. A name must begin with a letter or underscore. If parameter is a digit then it is a positional parameter. If parameter is * or @, then

all the positional parameters, starting with $1, are substituted (separated by spaces). Parameter $0 is set from argument 0 when the shell is invoked.

${parameter:-word}
If parameter is set and is not a null argument, its value is substituted; otherwise word is substituted.

${parameter:=word}
If parameter is not set or is null, then it is set to word; the value of the parameter is then substituted. Positional parameters may not be assigned to in this way.

${parameter:?word}
If parameter is set and is not a null argument, its value is substituted; otherwise, word is printed and the shell is exited. If word is omitted, the message "parameter null or not set" is printed.

${parameter:+word}
If parameter is set and is not a null argument, word is substituted; otherwise nothing is substituted.

In the above, word is not evaluated unless it is to be used as the substituted string, so that in the following example, pwd is executed only if d is not set or is null:

echo ${d:- `pwd` }

If the colon (:) is omitted from the above expressions, then the shell only checks whether parameter is set.

The following parameters are automatically set by the shell:

The number of positional parameters in decimal

- Flags supplied to the shell on invocation or by the set command

? The decimal value returned by the last synchronously executed command

$ The process number of this shell

! The process number of the last background command invoked

The following parameters are used by the shell:

CDPATH
The search path for the cd special command. See the section "cd" under "Special commands".

HOME
The default argument (home directory) for the cd special command.

IFS Internal field separators, normally space, tab, and newline.

MAIL
If this variable is set to the name of a mail file, then the shell informs the user of the arrival of mail in the specified file.

MAILCHECK
This parameter specifies how often (in seconds) the shell checks for the arrival of mail in the files specified by the MAILPATH or

MAIL parameters. The default value is 600 seconds (10 minutes). If it is set to 0, the shell checks before each prompt.

MAILPATH
A colon (:) separated list of filenames. If this parameter is set, the shell informs the user of the arrival of mail in any of the specified files. Each filename can be followed by "%" and a message to be printed when the modification time changes. The default message is "you have mail".

PATH
The search path for commands (see "Execution").

PS1 The primary prompt string, by default "$ ".

PS2 The secondary prompt string, by default "> ".

SHELL
When the shell is invoked, it scans the environment (see "Environment") for this name. If it is found and there is an `r' in the filename part of its value, the shell becomes a restricted shell.

The shell gives default values to PATH, PS1, PS2, and IFS, while HOME and MAIL are not set at all by the shell (although HOME is set by login(M)).

Blank interpretation

After parameter and command substitution, the results of substitution are scanned for internal field separator characters (those found in IFS) and split into distinct arguments where such characters are found. Explicit null arguments ("" or '') are retained.

Implicit null arguments (those resulting from parameters that have no values) are removed.

Filename generation

Following substitution, each command word is scanned for patterns (shell regular expressions), as described in regexp(M).

Quoting

The following characters have a special meaning to the shell and cause termination of a word unless quoted:

; & ( ) | ^ < > newline space tab

A character may be quoted (that is, made to stand for itself) by preceding it with a "\". The pair \newline is ignored. All characters enclosed between a pair of single quotation marks (' '), except a single quotation mark, are quoted. Inside double quotation marks (" "), parameter and command substitution occurs and "\" quotes the characters \, `, ", and $. "$*" is equivalent to "$1 $2...", whereas "$@" is equivalent to "$1" "$2"...

Prompting

When used interactively, the shell prompts with the value of PS1 before reading a command. If at any time a newline is typed and further input is needed to complete a command, the secondary prompt (that is, the value of PS2) is issued.

Spelling checker

When using cd(C) the shell checks spelling. For example, if you change to a different directory using cd and misspell the directory name, the shell responds with an alternative spelling of an existing directory. Enter "y" and press <Return> (or just press <Return>) to change to the offered directory. If the offered spelling is incorrect, enter "n", then retype the command line. In this example the user input is boldfaced:

$ cd /usr/spool/uucp

   cd /usr/spool/uucp?y
   ok

Input/Output

Before a command is executed, its input and output may be redirected using a special notation interpreted by the shell. The following may appear anywhere in a simple-command or may precede or follow a command. They are not passed on to the invoked command; substitution occurs before word or digit is used:

<word
Use file word as standard input (file descriptor 0).

>word
Use file word as standard output (file descriptor 1). If the file does not exist, it is created; otherwise, it is truncated to zero length.

>>word

Use file word as standard output. If the file exists, output is appended to it (by first seeking the end-of-file); otherwise, the file is created.

<<[—]word
Read the shell input up to a line that is the same as word, or to an end-of-file. The resulting document becomes the standard input. If any character of word is quoted, no interpretation is placed upon the characters of the document; otherwise, parameter and command substitution occurs, (unescaped) \newline is ignored, and "\" must be used to quote the characters \, $, `, and the first character of word. If "-" is appended to <<, all leading tabs are stripped from word and from the document.

<&digit
Duplicate the standard input from file descriptor digit (see dup(S)); similarly for the standard output using >.

<&- Close the standard input; similarly for the standard output using >.

If one of the above is preceded by a digit, the file descriptor created is that specified by the digit (instead of the default 0 or 1). For example:

...2>&1

creates file descriptor 2 that is a duplicate of file descriptor 1.

If a command is followed by "&", the default standard input for the command is the empty file /dev/null. Otherwise, the environment

for the execution of a command contains the file descriptors of the invoking shell as modified by input/output specifications.

Environment

The environment (see environ(M)) is a list of name-value pairs that is passed to an executed program in the same way as a normal argument list. The shell interacts with the environment in several ways. On invocation, the shell scans the environment and creates a parameter for each name found, giving it the corresponding value. Executed commands inherit the same environment. If the user modifies the values of these parameters or creates new ones, none of these affect the environment unless the export command is used to bind the shell's parameter to the environment. The environment seen by any executed command is composed of any unmodified name-value pairs originally inherited by the shell, minus any pairs removed by unset, plus any modifications or additions, all of which must be noted in export commands.

The environment for any simple-command may be augmented by prefixing it with one or more assignments to parameters. Thus:

TERM=wy60 cmd args

and

(export TERM; TERM=wy60; cmd args)

are equivalent (as far as the above execution of cmd is concerned).

If the -k flag is set, all keyword arguments are placed in the environment, even if they occur after the command name.

Signals

The INTERRUPT and QUIT signals for an invoked command are ignored if the command is followed by "&"; otherwise signals have the values inherited by the shell from its parent, with the exception of signal 11. See the trap command.

Execution

Each time a command is executed, the substitutions described in the previous sections are carried out. If the command name does not match a special command, but matches the name of a defined function, the function is executed in the shell process (note how this differs from the execution of shell procedures). The positional parameters $1, $2,...are set to the arguments of the function. If the command name matches neither a special command nor the name of a defined function, a
new process is created and an attempt is made to execute the command via exec(S).

The shell parameter PATH defines the search path for the directory containing the command. Alternative directory names are separated by a colon (:). The default path is :/bin:/usr/bin (specifying the current directory, /bin, and /usr/bin, in that order). Note that the current directory is specified by a null pathname, which can appear immediately after the equal sign or between the colon delimiters anywhere else in the path list. If the command name contains a "/", then the search path is not used. Otherwise, each directory in the path is searched for an executable file. If the file has execute permission but is not an a.out file, it is assumed to be a file containing shell commands. A subshell (that is, a separate process) is spawned to read it. A parenthesized command is also executed in a sub-shell.

Shell procedures are often used by users running the csh. However, if the first character of the procedure is a "#" (comment character), csh assumes the procedure is a csh script, and invokes /bin/csh to execute it. sh procedures should always be started with some other character if csh users are to run the procedure at any time. This invokes the standard shell /bin/sh.

The location in the search path where a command was found is remembered by the shell (to help avoid unnecessary execs later). If the command was found in a relative directory, its location must be re-determined whenever the current directory changes. The shell forgets all remembered locations whenever the PATH variable is changed or the hash -r command is executed (see hash in the next section).

Special commands

Input/output redirection is permitted for these commands:

: No effect; the command does nothing. A 0 exit code is returned.

. file Reads and executes commands from file and returns. The search path specified by PATH is used to find the directory containing file.

break [n]

Exits from the enclosing for, while, or until loop, if any. If n is specified, it breaks n levels.

continue [n]
Resumes the next iteration of the enclosing for, while, or until loop. If n is specified, it resumes at the nth enclosing loop.

cd [-L | -P] [arg]
   Changes the current directory to arg. The shell parameter HOME is the default arg. The shell parameter CDPATH defines the search path for the directory containing arg. Alternative directory names are separated by a colon (:). The default path is <null> (specifying the current directory). Note that the current directory is specified by a null pathname, which can appear immediately after the equal sign or between the colon delimiters anywhere else in the path list. If arg begins with a "/", the search path is not used. Otherwise, each directory in the path is searched for arg.

If the shell is reading its commands from a terminal, and the specified directory does not exist (or some component cannot be searched), spelling correction is applied to each component of arg, in a search for the "correct" name. The shell then asks whether or not to try and change directory to the corrected directory name; an answer of n means "no", and anything else is taken as "yes".

   The -L and -P flags are relevant to systems with symbolic links:

-L Preserve logical pathnames so that cd -L .. moves up one component towards the root along the current logical path.

-P Use a physical model for pathnames so that cd -L .. moves up one component towards the root by following the link to the parent of the current directory. This is the default behavior. For example, if /usr/include/sys/h is a symbolic link to the directory /sys/h, then cd /usr/include/sys/h; cd -L .would make /usr/include/sys the current directory; cd /usr/include/sys/h; cd -P . would make /sys the current directory.

If the -L option is specified to sh (or to set), the default behavior of cd is to use logical pathnames.

echo [arg]
Writes arguments separated by blanks and terminated by a new-line on the standard output. Arguments may be enclosed in quotes. Quotes are required so that the shell correctly interprets these special escape sequences:

\b Backspace
\c Prints line without newline
\f Form feed
\n Newline
\r Carriage return
\t Tab
\v Vertical tab
\\ Backslash
\n The 8-bit character whose ASCII code is the 1, 2 or 3-digit octal number n. n must start with a 0

eval [arg...]
Reads the arguments as input to the shell and executes the result-ing command(s).

exec [arg...]

Executes the command specified by the arguments in place of this shell without creating a new process. Input/output arguments may appear and, if no other arguments are given, cause the shell input/output to be modified.

exit [n]

Causes the shell to exit with the exit status specified by n. If n is omitted, the exit status is that of the last command executed. An end-of-file also causes the shell to exit.

export [name...]

Marks the given names for automatic export to the environment of subsequently executed commands. If no arguments are given, a list of all names that are exported in this shell is printed.

getopts

Is used in shell scripts to support command syntax standards (see Intro(C)); it parses positional parameters and checks for legal options. See getopts(C) for usage and description.

hash [-r] [name...]

Determines and remembers, for each name, the location in the search path of the command specified by name. The -r option causes the shell to forget all remembered locations. If no arguments are given, information about remembered commands is presented. "Hits" is the number of times a command has been invoked by the shell process. "Cost" is a measure of the work required to locate a command in the search path. There are certain situations which require that the stored location of a command be recalculated. Commands for which this is done are indicated by an asterisk (*) adjacent to the "hits" information. "Cost" is incremented when the recalculation is done.

newgrp [arg...]
    Equivalent to exec newgrp arg...

pwd [-L | -P]
Prints the current working directory. The -L and -P flags are useful with symbolic links:

-L Show the logical pathname to the directory preserving the route taken to get there.

-P Show the physical pathname to the directory. This is the default behavior. For example, if /usr/include/sys/h is a symbolic link to the directory /sys/h, then cd /usr/include/sys/h; pwd –L prints /usr/include/sys/h as the current working directory; cd/usr/include/sys/h; pwd -P prints /sys/h as the current working directory.

If the -L option is specified to sh (or to set), the default behavior of pwd is to use logical pathnames.

read [name...]
Reads one line from the standard input and assigns the first word to the first name, the second word to the second name, and so on, with leftover words assigned to the last name. The return code is 0 unless an end-of-file is encountered.

readonly [name...]
Marks the given names read-only; the values of these names may not be changed by subsequent assignment. If no arguments are given, a list of all read-only names is printed.

return [n]
Causes a function to exit with the return value specified by n. If n
is omitted, the return status is that of the last command executed.

set [-aefhknuvx [arg...]]
set takes the following options:

-a Marks variables which are modified or created for export.

-e If the shell is non-interactive, exits immediately if a command
exits with a non-zero exit status.

-f Disables filename generation.

-h Locates and remembers function commands as functions are
defined (function commands are normally located when the function is executed). For example, if h is set, /bin/tty is added to the
hash table when:

    showtty(){
    tty
    }

is declared. If h is unset, the function is not added to the hash table
until showtty is called.

-k Places all keyword arguments in the environment for a command,
not just those that precede the command name.

-L Causes the internal cd and pwd commands to use logical
pathnames by default rather than physical pathnames.

-n Reads commands but does not execute them.

-u Treats unset variables as an error when substituting.

-v Prints shell input lines as they are read.

-x Prints commands and their arguments as they are executed. Although this flag is passed to sub-shells, it does not enable tracing in those sub-shells.

— Does not change any of the flags; this is useful in setting $1 to "-". Using "+" rather than "-" causes these flags to be turned off. These flags can also be used upon invocation of the shell. The current set of flags may be found in $-. The remaining arguments are positional parameters and are assigned, in order, to $1, $2,...If no arguments are given, the values of all names are printed.

shift [n]
Renames the positional parameters from $2...to $1...If n is specified, it shifts the positional parameters by n places. shift is the only way to access positional parameters above $9.

test Evaluates conditional expressions. See test(C) for usage and description.

times Prints the accumulated user and system times for processes run from the shell.

trap [arg] [n]...
arg is a command to be read and executed when the shell receives signal(s) n. (Note that arg is scanned once when the trap is set and once when the trap is taken.) Trap commands are executed in

order of signal number. The highest signal number allowed is 16. Any attempt to set a trap on a signal that was ignored on entry to the current shell is ineffective. An attempt to trap on signal 11 (memory fault) produces an error. If arg is absent, all trap(s) n are reset to their original values. If arg is the null string, this signal is ignored by the shell and by the commands it invokes. If n is 0, the command arg is executed on exit from the shell. The trap command with no arguments prints a list of commands associated with each signal number.

type [name...]
Indicates, for each name, how it would be interpreted if used as a command name.

ulimit [n]
Imposes a size limit of n blocks on files written by the shell and its child processes (files of any size may be read). Any user may decrease the file size limit, but only root can increase the limit. With no argument, the current limit is printed. If no option is given and a number is specified, -f is assumed.

unset [name...]
Removes, for each name, the corresponding variable or function. The variables PATH, PS1, PS2, MAILCHECK and IFS cannot be unset.

umask [-S] [mask]
Sets the user file-creation mask to the value of the mask operand. If mask is an octal integer, the specified bits are set in the umask. Otherwise, mask should be symbolic mode (see chmod(C)), the new value of the file-creation mask being the logical complement of the file permission bits specified. If no mask is specified, the

current file-creation mask is printed. If -S is specified, the symbolic form is printed. See also umask(C).

wait [n]
Waits for the specified process to terminate, and reports the termination status. If n is not given, all currently active child processes are waited for. The return code from this command is always 0.

Invocation

If the shell is invoked through exec(S) and the first character of argument 0 is "-", commands are initially read from /etc/profile and then from $HOME/.profile, if such files exist. Thereafter, commands are read as described below, which is also the case when the shell is invoked as /bin/sh. The flags below are interpreted by the shell on invocation only; note that unless the -c or -s flag is specified, the first argument is assumed to be the name of a file containing commands, and theremaining arguments are passed as positional parameters to that command file:

-c string
If the -c flag is present, commands are read from string.

-s If the -s flag is present or if no arguments remain, commands are read from the standard input. Any remaining arguments specify the positional parameters. Shell output is written to file descriptor 2.

-t If the -t flag is present, a single command is read and executed, and the shell exits. This flag is intended for use by C
programs only and is not useful interactively.

-i If the -i flag is present or if the shell input and output are attached to a terminal, this shell is interactive. In this case, TER-MINATE is ignored (so that kill 0 does not kill an interactive shell) and INTERRUPT is caught and ignored (so that wait is interruptible). In all cases, QUIT is ignored by the shell.

-r If the -r flag is present, the shell is a restricted shell (see rsh(C)).

The remaining flags and arguments are described under the set command above.

Exit values

Errors detected by the shell, such as syntax errors, cause the shell to return a non-zero exit status. If the shell is being used non-interactively, execution of the shell file is abandoned. Otherwise, the shell returns the exit status of the last command executed. See the exit command above.

Examples

See "Solving problems with the environment" in the Operating System User's Guide and Chapter 11, "Automating frequent tasks" in the Operating System User's Guide for a general introduction to shell programming, and the development of an example script.

See "Tuning script performance" in the Operating System User's Guide for a general discussion of shell script efficiency considerations and some examples of generic scripts.

Notes

The command readonly (without arguments) produces the same type of output as the command export.

If << is used to provide standard input to an asynchronous process invoked by &, the shell gets mixed up about naming the input document; a garbage file /tmp/sh* is created and the shell complains about not being able to find that file by another name.

If a command is executed, and a command with the same name is installed in a directory in the search path before the directory where the original command was found, the shell continues to exec the original command. Use the hash command to correct this situation.

If you move the current directory or one above it, pwd may not give the correct response. Use the cd command with a full pathname to correct this situation.

When a sh user logs in, the system reads and executes commands in /etc/profile before executing commands in the user's $HOME/.profile. You can, therefore, modify the environment for all sh users on the system by editing /etc/profile.

The shell doesn't treat the high (eighth) bit in the characters of a command line argument specially, nor does it strip the eighth bit from the characters of error messages. Previous versions of the shell used the eighth bit as a quoting mechanism.

Existing programs that set the eighth bit of characters in order to quote them as part of the shell command line should be changed to use of the standard shell quoting mechanisms (see the section on "Quoting").

Words used to specify filenames in input/output redirection are not expanded for filename generation (see the section on "Filename generation"). For example, cat file1 > a* creates a file named a*.

Because commands in pipelines are run as separate processes, variables set in a pipeline have no effect on the parent shell.

If you get the error message:

    fork failed—too many processes

try using the wait(C) command to clean up your background processes. If this does not help, the system process table is probably full or you have too many active foreground processes (there is a limit to the number of processes that can be associated with your login, and the number the system can keep track of).

Warning

Not all processes of a 3 or more stage pipeline are children of the shell, and thus cannot be waited for.

For wait n, if n is not an active process ID, all your shell's currently active background processes are waited for and the return code is 0.

Files

/etc/profile
  system default profile, read by login shells before

$HOME/.profile
  read by login shell at login
/tmp/sh*
  temporary file for <<

/dev/null
  source of empty file

APPENDIX B

Using the vi Editor

Overview

The visual editor is a full screen editor and is invoked with the Unix command *vi* followed by a file name. A new file is created when the file name does not exist.

Within the visual editor, there are three modes of editing. The command mode allows you to enter command keystrokes to perform specified functions. When you are in insert mode, anything you type is interpreted as text and displays on your screen. The Esc key exits a command. Although not all commands require you to press Esc to exit, it is good practice to always press the Esc key when completing any command. The edit mode may be performed from the editor status line. The colon will take you to the status line at the bottom of the current screen where you type a command string. Generally, the command strings used with the colon apply globally, although they can sometimes be limited with a parameter.

Many commands are performed on a character, a word, a line, or on selected text. The editor interprets the end of a word as the last character before a space or the last character before a special character such as a period or slash. The editor identifies a line as a group of characters ending with an end of line or end of record marker such as a carriage return.

View the hidden characters such as end of record markers within a file by turning on the hidden codes display. To do this, in command mode type

`:set list`

The hidden characters will display to your screen. The dollar sign indicates the end of the line or record. Display of hidden characters often identifies problem areas within files such as imbedded tabs or extra carriage returns.

Novice users might want to use vedit instead of vi. The vedit editor sets the screen to showmode which displays mode information at the bottom of the screen. For example, it will display INSERT mode when you are typing text and COMMAND mode when you can type commands.

Keep in mind that the visual editor is case sensitive. Command functions use the uppercase and lowercase alpha keys.

Customizing the Editor

Invoking commands when starting vi

Open the visual editor and invoke a command at the same time by using the –c option. For example, to open the file *sample* and place the insertion point at the end of the file, type:

`vi -c Shift+G sample`

To open the editor window with a size different from the default, specify the –w option followed by the number of lines desired. For example, to open the file *sample* in a 15 line window, type:

`vi -w15 sample`

Setting Editor Defaults

The visual editor uses the EXINIT environment variable for default configuration settings. To override the default settings, place a file named .exrc in your $HOME directory. The visual editor will invoke the settings you specify within the file. The available settings are listed under *Options* in the vi man pages.

To invoke the options ignore case and error bells for all editing sessions invoked with vi, place the lines within the .exrc file. The commands would exist in the file *.exrc* as follows:

```
set ignorecase
set errorbells
```

Navigating in the Screen Editor

Using Navigation Keys

There are several ways to move around in the editor screen. Depending upon the type of terminal you are using, the arrow keys may not work for navigation.

When I started using vi on a dumb terminal, the arrow keys did not work within the screen editor. Since Unix uses so many different terminal types, it is a good idea to learn the corresponding alpha keys so that you will be able to navigate under all conditions. I also prefer to keep my fingers on the alphabetic keys. Once you begin to use the keystrokes, they will become second nature to you.

The corresponding key for the Up Arrow is lowercase k. In command mode, pressing the k one time will work the same as pressing the Up Arrow one time. Lowercase t will place your insertion point on the preceding line. The keys will repeat in the same manner as the arrow keys. The following alpha keys equate to the arrow keys:

Navigation Keys
Key Definition
j   Down Arrow

k   Up Arrow
h   Left Arrow
l   Right Arrow

It is important to note that the alpha navigation keys are lowercase only. The uppercase keys have different functions. For example, the Shift+J will join lines together rather than move your insertion point to the next line which is the function of the lowercase j.

The navigation keys will not move the insertion point past the end of the file.

Navigating by Page

As with the arrow keys, the Page Up and Page Down keys may not be defined to work within vi. To move forward and backward one page at a time rather than one line at a time, use the following keystrokes:

Ctrl+F to move forward one page
Ctrl+B to move back one page

Navigating by Line

The dollar sign moves the insertion point to the end of the current line. Pressing the 0 key moves the insertion point to the first position of the current line. The plus sign moves the insertion point to the first character of the next line and the minus sign moves the insertion point to the first character of the previous line. Use the left parenthesis to place the insertion point at the beginning of the sentence or the right parenthesis to place the insertion point at the end of the sentence. A sentence may not be the same as a line.

Navigating by Line Number

To move to a particular line in the text, use the colon followed by the line number. For example, to go to line 25, type

:25

The insertion point will move to line 25. If at any time you would like to view the line numbers in your file, type

```
:set number
```

and the line numbers will precede each line. The line numbers are for informational purposes only, and will not be saved with the text at the time the file is written.

If you simply would like to know the number of lines in the file as well as the line number of the current line, type Ctrl+G.

To move the insertion point to the of the file, within command mode type Shift+G. The insertion point will move to the first character of the last line where text appears. The Shift+G can also be used to move to a line by typing the line number followed by G as follows:

```
25G
```

The insertion point will move to line 25.

Navigating by Word

The commands Shift+W and lowercase w move the insertion point to the beginning of the next word. Shift+B and lowercase b move the insertion point to the beginning of the current word. Shift+E and lowercase e move the insertion point to the end of the current word. The uppercase commands, Shift+W, Shift+B, and Shift+E ignore special characters such as punctuation when interpreting word length.

Navigating by Search Text

To find a string of text, in command mode type slash followed by the search string. For example, to search for the words "program name" type

```
/program name
```

When you press enter, the insertion point will find the next occurrence of the words *program name*. Press lowercase n to find the next occurrence. To go back to the previous occurrence, press Shift+N. The search feature will automatically wrap to the beginning of the file after reaching the end and will continue searching. To search backward instead of forward, use the question mark in the place of the slash.

Using Basic Editing Commands

The following tips will be helpful to you when editing in the visual editor:

The cursor is the insertion point.

Text editing commands are alphanumeric. Alpha commands indicate the function to be performed. Generally, numeric digits used with commands indicate how many times or to what extent to execute the function.

The period function repeats a performed edit at the insertion point.

Ctrl+u undoes the last performed edit. Shift+U removes all of the edits performed on the line during the current editing session.

Inserting New Text

Using the Esc key will end the insertion for all of the insert commands.

Shift+O opens a blank line previous to the current line for text insertion. The existing text will shift down to display a new blank line. As you continue to type and the text wraps, the existing text will continue to shift until the insertion is complete. Lowercase o acts the same way, however, the blank line is opened below the current line.

Use lowercase i to begin inserting text on an existing line. When the insertion point is at any location on a line, using Shift+I will move the insertion point to the beginning of the current line and place you in text insert mode. Lowercase a will begin inserting text after the insertion point. Shift+A acts like Shift+I, only the insertion point is at the end of the current line.

Changing Text

The commands used to change text do not place you into insertion mode, but rather type over the existing text. To change text, place the insertion point on the first character of the word or phrase where the change begins.

By Character

To replace one character use the lowercase r command. Use the Shift+R to replace text indefinitely. Typed text will continue to replace the existing text until command mode is exited. To change one character, use the lowercase s command. This will change one character and then place you in insert mode. You can type a number with the s command to change a number of characters, and then be placed in insertion mode.

By Word

To change a word, use the command lowercase c+w. You will be able to tell you are in change mode by the dollar sign which is placed at the end of the word you are changing. Press the Esc key to exit the command. This will replace the existing word with the new word regardless of the length; the unchanged text will be adjusted to accommodate the varied word lengths.

Replacing Recurring Text

To replace a word or phrase that occurs several times within a document, use the search and replace command string. The %s performs the search and replaces the first string with the second string. The last parameter indicates the extent of the replace. For example, to globally replace the word *temp* with the word *tmp*:

```
:%s/temp/tmp/g
```

The % can be replaced with line numbers if you only want the changes to occur on certain line numbers. If you only want to change *temp* to be *tmp* on line 10 to the end of the file:

```
:10,$s/temp/tmp/g
```

Special characters within the command string must be preceded by as backslash to be treated as literals. For example, to replace the first occurrence of the phrase */usr1/temp* with */usr1/tmp*, use the following command string:

```
:%s/\/usr1\/temp/\/usr1\/tmp/1
```

The use of special characters can also be accommodated by using the question mark as a delimiter in the string. This will cause all of the special characters to be interpreted literally. For example, this command will replace */usr1/temp* with */usr1/tmp*:

```
:%s?/usr1/temp?/usr1/tmp
```

Deleting Text

Delete text by character, word, line, or multiple lines. When using a terminal interface program, the cut feature deletes text, too.

By Character

The lowercase x deletes one character at a time beginning at the insertion point. The Shift+X deletes text behind the insertion point. Both of these methods rejoin the surrounding text. Use a number with lowercase x to delete a number of characters. In command mode, to delete 10 characters from the insertion point forward:

```
10x
```

By Word

Use the command d+w to delete a word.

By Line

To delete the current line of text, type lowercase d+d. Repeat the command to delete multiple lines or specify the number of lines prior to executing the delete. For example, to delete 25 lines of text including the current line type:

```
25dd
```

Copying and Moving Text

Personal computer interfaces provide the capability to cut-copy-and-paste using the Clipboard. However, since many Unix installations utilize dumb terminals, vi provides the functionality within the editing functions to accomplish these tasks.

When using the cut-copy-and-paste Clipboard in lieu of the vi commands, it is necessary to open an insert area when pasting text in the visual editor. For example, open a new line with Shift+O, an insert area with lowercase i, or an append area with lowercase a before performing the paste function.

Selecting and Copying Text

The yank function places selected text into memory. The put function places the text located in memory into the document at the insertion point. (It is not necessary to open an insertion area before performing a put.)

Yank and Put Commands

Keys	Definition
yy	yank number of lines
yl	yank number of characters
p	put the buffer text after the insertion point
P	put the buffer text before the insertion point

For example, to yank the first two lines of text, place the insertion point on the first line, and in command mode, type 2+y+y. The command copies the two lines into the buffer. To copy the selected text to the last line of the document, move the insertion point to the end of the document and type lowercase p. The copied text will display at the end of the document. Repetition of the put command will continue to place the buffered text at the insertion point.

When you need buffers in addition to the default memory area, specify your own by using the quotation mark and a lowercase letter. You have up to 26 buffers that you can use. Reusing a buffer will clear out the existing text and put new lines into the buffer. For example, to place 10 lines into buffer *a* you would type the following command:

```
"a10yy
```

To retrieve the 10 lines out of buffer *a*, use the put command:

```
"ap
```

To reuse the buffer without clearing out the existing text, use the equivalent uppercase buffer name. The use of the uppercase letter indicates you wish to perform an append. To place 10 additional lines into the buffer lowercase a:

```
"A10yy
```

To retrieve the original 10 lines as well as the appended 10 lines out of buffer *a*, use the same put command:

```
"ap
```

Exiting from the editor clears all of the buffers.

Using Mark to Select Text

By marking a block of text, you can easily delete or yank it. Marking the text relieves you from having to count how many lines to delete or yank. To mark a line, use the lowercase m plus a letter. To mark the current line as *a*, type the following command:

```
ma
```

You can then access that line by using the single quote command. To go to the line marked *a*, type:

`'a`

To yank all of the lines from the current line to the line marked *a*:

`y'a`

To delete all of the lines from the current line to the line marked a:

`d'a`

Reading an existing file into the editor

The following command will read the file *sample* into the file currently being edited and display it at the insertion point:

`:r sample`

Keep in mind that you are still editing the original file and the file *sample* still exists unchanged in its entirety as a separate file.

The following command will close the current file without saving changes and open the file *sample* for editing:

`:e! sample`

The exclamation point following the lowercase e suppresses the warning message from vi created when you quit without saving revisions. The exclamation point is not needed if revisions were not made to the current file.

Saving the file

The visual editor creates an edit copy and the invoked file is not changed until it is written. To exit from a file and save revisions if they exist, use Shift+Z+Shift+Z. The write and quit command can be used to rewrite the file under all conditions as follows:

`:wq!`

Saving As

When you need to save the revision as a new file and leave the original file unchanged, use the write command to save the text to a new file name. For example, you are modifying a file named *guide* and you want to save it to a new file named *text*, use the following write command:

```
:w text
```

The write saves the revision to a new file named *text* and does not rewrite the file named *guide*. However, the current file is still *guide*, and the quit command must be used to exit the file without saving the changes.

Specifying line numbers before the write command limits the text written to the new file. For example, to save line numbers fifteen through fifty only, use the following write command:

```
:15,50 w text
```

The write saves lines fifteen through fifty to a new file named *text*. The editor will alert you when a file already exists and will be overwritten. An alert does not occur when writing to the current file being edited.

Quitting without Saving

To exit the visual editor without saving the revisions, use the following command:

```
:q!.
```

The quit command exits the editor without saving and the exclamation point overrides any errors or warnings generated by Unix. The Shift+Z+Shift+Z command will exit without performing a save only when the file has not been modified.

Recovering a File

If the vi editing session is halted due to a system error, retrieve the previously saved version with the following command from the Unix command line:

```
vi -r file
```

Use the Unix recover command to retrieve the temporary edited version saved in the tmp directory.

```
recover file
```

INDEX
(Topical)

INDEX

(Alphabetical)